UNLEASHED PROMISES
of
Merciful Love

A Compellation of True Life Mixed with Biblical Stories

Joyce A. Leonard

Unleashed Promises of Merciful Love

Copyright © 2022 by Joyce A. Leonard. All rights reserved.

No part of this publication may be reproduced, stored in a retrieval system or transmitted in any way by any means, electronic, mechanical, photocopy, recording or otherwise without the prior permission of the author except as provided by USA copyright law.

The opinions expressed by the author are not necessarily those of URLink Print and Media.

1603 Capitol Ave., Suite 310 Cheyenne, Wyoming USA 82001
1-888-980-6523 | admin@urlinkpublishing.com

URLink Print and Media is committed to excellence in the publishing industry.

Book design copyright © 2022 by URLink Print and Media. All rights reserved.

Published in the United States of America
Library of Congress Control Number: 2022910555
ISBN 978-1-68486-206-1 (Paperback)
ISBN 978-1-68486-199-6 (Digital)

27.05.22

CONTENTS

Introduction vii
Acknowledgements xi

Chapter 1:   Malicious Accusations 1
Chapter 2:   Flirting with Sin 7
Chapter 3:   "You Shall Not Surely Die" 11
Chapter 4:   "Blind Faith or Delusional Sacrifice" 15
Chapter 5:   "Friendly Fire Within the Church" 25
Chapter 6:   Blessing or a Curse? 30
Chapter 7:   The Choices in a Decision 41
Chapter 8:   Preparing to Meet God at the Mountain 58
Chapter 9:   The Silence of the Ticking Clock 71
Chapter 10: "Search for Me with all Your Heart" 82
Chapter 11: A House of Tears 90
Chapter 12: "Whistling Girls and Crowing Hens" 94
Chapter 13: A Bittersweet Love Story 102
Chapter 14: What Can A Dream Mean? 108
Chapter 15: Love Him Now, Love Him Again 116
Chapter 16: The Lamb Was Slain 123
Chapter 17: We All Loved Lucy 131
Chapter 18: Condemn One, Condemn All 142
Chapter 19: Where is the Healing Balm of Gilead? 153
Chapter 20: The Legend of a Name 162
Chapter 21: Cast the First Stone 175
Chapter 22: Tongues of Men and Angels 180

Chapter 23: It's Time to Fly 187
Chapter 24: Hear No Evil, See No Evil, Speak No Evil 195
Chapter 25: His Hand was on Me 203
Chapter 26: Profession or a Calling 211
Chapter 27: Mothers, Mothers and Mothers 222
Chapter 28: "Don't Worry, Be Happy!" 228
Chapter 29: The Christmas Dream 233

Most Scripture is NKJV unless otherwise labeled

Scriptures & Quotes used

Introduction—Philippians 3:17-21 Amplified—Isaiah 14:12-14 NKJV—Revelation12:4,7-9,12—Ephesians 6:10-12
I Samuel 17:47 b, II Chronicles 20:15, Eccl 12:9

Chapter 1—Quote by Walter Scott/ quote COL (Christ's Object Lessons) by EG White pg. 172—Romans 8:28

Chapter 2 DA (Desire of Ages) by EG White pg. 148

Chapter 3 Genesis 3:1—Genesis 3:3—Genesis 3:6 (NKJV)

Chapter 4 Leviticus 18:5—Genesis 16:2—Genesis Chap. 17—Genesis 22:2—Proverbs 3:7 Romans 4:3, 8:31—James 2:23—Genesis 22:7 & 8 John 3:16—Genesis 22:12 & 13

Chapter 5 Ephesians 4:25, Ephesians 2:13-16

Chapter 6 Proverbs 1:1-3 EW (Early Writings by EG White pg. 17—Numbers 22:9,12,18,20,21, II Samuel 17:23—I Kings 2:40—SDA Commentary Vol. 1, pg. 902 Numbers 22:25, 28,31—James 3:8-11 Numbers 24:2-9

Chapter 7 Isaiah 30:21, Matthew 25:43 SM (Selected Messages Book 1) by EG White pg. 123, Psalms 103:20, Psalms 103:2-4

Chapter 8 Psalms 8 Isaiah 42:8, Exodus 19: 10-15,16-19 P & P (Patriarchs and Prophets) by EG White pg.305, 306, Exodus 20:3, I Samuel 15:22, Exodus 20:19-21

Chapter 9 Ecclesiastes 3:1, 7b-8, Proverbs 7:6-27 (paraphrased), Matthew 16-26 last part, Psalms 42:5

Chapter 10 Quote Brenda Walsh, Numbers 10:33, Psalms 44:21, Psalms 76:6, Psalms 139:23, Psalms 46:10, Eccl. 7:25, Jeremiah 17:10, 29:11-14

Chapter 11 Romans 8:28, Psalms 56:8, I Samuel Chapter 25, Isaiah 65:17, 19

Chapter 12 James 3:13 II Samuel Chap. 1, Romans 3:23, Revelation 3:19, II Samuel 14:25, Isaiah 14:13-14, Romans 8:31, I Timothy 4:7

Chapter 13 Song of Solomon 2:4

Chapter 14 Proverbs 3:6, Genesis 37:3, 7, 9 Joel 2:28-29

Chapter 15 Ezekiel 33:31, I Corinthians 12:28, Daniel 10:16-17, Revelation 3:16-17 (paraphrased), Ezekiel 24:16, Jeremiah 23:29, II Peter 3:9, Ezekiel 3:11, James 5:16, Matthew 6:33

Chapter 16 Revelation 5:12, Matthew 26:50, Joshua 24:15, Matthew 27:46 (The account written was all paraphrased)— the actual account can be found in Matthew 27, Mark 15 & 16, Luke 23, and John 18 & 19

Chapter 17 Proverbs 31:26-27

Chapter 18 Luke 6:37, Job 9:20, 34:21, 34:31-33 NIV, Matthew Chap. 7, Luke 6:37-38, Titus 2:8, Matthew 12:37, I John 2:1, Romans 6:23

Chapter 19 Jeremiah 8:22 Mark 5:7, 1-17, Hosea 6:8, Jeremiah 46:11, Jeremiah 30:17 (Message)

Chapter 20 Quote Harry Truman March 1946, Judges 11:2, Matthew 1:5,6, & 16, Joshua 2:1-24, SDA Commentary pg. 184, Joshua 1:9, 14, 20; 6:4, SDA Bible Commentary pg. 199, Joshua 24:15

Chapter 21 Proverbs 24:1, John Chap. 8:7 (KJV), Numbers 32:23,

Chapter 22 Quote Mother Theresa, Ephesians 4:26-27, Romans 14:12-13, Psalms 32:9

Chapter 23 Luke 12:6, 9

Chapter 24 Isaiah 1:16, Psalms 34:7, I Corinthians 2:9

Chapter 25 Psalms 103:2-3,

Chapter 26

Chapter 27 Quote Dewitt Talmage, Matthew 14

Chapter 28 I Peter 5:7, Genesis 3:8-10, Genesis 22, Genesis 37, Matthew 6:27,32 Psalms 37:1-7

Chapter 29 Psalms 37:4

INTRODUCTION

"For there are many, of whom I have often told you even weeping, that *they* are enemies of the cross of Christ; whose end is destruction, whose god is in their stomach (their *appetites*, their sensuality) and they glory in their shame, siding with earthly things and being of their party.

> "But we are citizens *of* the state (commonwealth, homeland) which is in heaven, and from it also we earnestly and patiently await (the coming of the Lord Jesus Christ (the Messiah) as Savior, Who will transform and fashion anew the body of our humiliation to conform to and be like the body of His glory and majesty, by exerting the power which enables Him even to subject everything to Himself" *Philippians 3:17-21 (Amplified)*.

With all the many trials I have encountered and been in throughout my life and having already written a third of my life, "A Journey of Trials Strengthened Through Faith" for the world to read and examine; the next part of my life is far too complex to share on the pages of a book. It would involve lives that have hopefully changed and are preparing for the citizenship of heaven. It is my conviction that the very issues I have experienced and gone through, can only be expressed in bits and pieces, while leaving out names and places to protect those who had taken part in some of the unrighteous paths that have been walked as well as in lives that I have been privileged to acquire information. I want this book to begin with stories that show how Satan starts with subtle remarks, coy sayings that infiltrate the mind and sets the attack with the ultimate goal to destroy.

The stories within the pages ahead may make some gasp or become angry while some may laugh, but as the stories unfold, you must remember it all began with a war in heaven. That was where the lie originated within the perfect angel, Lucifer. He began rumors and gossiped while using his freedom of choice to have a desire to become like the Most High and overthrow the throne of the Living God. Lucifer boasted that he was going to exalt his throne above God. Then God speaks to His fallen angel in Isaiah 14:12-14 (NKJV).

> "'How you have fallen from heaven,
> O Lucifer, son of the morning!
> How you are cut down to the ground,
> you who weakened the nations!
> For you said in your heart; I
> will ascend into heaven,
> I will exalt my throne above the stars of God;
> I will sit on the mount of the congregation
> on the farthest sides of the north;
> I will ascend above the heights of the clouds,
> *I will be like the Most High.'"*

And the earth has trembled since that day when Lucifer with one third of the angels were cast out of heaven in a war that far surpasses any war fought on planet earth. It was not a war of guns and combat but a war of truth. A war that held unacceptable ideas that Lucifer started with a lie among angels who listened as he conveyed his own thoughts and ideas. A war against the Creator God and His authority.

In Revelation 12:7 (NKJV) it states, "Michael fought with the dragon." Michael is Jesus Christ, Himself and Lucifer became the dragon. It continues (verse 8), "they (the dragon and his angels did not prevail, nor was there a place found for them in heaven any longer." (V. 9), "So the great dragon was cast out, that serpent of old called the Devil and Satan who deceives the whole world, he was cast to the earth and his angels were cast out with him." Revelation 12:4 (NKJV) points out "He drew a third of the stars of heaven and threw them to the earth." This represents Satan's angels. One third of the angels of heaven who had been in the occupancy of heaven believed the lies of Lucifer, who now became the devil, Satan, the Dragon. So, these demons are on this earth raging the battle that still infiltrates the mind, in an intense conflict to take control of humans and their frailty Do we believe the lie, or do we trust God? "For the devil has come down to you, having great wrath, because he knows he has a short time" (Revelation 12:12 NKJV).

In the following pages I want to show you in terms of human interest that Satan can deceive even the very elect of God, if they should for a moment let go of His truth and take on another manifestation of a lie, just as it began in heaven and cause friends, loved ones, and even you, yourself to believe the lie and act on it. Once the action has been taken then it becomes a sin.

But we are not in this battle alone. This battle is far beyond what we can comprehend for in Ephesians 6:10-12 (NKJV) counsels "…be strong in the Lord and the power of His might. Put on the whole armor of God, that you may be able to stand against the wiles of the devil. For we do not fight against flesh and blood, but against principalities, against powers, against rulers of darkness of this age, against spiritual hosts of wickedness in heavenly places."

Our enemies are God's enemies. Yet, He shed His blood for each one and that is how the Christian must view the atrocities of each of the stories before us. I am hopefully intermingling Bible stories and corresponding them with stories of today that will awaken your imagination and inspire you to stand fast because this battle does not belong to you but to the Lord and He will go before you (I Samuel 17:47 b, II Chronicles 20:15 last part NKJV) if you listen to hear His still small voice and trust Him with all your heart. "That which has been what will be, that which is done is what will be done, and there is nothing new under the sun" Eccl 1:9 (NKJV).

ACKNOWLEDGEMENTS

My brother, Stanley M. Wetmore is an artist. He was given a talent by God that he uses with his tremendous imagination and creates artistry in many forms. He is the designer of the cover of this book, and he also drew the picture of Christ and the many forms of evil that are portrayed within the chapters. I am thankful for the talent he has and grateful to him for allowing me to use them in my book.

I am also grateful to Hillary Cuffori for her talent in making sure corrections were done and worked tirelessly in helping me to get this ready for publishing. She is a nurse who specializes in working with those suffering their last days in hospice. She is a talented, special woman God put in my path. Thank you, Hillary, for all you have done to help make this book a reality.

CHAPTER ONE

Malicious Accusations

"Oh, the tangled web we weave when we practice to deceive!"
(Walter Scott)

The sun was beautifully shining this particular day in May and spring was in the air. There had been three consecutive chilly days, which was unusual for mid-May. Roberta was putting all her burdens behind her today and planned on a good day because each day is the beginning of forever. She started out on her school bus run and one of her eighth-grade boys wanted to know if he could come over to her house and spend the day with her brother, who was close to his age, as they were having a field trip this day and he didn't want to go. Roberta asked, "Is this okay with your folks?" This boy was under his sister's guardianship, just like her brother was with her, and he answered, "My sister doesn't mind, if it is alright with you." Roberta replied, "If you come to my house, you have to work." He retorted in astonishment, "Work?" She responded back at him. "That's the deal, I have a bus that needs cleaning, and it would be helpful if you and my brother could clean it for me, as I have a kindergarten field trip tomorrow." He whined again, "Aw, come on, work?" "That's the deal," she repeated. "If you don't work you don't stay," the requirement was reinforced.

It was several stops later and one of the pick-ups was a friend of this particular boy. When he hopped on the bus, he looked at his friend and asked, grinning ear to ear, "Is it all set?" Jimmy affirmed, "Yeh, but we have to work." Paul. Retorted, "I don't care, I will do anything as long as I don't have to go to that boring field trip." Roberta's first run was finished except for the few stragglers that were going to her house to work, and she continued for the second run as she didn't have time to argue with these boys who were determined to get out of the "boring field trip!" The second run was finished, and she was heading home with the bus as her son was home from school with a bellyache. She needed to see how he was doing.

On her way home, the bus started acting up, and she thought it might be the power steering as it was getting difficult to turn the steering wheel and it took all she had to maneuver it. Once she was home and inside, she called the bus garage and relayed the message to the mechanic on duty. He relayed the message to her boss, who was on his way in town to the inner cities. She heard his voice boom back over the two-way radio to the mechanic, "Tell her to get the bus back to the garage!" She timidly asked if the bus would be ready for the kindergarten run and again heard the grumpy answer, "I don't know, she will have to wait until I get back." Roberta called out to her school skippers, "Come on boys, "I must take the bus over to the bus garage. If they get it fixed in time, you can clean it for me when, we get back." The boys got in the bus quite disappointed. Her brother stayed home with her son. When she arrived at the bus garage, the mechanic said the school called and wanted her to call back. "Which one?" she questioned since her son was home sick.

"Local," he answered. She called and asked for the principal. Roberta affirmed who she was, and the principal asked, "Did Paul and Jimmy take your bus today?" A lump formed in her throat, and she thought, "Oh no, the boys are in trouble." She did not think ahead to the consequences for herself. She was thinking of the boys, and she heard herself say, "No, they didn't." The principal echoed back her answer, "They didn't?" He continued, "Then I will have to notify their parents, as they are missing."

She walked over to her van where the boys were happily waiting and tore down their sunshine. She let them know of the conversation she had with the principal. Paul turned white and said frantically, "I have to get back to the school now." Roberta agreed and took him back and dropped him off.

She looked at Jimmy and asked, "How about you?" He answered, "No, my sister knows where I am, and I am staying." Roberta was now leery of their answers, and questioned again, "Are you sure?" He answered quite assuredly, "Yeh, I told her I was coming over and spend the day with your brother, my buddy." She felt at ease and answered with a sigh of relief, "Okay." She dropped Jimmy off with her brother and went back to the local restaurant to have coffee with a friend. It was 10 a.m. and she knew she would have to start the bus run in an hour. That didn't leave her much time to get anything done at home. Roberta had her brother and his buddy busy grinding laundry and straightened up the living room, while listening to her son complain about his belly, however he was able to devour a bowl of cereal in a single bound. That was most likely how he acquired his bellyache.

The phone rang, she answered and the voice on the other end, asked, "Is Jimmy there?" Roberta answered, "Yes, he is and handed the phone to him. Listening to his end of the conversation, she could tell that his sister did not know he was at her house. The principal had called her, and it wasn't long before his sister, tore into Roberta's yard. She went to speak with her. Their conversation was not an unpleasant one, in fact they discovered that Jimmy had only told a half truth, which is a lie no matter how you look at it. The devil always tells half-truths and makes it sound like it is okay when it really isn't.

Before Roberta made it back to the bus garage, her boss called her and asked some pointed questions. She could tell by the tone of his voice he was ready to read her the riot act. They got through round one, and then he switched gears on her and told her to take Bus # 9, and then went back to what they had been discussing. He asked, "what is going on anyway?" Their conversation ended abruptly as Roberta had to go on her bus run. During her route she heard her boss' voice crackle over the two-way radio, "Bus 9, your bus is finished, stop in here before you leave."

When she returned to the bus garage, she parked the bus and walked apprehensively to his house. As she reached the door, he called from inside for her to come in. He seemed to have a different demeanor about him. He had a softness in his voice and gently asked her to sit down. As she sat down, she said, "That bad huh?" He nodded his head in affirmation. He began to unfold the charges from Paul's mother, such as kidnapping, abducting, seducing, and molesting her son. He was serious as he spoke, and Roberta sat with mouth agape in stunned shock.

"Kidnapping, abducting and what?" she blurted. It seems the principal was adding insult to injury with innuendos of smearing her character that since she was a divorced woman and may be involved with lurking after innocent boys' bodies that have hardly been weaned from their mother's breast. Roberta could feel the heat on her face flush from anger, hurt and absolute horror as her boss placed the facts before her with gentleness. He counseled that she couldn't fight "city hall" and rather than to be raked over the coals, and stripped of all self-respect, she should quietly bow out of the situation, and he would cover her tracks until the dust settled.

She was still in a state of disbelief and bewilderment as she left that afternoon for her last bus run. She watched each child as they got off the bus and it took all the stamina within her to hold back the tears as she bid each child goodbye. They didn't know it was good-bye. A lump had formed in her throat, while her heart was shattered. She loved those noisy, troublesome kids that were so full of life. School bus driving was her life, waving to different people and exchanging familiarities with parents she saw each day, came to a screeching halt and a bitter end.

This was a silent verdict within an empty courtroom that had no trial. Not once was she faced with her accuser. Not since that day has any kind of repercussions ever taken place pertaining to that day, and no word since then to confirm or deny that it ever took place. She was asked why didn't she fight this? She had just been set free from an abusive marriage and was in the valley of low self-esteem. She felt worthless and the accusations against her seemed too harsh to overcome. She felt she had no recourse because who would believe her, a divorced woman who couldn't hold her marriage together?

Her boss made it sound so ominous, a man of means and influence didn't think there was any recourse for her, so she felt she had no choice. "While the world is progressing in wickedness, none of us need flatter ourselves that we shall have no difficulties. But it is these very difficulties that bring us into the audience chamber of the Most High. We may seek counsel of One who is infinite in wisdom" (Christ's Object Lessons, p. 172 by E.G. White).

Roberta had to believe that God was going to open a door for her, and all she had to do was wait on Him, as difficult as it may seem and it was...but in His time, "All things (would) work together for good to those who love God and are called according to His purpose" Romans 8:28 (NKJV).

CHAPTER TWO

Flirting with Sin

"That which it offers may please the eye and fascinate the
senses, but it proves unsatisfying.
The wine turns to bitterness, the gaiety to gloom.
That which was begun with songs and mirth ends in
weariness and disgust"
(Desire of Ages by EG White, page 143).

What do you fall in love with when you sleep with the enemy of your soul? The flashing flutter of eyelids, the intimacy that sends thrills of touching and exploring the untouchable, and the sin becomes comfortable and no longer feels like sin. Many find themselves in a rebound situation and take on a relationship with the attachment ov lust and sin is the underlying factor that rears its ugly head.

Jennifer, now divorced, became infatuated with the murmurings and the cooing's of the man who would spiral her life into despair. She had no intentions of marriage, after all she had been in an unfaithful, marriage and now her captivity was over, and she was about to embark on another adventure, and it didn't involve marriage. Yet, she desired the attention of the other sex, and it was a lustful attraction that left her in a controversy of her moral values and her desire to be loved. He held an attraction of spirituality she wanted to endorse but he was also judgmental of her beliefs and voiced them.

He had redeemed his former habits and had begun smoking and using marijuana. This was against what Jennifer was ever part of and against what she believed to be right. Often, she accompanied him as he visited family members and friends who also took part in this practice. They would come together to watch a movie on the television and during the program they would begin to laugh hilariously over nothing at all or stay in stymied silence! Everything was a delayed reaction. When Jennifer would try to reason their behavior, they would come back at her with "don't knock it if you haven't tried it."

Then came the fateful day when Jennifer became angry with her lover over something that was said, or he had done. Somehow his sister became involved in the situation and there was the voice of sympathy. Satan is always ready to condone sin and then condemn you for being taken in by it. She said, "Let's go to the Lounge for a drink." In Jennifer's anger, she thought this would teach Victor a lesson that she didn't need his insults or whatever else he handed out, went along with her and sat at a small round table, while his sister ordered a black Russian drink. Jennifer was unfamiliar with what this drink had in it but sat sipping on the liquor and when her friendship with his sister seemed more in harmony, then Satan went in for the kill. "Aw come on, have a cigarette." Jennifer had given up smoking seven years prior, yet her anger was still seething with emotion, and she quickly snatched it up and inhaled deeply as her comrade of sympathy lit it for her. Funny how we think we are hurting the one that has hurt us when we fall into the trap of temptation just for a minute.

If that wasn't bad enough Jennifer decided to try marijuana. When she finally returned home and found Victor there and he saw her light up a cigarette, he really gloated that she had become a puffer, while laughing that she had fallen from grace. Her anger became defensive and embittered by the demons that make one feel like they are in their rights to retaliate and begin to dig the ditch of sin deeper. He offered her a hit off a joint he had just acquired. They laid down on the bed and while laying down and basking in the sinful adventure, Jennifer instantly felt strange. Her throat began to feel dry. It was so dry, she couldn't swallow, or even find any saliva to moisten her throat. It was as if it was swollen shut.

Simultaneously, it was as if she were looking down at herself lying on the bed and could not move. She felt her breathing begin to stop as soon as this happened. Victor recognized her condition immediately, and he dragged her off the bed and down over the stairs. She felt like a rag doll that had no control over her limbs. He poured milk into her mouth trying to force her to swallow. He continued frantically to bring her out of this trance that had overtaken her and since he had used drugs in the past, he quickly realized the joint had been laced with PCP (angel dust) and he was aware of the symptoms. He doused her face first into the watery snow that had been melting. Jennifer was aware but had no voice to speak. There was nothing she could do to bring herself out of this state of mind she was in. She was in a hallucinating grip that left her in fear of dying.

He placed her in his vehicle and within the twenty-minute drive to the emergency room she watched the snowbanks on each side of the road, which seemed to be closing in as they traveled and became fearful that they would not make it through such a narrow opening. It was on the last couple of miles before reaching the hospital that she finally was able to speak and breathe normally. She never made it to the emergency room but by the grace of God she was set free from that horrible curse created by her own anger. It had become the battlefield within her mind, which placed her in a situation of near death. Yet, God never let go of her even within her sinful state of mind.

CHAPTER THREE

"You Shall Not Surely Die"

"Now the serpent was more cunning
than any beast of the field…"
Genesis 3:1 (NKJV}.

A serpent is a large and usually poisonous snake. God created the Garden of Eden, and everything was perfect because God does not create anything that isn't perfect. The air was crystal clear, and the animals were flawless. Adam and Eve lived in a perfect environment. The sky was always cloudless, and the sun was always sparkling—never too hot and never too cold. There was much to be attended to, for Adam and Eve had to be sure the animals were named and cared for. They probably played with the lions and laughed with the hyenas. There was no need for fear of any sort because they had the presence of God and visited with Him every day when He came to the Garden in the "cool of the day" (Genesis 3:8 NKJV).

They had access to every fruit and vegetation within the Garden, but they were not to take of any of the fruit from the Tree of Good and Evil within the midst of the Garden called the Tree of Knowledge (Genesis 2:17 NKJV). They could eat of any tree from the garden except the tree within the midst of the garden! So why with all the perfect things in the Garden, would God put one thing that they were not to touch? It was a test to obey God or not. Basically, that was it! Simple. It was there within all the perfection of the Garden that the serpent lurked. It wasn't an ugly snake but probably had multiple colors and transparent wings, and its beauty was spectacular, along with the fact he spoke, which made the serpent even more intriguing and possessing a greater ability to deceive.

It seems Eve wandered away from Adam and that is another story of straying too far away from your mate and not being attentive to their needs. The allure of the serpent can come in many forms, and it has materialized in many manifestations down through the ages. As the serpent spoke and they had a conversation concerning the fruit of the tree "in the midst of the garden," the serpent enticed Eve in his craftiness to believe a lie and she fell for it. Satan's form of beauty with convincing knowledge and impressive reasoning enticed Eve with dangerous thoughts. She hadn't wandered far from Adam but was far enough away to be mesmerized with the subtle conversation with the snake.

Communication is key and is what brings two together in the first place. Of course, there are always mitigating circumstances that are in every story and rationalization or extenuating circumstances that unfold, but they all began with believing a lie. After all, this was how a third of the angels were cast out of heaven and so Satan was on a mission to prove God wrong, since he knew full well the Word of God was true and God does not change. Since Satan, himself became the fallen angel, tossed out of heaven, devoid of God's grace because he made war with God and became the prince of this world, Eve gave in.

The fruit looked luscious and in fact it looked better than all the other trees in the garden. It was plumper, and juicier. It had a color about it which was more brilliant than all the other fruit. Yet, she heard the echo of the words from God that were repeated in her ears, "Do not touch or eat of the tree in the midst of the garden or you will surely die" (Genesis 3:3 NKJV).

That was unbelievable as she listened to the serpent's convincing purr that she would be made wise. Her husband, Adam was close by but instead of counseling with him and asking, "What do you think?" she went ahead and took the fruit and passed it to Adam (Genesis 3:6 NKJV). The command from God was not to even touch it, let alone eat it and her hand had already touched it, and she had not been struck dead yet! Well maybe, just maybe this serpent knew what he was talking about. So, without further thought on the subject—I mean what would one bite do? She took the first bite and Adam joined her.

Today, all it takes is one piece of candy to lead to a whole bag, or one drink of alcohol to enter alcoholism, or one extra helping to continue into gluttony. It only takes one moment of self to end up in selfishness. What was Adam thinking? There they were "in the midst of the garden." She was talking to this serpent. Everything happened so fast. He could have said "No Eve, don't do it. Remember what God has said." But he did not. Eve, his beautiful Eve, disobeyed God, and there was nothing he could do about it. Well, that was another lie. He loved Eve so much he would rather die with her than to lose her. God could have created another mate for Adam had he not given in and believed that there was no other alternative. There is always a way of escape from a temptation if we trust God and wait for Him to do His good will and pleasure in us. Always. So, Eve's sin was believing a lie and Adam's sin was believing God couldn't do anything about it. From that day forward sin entered this earth. The curse was pronounced on us who live under the curse and struggle to keep God's commandments and trust Him no matter what. It was from that moment on that the leaves began to wilt and die on the branches, that flowers faded in their color and lost their radiant beauty within a short time. And the effects of life changed from that day forward and from that day to this it has become worse as time has progressed.

A lie is a lie is a lie and a sin is a sin is a sin. You can't change it and if we do not repent, we will surely die the death of damnation. But there is the merciful love of God still waiting to transform, renew and to be born again so that we may enjoy the benefits of heaven and never again be seduced by the lie that once began in heaven. God is preparing a people that will trust Him regardless of the circumstances so that He knows that heaven, itself, will be safe from ever having that lie manifest again. Its occupants will be able to have their citizenship where God is the God of His people.

CHAPTER FOUR

"Blind Faith or Delusional Sacrifice"

"You shall therefore keep My statutes and My judgments, which if a man does, he shall live by them; I am the Lord" Leviticus 18:5 (NKJV).

Sarai had no children and there didn't seem to be any hope of having any. Yet, God had promised Abram that he would have a child to be his heir and Abram would be the father of many nations. Sarai and Abram didn't quite understand the process of God or how He was going to give them a son when they were way past childbearing years, so the decision was made by Sarai for Abram to take her Egyptian maidservant and have a child with her. In other words, for her to be a surrogate for Sarai since Sarai could not have children and once the child was born it was Sarai's thought that she would obtain children through her handmaiden *(Genesis 16:2 NKJV)*.

When we take things into our own hands and think we are helping God out by making our own rules and putting them into place, there is always a catastrophe ahead. But here we go again with Satan standing nearby to make sure God's plan failed. When Hagar, the Egyptian handmaiden conceived Abram's child, then there was animosity between the two women and jealousy arose. It was not a pretty picture. Abram had failed God's test of patience and waiting on Him. But God always has an alternate plan ready. Once we realize our mistake and ask for forgiveness, things can go forward with the divine detour provided.

The Obsession of Flesh and Blood

None of the following weeks made any sense and the lapse of time just blurred from one day to the next with no sequence of days or nights. They were all run together. Jenny didn't sleep and when she did it was fitful and ended by waking in tears. Food was a thing to stay alive. There was no enjoyment in eating and swallowing became a conscious effort. Within her mind she kept hearing, "You must eat to live." It was difficult to swallow so she would massage her throat to get the food to go down. She had forgotten how to pray or even that for which to pray. Her children bounced in and out of the house with their own agenda and no one seemed to understand or realize the emotional pain she was experiencing. Motherhood did not seem to be doing a particularly good job.

Her daughter had once been involved in spiritualism and its unsanctified influence left her in a battle against evil that she was not aware of, and it seemed no one else really understood the effects of its deeply indulgent results. The Ouija Board was just a game, or was it? Her daughter flaunted herself continuously in front of her stepfather and gleefully taunting her mother with words that cut deeply. Jenny overheard her whisper in seductive tones to her stepfather, "My mother can't give you a baby, but I can." She would display her own baby pictures to him and teasingly coo to him what a child of theirs would look like. She was sweet sixteen and her laugh became anything but sweet.

Jenny's own daughter, her own flesh and blood. Jenny's knight in shining armor became increasingly belligerent toward her. He was becoming obsessed with having his own "flesh and blood" child. Jenny's faith was waning and there seemed to be no faith at all. Plots and whispers were beginning to be put into action slowly and every strategy in their mind came out as a purified reason that this was the right way to go. As bizarre as it all seemed her thoughts were not considered.

Jenny's sanity was threatened, and her life was being manipulated. The man she felt was her savior of sorts had reasoned along with her daughter that the Bible account of Abram, Sarai, and Hagar in Genesis 16 made this theory okay. In the Biblical account Abram took Sarai's handmaiden, Hagar to have the promised child since Sarai was barren. Now Jenny was barren since she had her uterus removed due to a disease that claimed her ability to bear more children.

As the account continues Hagar became despised in the eyes of Sarai and had to flee from Sarai's face as her child was not intended as the promised child. Jenny was manipulated into being the intercessor in the action of transferal of sperm. Jenny had presence of mind enough to convince her daughter that this was wrong, and she should keep the secret that the transferal of sperm did not take place.

Then all of Jenny's worst fears materialized. All the kids were somewhere with friends, except her oldest. She had run away and of course "the deliverer" had to find her to rescue her. Jenny's other daughter confided in her mother that she thought this had been planned. After all Number One was captivated with "the deliverer" and was certain he would go after her. She thrived on his attention and would do anything to secure it.

What does one do when God is not in the center of your life and the world throws you a curve ball? Well, you take matters in your own hands and find a place to drown your sorrows and lick your wounds. A good bottle of coffee brandy and a long drive. A quiet spot next to the lake where boys were laughing while riding bicycles and men were fishing, people laughing, talking, and visiting. The world was careening on a collision course and Jenny was in the middle of it. The water was peaceful, lapping ripples against the shoreline that spelled solace.

Earlier her screams had been so loud she was sure the heavens would move out of their course and maybe, God would hear her. After all He heard Hagar when she cried alone in the deserted place. But that was then, and this is now, and no one heard her screams, and she was certain God didn't either.

Then The Promised Son Was Born

Eventually Abram had Isaac by Sarai, even though he also had Ishmael by Hagar. God blessed both children. Then Abram became Abraham and Sarai became Sarah. God gave them these names signifying their heritage of being the "father of many nations" promised by God in *Genesis 17 NKJV* and Sarah being the "mother of nations."

Isaac was born and became a strong boy, obedient to his father. He had a willing heart and was trained to keep the commandments of God. It was early in the morning when Abraham packed up and headed north for Mount Moriah. He heard God's voice and knew it was God speaking to him since he was very familiar with His voice and there was no mistaking God's command. When you hear God's voice once, you never forget it. God had promised that Abraham's descendants would number as the stars in the sky. And now since He made good on His Promise, God, Himself was asking Abraham to sacrifice his only son to Him on an altar. It was clear "*...Take your son, your only son, Isaac, whom you love, and go to the land of Moriah, and offer him there as a burnt offering on one of the mountains of which I will tell you" Genesis 22:2 (NKJV).*

Have you ever asked yourself, "Didn't Abraham question God's sanity?" Didn't he say, "But God, I will do this for You or that for You but not my son, my beloved son!" After all, wouldn't any good parent try to put their own life ahead of their child?

It seems that it wasn't uncommon for a ritual in the Canaanite practice to offer their first born to a deity. But God prohibited such a practice as stated in *Leviticus 18:21 (NKJV)*. The bottom line was God was testing Abraham because Abraham had messed up a few times before—first with giving in and having a child with Hagar and then earlier sending his wife off to Abimelech, King of Gerar, and saying it was his sister! Fortunately, the hand of God moved to save Sarai from a sinful interlude as God came to Abimelech in a dream and told him the truth so that he never touched Sarah! What was Abraham thinking?

In checking out the Hebrew word "nissah" we learn that it has many forms meaning to test, prove, and to be tried, which are all various combined forms of the word tempt. So, we can safely conclude that God was testing Abraham's faith.

We become "wise in our own eyes" (Proverbs *3:7 NKJV)* and take matters into our own hands, when we are listening to the voice of the enemy and not waiting on the Lord. We then are suffering the consequences of our sin have all faced the consequences of our practices and found ourselves in a position of blind faith or delusional sacrifice. What is your most prized possession that you would have to give up if God asked you to. Would it be your job, your marriage, your home, your career, your savings, or your children?

I am sure Abraham wasn't sleeping very well. What have you done when you had nights you couldn't sleep? When my children were little, I used to tiptoe through the house and in their rooms and watch them sleep with tender thoughts and wondered if they would ever understand their mother. Would my mistakes become their curse? I have looked out into the darkness of the vast sky dotted with stars and prayed to the God of my parents, my God and reached out to grasp something that I couldn't touch or feel, yet I must trust for answers. I am sure Abraham was not much different. He probably looked at his sleeping son and agonized over the unknown and then his wife...could he tell her, did he? If he told her, she may think he was delusional and fight him on it. He must go forward and remember that God would give back whatever he may lose and be prepared to meet the test.

I believe that Abraham rehearsed and reviewed his life and all his mistakes rationalizing everything. I am sure he thought back on the many conversations he had with God and how God's hand had been over him time and time again. Satan was right there making sure Abraham doubted Jehovah and questioned everything and would fail this test too! I am sure he thought back on those mistakes and realized his thoughts certainly fell into the pit of despair and what he felt was right and turned out to be a horrible mistake. God doesn't ask us to do anything without a reason no matter how unreasonable it may seem.

It was a long hike to the land of Moriah and with rough calculations and the help of a Bible map, I guesstimated it to be 70-80 miles from his home. It was three days' travel over treacherous terrain. Abraham had taken two male servants with him and Isaac. They had an ass packed with firewood for the offering and all that they needed except the sacrifice.

There were no grazing lands nearby to have a lamb or other offering supplied. But no one spoke a word. It was a silent walk. I am sure Abraham was doing the heaviest thinking. He was probably going over and over in his mind, "have I heard God, right?" or just delusional thinking? He had to make the decision to do as God had asked or accept his own reasoning.

God promised to designate the exact location and just ahead of them was the cloud of glory hovering over the mountain, the place of sacrifice. This was where the journey stopped with blistered feet in dusty sandals and an aching heart. The same situation in another century and here we are—"If God is for us who can be against us? (*Romans 8:31 NKJV)*. If our actions are for the benefit of others, regardless of what anyone may think, we must remember, God can restore. He can replenish. He can give back. It is His timing.

Maybe Isaac glanced up at his father with that childlike innocence with a smile that reflected trust. After all, he had been on many treks with his father to distant altars that his dad erected along the way during his wanderings. There was always a story to tell at each one. Even at Abraham's age there was no weakness in his countenance, no faltering, no murmuring. Even though he was carrying a burdensome weight that overshadowed the secret he was carrying, deep down he believed God would bring Isaac back to life and restore the sacrifice. This was counted to him as righteousness (Romans 4:3 & James 2:23 NKJV).

What is counted as righteousness for you? Trusting God, no matter what? Standing up against the enemy and his lies and refuting all that he says no matter how convincing it may be? Stepping out of your comfort zone into the realm of impossibilities, enduring the unthinkable in situations you have had it with and want it to end now?

Now Isaac breaks the silence as they part from the two male servants and head up to the last decent of the mountain. *"My father! ...the fire and the wood but where is the lamb for a burnt offering?"* Genesis 22:7 (NKJV). Abraham answered with tears in his voice (I am sure), (v8) *"My son, God will provide for Himself the lamb for the burnt offering."* Abraham's heart must have melted to hear such trust in his son's voice accepting implicitly his father's answer as they finished their journey.

The final scene unveils. The moment Abraham must tell his son that he is the sacrifice; What did he say? The Bible doesn't say but we can speculate that it may have gone something like this, "You are my seed, and you were given to your mother and I as a promise from God in our old age. You were a gift, and this is just a test. God will restore your life back to me because there is nothing impossible with God and He has asked me to give you as the sacrificial offering."

Isaac could have run or argued the point or even overpowered his aging father, but his faith and trust was as complete as his father's was in God. To lose a child due to a dreaded disease, SIDS, or a tragic accident, even a separation of denial with hostilities which are a piercing, gripping pain for any parent to endure. Abraham had faith while raising the knife to take his own child's life and to expect it to be restored with a faith that blindly has not any tangible evidence of happening is a scene that heaven must have gasped to watch. The heart wrenching sobs, the moans of agony as Abraham bound his precious son on the altar, we can only imagine for there is no account of that scene.

When my grandson was found in his crib in the arms of death at two months old, I watched my own son grow cold inside as he lost hope in Jesus to restore his son in the earth made new. Still, I clutched in faith that the sacrifice made at Calvary on the hill known as Golgotha was not in vain and the sting of death will not be the victory, for *"God so loved the world that He gave His only begotten Son, that whosoever believes in Him should not perish but have everlasting life" (John 3:16 NKJV).* Isn't it amazing that from Mount Moriah just a little further to the northwest is the hill of Golgotha? This was where the true sacrifice was made in faith to redeem all who believe and trust God for everlasting life and rebuke the devil and his lies.

There were tears of utter joy, when the arm was raised with the knife clenched in his hand and the Voice of God was unmistakably heard, *"Do not lay your hand on the lad or do anything to him; for now, that I know you fear God, since you have not withheld your son, your only son from Me" (Genesis 22:12 NKJV).*

"Then Abraham lifted his eyes and looked, and there behind him was a ram caught in the thicket by the horns. So, Abraham went and took the ram and offered it up as a burnt offering instead of his son" (Verse 13 NKJV). Have you gone through a trial that was the consequence of a sin from listening to Satan's lie? And on your way up to the mountain to give your burnt offering of whatever the Lord had asked you to give, are you sure there will be a ram in the thicket for you? And what if there isn't? Are you still willing to let go of what you felt was irreplaceable? You will have to answer that for yourself. You don't lose with God. The blind delusional faith is willing to wait, willing to give it all, willing to be tested and willing to accept God's will

BLIND FAITH

When you cry out fervently, "Oh my God."
When you press for His answer, the sign of His nod,
For this test, this trial seems to be more than you can bear,
And you plead, don't you understand? Don't You care?
Oh yes, He cares for you are a child of the King,
And He has asked for your burdens and requests to bring,
Accompanied by blind faith that can do anything,
As you empty your dreams before Him and in praises sing.
Come to the mountain and place the cherished gift,
Upon the altar of sacrifice and let your burdens lift.
For the Covenant Keeping God will give back and supply,
For He can restore, and He does not lie.
When the waters of affliction begin to rise high,
He promised they would not overpower me; I would not die.
When he asked me to give up all that I dream,
He promised He would strengthen me, He would redeem.
In tears of sorrow for myself, I finally let it all go,
I decided to wait and prove His Word
till my heart would know.
And His promises were made good, and His peace returned.
The lesson in faith, He gave was well learned,
For you cannot second guess the Voice of His Word.
Just reach out and touch what your heart has heard.
He grants the extra measure of faith to all who touch.
His children, His heirs for whom He loves so much.
By Joyce A. Leonard August 13, 1999

CHAPTER FIVE

"Friendly Fire Within the Church"

*"Be Kind to one another, tender-hearted, forgiving one another,
Even as God in Christ has forgiven you"*
Ephesians 4:25 (NKJV).

So many who walk in the front door of the church are excited to take their baptismal vow into the watery grave of acceptance into Christ Jesus, the absolute epitome of love and acceptance, forgiveness, and hope. Let's not forget the hope that we will one day see our Savior face to face. It isn't long after this transpires that the nurturing and acceptance of the self-righteous member's rule book begins to spiral into seeing the "speck" of some sinful act in the newly adopted brother or sister forgetting the log in their own eye! Now comes their infinite power to overrule, and control as they unwittingly become Satan's advocate within the church.

Friendly fire is one who sweetly says, "You should sit in the back of the church with your children so that you don't disrupt the service by their actions." Friendly fire is the one well-intentioned member who says, "you have become deaf to the humming of your child during the church service, and it is annoying." Friendly fire is when you attend a conservative church that shuns jewelry and gaudiness of any form and sees a younger member of the church whose husband left her and she grieves their separation, so wears his wedding band on a chain around her neck. Then whispers begin. And what about the friendly fire of another young woman who runs to those in leadership with emotional pain in her heart, pleading for them to pray with her for her wayward husband and is met with the remark, "He made his bed now let him lay in it."

Friendly fire is when you are working for Jesus within the church for the good of others and the love of God when another member takes advantage of your good virtues and steals your talent and makes it theirs then lets you know of your many mistakes. Friendly fire comes in many forms and when it happens, the child of God is slowly, methodically, being attacked by the enemy within the church, under the "friendly fire" of the very brother or sister that you have trusted.

Without being grounded in the Word of God and trusting Him regardless, that dear member can slowly leave the church feeling disgraced, unwanted, and invaluable and isolated from the church and God. Throughout the years, the one quote that continues to manifest itself is, "Don't look at the people, keep focused on Jesus." But with all respect to those who say this, at one time or another, when we are babies in the church, it is the people, the leaders in the church that nurture us to know our loving Jesus and see how He endures the "friendly fire" of those who nailed Him to the cross. Because they believed they were doing the right thing, getting rid of this heretic who was demeaning their control and changing the attitude of the church, putting love first and forgetting that all the avenues of darkness are not done away with in one day when you take on the baptism and die to self in the watery grave. Now you are falling prey to the enemy and moving under Satan's control. Isn't that what those within the church do when they are not standing firm in the love of God and can only see the mistakes?

"...in Christ Jesus, you who were once away, have been brought near by the Blood of Christ. (v.14) For He, Himself is our peace, who has made the two one, and has destroyed the barrier, the dividing wall of hostility. (v.16) in part—...to reconcile both to God through the cross, by which He put to death their hostility" Ephesians 2:13-1 (NKJV).

Jesus, Himself underwent the "friendly fire" within the church by being about His Father's business. In *Matthew Chapter 23* Jesus condemns the scribes and the Pharisees by their hypocritical attitudes. It is the love, the unconditional love of God that changes the world including those within the church. After all, the church is just a "hospital for sinners."

It seems when you live in an unjust situation and each day you are reminded of the evil lurking at your doorstep even with the very ones you love and trust, it is often difficult to separate their sins and their behavior from the person themselves.

Remember that it was the absolute sacrifice of Christ Who gave His life to save each of us who fall from grace, yet we are under the attack of the demons who take control of the bitterness that drips and the ever-present resentment that manifests itself. Without realizing it you begin to walk in the bitterness and become paralyzed to what is really happening. Resentment continues to mount, and you begin to wade in a pool of disgust, anger filled with self-righteousness. You have now become like the Pharisees within the church. The very ones Jesus dealt with and called "friend."

The enemy has grasped hold of you with his claws and punctured your heart so you cannot feel anything but your pain. In that pain, you lash out and can respond only with characterized cynicism because you want others to hurt like you are even if they have not caused your pain to begin with. One wrong word or action and revenge stirs within the heart that has for a moment lost sight of His sacrificial love.

A friend I knew who battled with this, once said, "I searched the whole Bible through, and nowhere did it say I had the right to vengeance." Yet, the cycle continues to recycle until the day you allow the bitterness to empty with repentant tears and cry—O God, forgive me! Jesus called His enemies "friend" even to those within the "friendly fire" of the church. So, my Father, forgive those who have hurt me and help me to forgive them, too.

Help me to see beyond the attack realizing they also are in desperate need of healing, for they too feel the effects of Satan's lies and have fallen prey.

"THE FACE OF GOD"

I saw gentleness carved within the lines of His face.
I saw the laughter sparkling through
the eyes that had found Grace.
I saw long-suffering mingled within His tears.
I saw goodness displayed as the value of His years.
I saw peace wrapped up among all of these,
For He encountered God each day upon His knees.
Look to the wise who confess their strength from above.
Look to the meek and lowly who display the virtues of love.
Watch the frame of one who walks with Him,
And listen to the voice of witness that doesn't falter or dim.
My friend, you will clearly see abroad—
And recognize the face of God.
The same Spirit that sanctifies the life of a fallen soul,
Can transform the body with the Spirit's control.
The Savior calls, "Come unto me, those weary of heart."
Relinquish your burdens and from evil depart,
So, you may reflect among others where your footsteps trod,
That you have witnessed the face of God.
By Joyce A. Leonard ~ April 25, 1998

CHAPTER SIX

Blessing or a Curse?

*"To know wisdom and understanding, to
perceive words of understanding
To receive instruction of wisdom, justice, judgment, and equity.
Proverbs 1:1-3 (NKJV).*

There he was just waiting to be set free to go outside. His big eyes seemed to be pleading with me to just let him go. He reached up and batted the doorknob with his huge paw and gave me the most pathetic cry. I reasoned with myself that I just couldn't let him out. I had just lost a beloved pet to the dangers of the road. I couldn't bear to risk losing this one that came into our lives just a week and a half ago. I gave him food and shelter, comfort, and lots of love, yet it didn't seem to be enough. He was already two years old when he became part of our lived. He was a Maine Coon cat, already weighing 14 lbs.

It occurred to me as I stood there with hand on the doorknob and lump in my throat, caught between should I or shouldn't I, that our Savior must have a similar dilemma. When one of His children has tasted the pleasure of sin and want, to continue in that lifestyle, He lets them go, for He has given them the freedom of choice.

My precious cat wanted to go out. He wanted his freedom because he had had his freedom before he came to live with us, and it was calling him back. No amount of coddling and provision seemed to matter. So silently, I prayed "Lord, take care of Higgins. Bring him back safely each time." God answered that prayer . . . . of faith and watched over my cat until he had feline shutdown acquired from old age and I had to have him put to sleep.

God gave him a second chance to live for 16 more years. He gives you and I a second chance to life each day. Sometimes we are aware of it and sometimes we aren't. We seemed to become more aware of what the value of life is when we have had a near death experience or if a tragedy has occurred and sets us to thinking what our real priorities are in life. How often do we approach daily life with the concept that each day is a new beginning a second chance? How often is the new beginning held sacred?

We are on probation waiting for the finalization of earth's history and the return of Jesus Christ. And what does the Bible say to do while we wait for that event? *"Those who sow in tears shall reap in joy. He who continually goes forth weeping, bearing seed for sowing, shall doubtless come again with rejoicing, bringing his sheaves with him" Psalms 126: 5 & 6 (NKJV).* Yes, they work hard and sometimes the planting of the seeds can be a strain, but the harvest is worth the time and effort.

In the book, <u>Early Writings</u> by EG White page 17 is penned, *"We tried to call up our greatest trials, but they looked so small compared with the far more exceeding and eternal weight in glory that surrounded us that we could not speak to them out, and we all cried out 'Alleluia, heaven is cheap enough!'"* Anyone placed on probation under an officer of the Court is required to report periodically plus they have a certain set of rules that must be adhered to, or they can be found in violation of those rules and be returned to jail for violating them. There is no freedom to come and go as they may choose, only if given special permission.

God allows us freedom of choice, even though we are under probationary risks to serve the world and its prince of darkness if that is our choice. Many want both ends and the middle. They want to hold Christ on one hand and still have their way with the fellowship of the world on the other. Only obedience to God is the true sign of discipleship.

If you profess Christ and Him only and He calls on you to serve, then you must be ready to do as you are called no matter where it takes you, or what you are called to do for there is no running away when you have claimed to be a child of the King.

Balaam thought he could run away like Jonah and David. God called them and others like them to do His work not because they were so important that He couldn't do without them, but because He loves us, He uses the special talents He has given each one of us to be the heavenly influence on the people around us that have not had the experience of meeting an angel in the roadway, or sitting in the belly of a great fish or falling prostrate in deep contrition after a deadly sin was committed or even when I decided to walk in my own willful way.

Let's begin. Balaam's name means to "swallow up," or to "violently destroy." And Balak means "devastator"; "to ravage" or "to wreak havoc by violent destructive action." Balak was king over the Moabites. The Moabites were afraid of the Children of Israel because they saw what they had done to the Amorites and there were many of them! King Balak was

Unleashed Promises of Merciful Love

a follower of darkness. He believed in black magic and devil possession. Even though he practiced these arts in idolatry, he realized he needed more than human help to get rid of these Israelites that had come up out of Egypt and had humbled even the great Pharaoh, himself! He had heard about the effective powers of Balaam. The Moabites and the Midianites were traditionally enemies but when it came to the Children of Israel, they were in sync and united as they plotted together a scheme to destroy them. This whole course of action was just a form of good business in their behalf. They were prepared to approach Balaam with an offer that would be hard to resist if he would just come and place a curse on Israel for them. After all, it wasn't kosher to ask a favor without being prepared to pay handsomely for the deed.

Balaam had been a true prophet of God. You could say, he was sort of running away from his calling by using the talent God had given him for perversion in worldly gain. He had once had a good relationship with God, so his reputation had preceded him that he did play both ends in the middle. Princes from King Balak were sent along with elders from the Midians to Balaam with their proposal to offer him, that if he would use his power to curse Israel, so they could defeat them and drive them out of the country.

Balaam was shrewd. He invited his guests to spend the night while he said he would inquire of the Lord as to what His consent might be. Balaam knew that once God gave a blessing, no human being on the face of the earth could reverse it. But he didn't let them know this. He played their game carrying deceit in his heart. God came to Balaam that night and asked, "Who are these men with you?" as if God needed to ask who they were! (Numbers 22:9). This was just a disciplinary question, hoping to bring Balaam to his senses about the situation at hand and help him to realize he was treading on dangerous ground. Balaam was using all his ways of manipulation on God, but it didn't work and neither does it work for you or me. God said directly to Balaam, "Do not go with them. You must not put a curse on these people, because they are blessed" (Numbers 22:12 NKJV).

Of course, Balaam, refused their offer the next morning repeating the words of God to them. He still didn't let on that he could not reverse the blessing of God but by saying that "The Lord has refused to let me go with you." (Verse 13), they misinterpreted his meaning. They took this to imply that perhaps the anti-wasn't high enough! They went back to King Balak and gave an account of all that went on and King Balak was sure if more prestigious princes and a greater number were sent than before this would give honor and respect to Balaam that he had not been shown before. As for payment, all he had to do was name his price. Money & fame were of no object for his services.

It is risky business to hear God's voice and do the opposite of His command. When God speaks, He expects you are going to obey and if you don't you do pay the consequences of your actions. My dad was much like that. It was really "risky business" to do the opposite of what he had told you to do or not to do and then go on your merry way and expect that you could weasel your way out of the situation later with a fake "I'm sorry" and trade off the act with a weak confession. Balaam was in the process of creating his own risky business and falling into Satan's trap.

He couldn't seem to be straight forward with King Balak because his greatest sin was "greed." His answer reflected his thoughts. "Even if Balak gave me his palace filled He couldn't seem to be straight forward with King Balak because his greatest sin was "greed." *I could not do anything great or small to go beyond the command of the Lord my God"*

Numbers 22:18 (NKJV). His inference in calling Jehovah "my God" implied a personal relationship with God and perhaps powers of persuasion over the Almighty.

Balaam knew God could control his actions, but not his thoughts. He went through the same sequence of events with the second proposal, as with the first. He led the messengers to believe that he would approach God and see if He just *might* change His mind! This was just another form of a lie.

Have you at one time or another tried to manipulate God? Let's think about some ways that, might be done. Perhaps we may promise Him that once a financial crisis has passed and our lives are in order that then we will serve Him without holding back. Or just one more thing to accomplish so we can be relaxed in our service to God, without feeling any pressures. Maybe it is tithe, but just as soon as we get on our feet, we will pay that faithful tithe or perhaps we do pay tithe, but we just can't afford offerings to support the church right now. Are you manipulating God to forgive you for your shortcomings and accept your terms rather than His?

David prayed *"Who can understand his errs? Cleanse me from secret faults. Keep back thy servant also from presumptuous sins; let them not have dominion over me. Then shall I be blameless, And I shall be innocent of the great transgression" Psalms 19:12 & 13 (NKJV).* We need to keep that close on our lips that we wouldn't fall under the sin of taking God for granted and giving way to the secret sins of our heart.

God's answer to Balaam was this, "If the men come to call on you, rise up and go with them, but only the word that I speak to you—that you shall do" (Numbers 22:20 NKJV). We could say here "Well, God told him to go!" But dear friend, by going, he was sending a false message to King Balak, the princes and the elders. He was allowing them to think that

God had been swayed by Balaam and he could indeed curse Israel so he would be receiving the riches that King Balak had promised. I would say that God was testing Balaam and he failed the test.

"*Balaam got up the next morning, saddled his donkey and went with the princes of Moab*" Numbers 22:21 (NKJV). The fact that he saddled his donkey implies tragedy as in several places in the Old Testament, rebellion seems to be preceded by a short journey and the saddling of a donkey. (Further study in this connection is found in II Samuel 17:23; I Kings 2:40).

God was not happy with Balaam going directly against His will. The fact that God said "NO," the first time in *Numbers 22:12* should have been the end of the matter, but the continuation of Balaam's self-will was about to bring tragedy on himself. Balaam's rebellious heart was determined to walk in his own willful way. God may permit us to follow our own desires and suffer out the consequences if we just refuse to listen. This was the situation with Balaam. "*Balaam is an example of a prophet who prostitutes his calling, seeking to make gain of his Divine gift*" (S.D.A. Commentary Vol. 1, pg. 902).

The Angel of the Lord, who may have been the Lord Himself stood in the road to oppose Balaam as he headed out, two servants with him. The donkey saw the angel standing there with his sword drawn, so she turned off the road taking Balaam off into a field. He was very angry with his donkey. He beat her until she got back on the road again and they continued the journey. Again, the donkey saw the Angel of the Lord standing this time by the narrow pathway between two vineyards. The animal pressed close to the wall to squeeze by the angel but in the process crushed Balaam's foot!

Now Balaam was infuriated, beating her again *(Numbers 22:25 NKJV)*. The donkey once more saw the Angel of the

Lord who had moved further ahead to a place so narrow, there was no way the donkey could get by. There simply was no place to turn, neither right nor left. So, the donkey laid down right where she was. This time Balaam was livid. Once again, he began to beat her.

The Bible says, "The Lord opened the mouth of the donkey…" (v.28). "What have I done to you, that you have struck me these three times? Doesn't it seem strange to you that I have acted this way? Did you ever stop to think there might be a reason?" Balaam answered the donkey, "I am so angry at you right now, if I had a sword, I would kill you right here and now!" (paraphrased). The Bible doesn't say that he was surprised to have the donkey speak to him. That alone would make me stop my anger. Instead, they carried on a conversation! The best that I can figure is the servants must have been way ahead and perhaps this was why Balaam was hurrying along so to catch up. They obviously were oblivious to the situation as Balaam had been.

Men still come face to face with angels on pathways of sin and shame. They are often stopped in their mad course, and like Balaam, they do not understand. Plans, pleasure, and business come to a standstill, and the ungodly wonder why. The faithful donkey had seen the Angel of the Lord and tried her best to avert him. When she saw the hopelessness of the situation at the intersection, she laid down.

Finally, Balaam realized.

He came to his senses. Balaam's eyes were then opened, "…and he saw the Angel of the Lord standing in the road with his sword drawn. So, he bowed low and fell face down" (v31). The sword being drawn was a sign of attack, so he was petrified. Balaam began to confess, "I have sinned. I did not realize you were in the road to oppose me. Now if I have displeased you, I will go back." It's like saying, after being caught in the act of defiantly doing your own thing regardless of what anyone else thought even God, "Okay, okay, if you really don't want me to do that now, then I won't." Of course, you won't. You won't out of fear—fear for your life, fear for your reputation, fear that someone will know your real motives or some other agenda. But God wasn't about to let Balaam get off that easy, and He won't let you or me off that easy either.

Balaam had to learn a valuable lesson. He had to learn you don't play with God. Despite Balaam's selfish, greedy heart, he used him to bless the nation of Israel before King Balak, all the princes of Moab and all the elders of Midian not once but four times throughout *Chapter 23*. God spoke through Balaam, and he had no choice but to say the words that God put in his mouth.

"But no man can tame the tongue. It is an unruly evil, full of deadly poison. With it we bless our God and Father, and with it we curse men, who have been made in the similitude of God. Out of the same mouth proceeds blessing and cursing. ... Does a spring send forth fresh water and bitter from the same opening?" James 3:8-11 (NKJV).

Like Balaam, I once had run away from God. I blamed God's people for my failures and even convinced myself into believing I was right, and they of course were wrong. Times were tough. The grocery bill was high and often there weren't groceries at all. I thought it was a good idea when some friends suggested I raise a pig so there would at least be plenty of meat to feed my children during the winter months. I didn't have a freezer or a place to raise a pig, but they were kind enough to offer their barn to raise my pig while they also raised one, plus, they would allow me to use their freezer for the surplus meat. I had been taught as a child to follow all the laws of God including the criteria set in Leviticus, chapter 11 that defines the clean and unclean meats.

Since I had set my course in the world, I had tasted some of the "unclean" meats. Many reasoned when I told them of my beliefs that "nothing was defiled as long as it was blessed by God." The reasoning was if I said my blessing, God blessed it! And then there was other reasoning such as, "that was done away with because we aren't Jews." I began to delude myself. I thought well, my parents were too strict, it was their beliefs, and this was their teaching not mine! The Bible says, "in times of ignorance, God winks!" (Acts 17:30 (KJV). But I was not totally ignorant of the situation.

Day after day, I fed the pig, supplying its food, so it could be nice and fat in time of slaughter. And it grew to be a big pig. It was getting closer and closer to slaughter time. It seemed all my friends did was talk about the pigs! Slaughter time was soon, and I came under conviction. I spoke what the Spirit wanted me to say even though I didn't want to say it because once I made the statement, I had to back it up and tell all the rest that went with it and I couldn't help myself as I blurted out, "I can't eat the pig."

Everyone looked at me in bewilderment. "What? Why?" I had to confess the reason "why" as we searched the Scriptures together, I realized that not only were my parents right, but God was speaking to me louder and louder as the pig got fatter and fatter. God was allowing me another chance to serve Him in total obedience. I gave the pig to my friends that I had paid for to fatten and later they also fell under the same conviction as they studied it out with me.

God often uses our weaknesses to bring us to our senses. He brings us low before Him. Let us be sure that we are bowing low out of reverence, respect, and love for a powerful, mighty God and not out of hopeless fear for our sins. "When Balaam looked out and saw Israel camped tribe by tribe, the Spirit of God came upon him, and he uttered his oracle:" Numbers 24:2-9 (NIV).

> "How beautiful are your tents, O Jacob, your dwelling places, O Israel! Like valleys they spread out, like gardens beside a river, like aloes planted by the Lord, like cedars beside the waters.
> Water will flow from their buckets; their seed will have abundant water.
> Their king will be greater than Agag; their kingdom will be exalted.
> God brought them out of Egypt; they have the strength of a wild ox.
> They devour hostile nations and break their bones in pieces. With their arrows they pierce them.
> Like a lion they crouch and lie down, like a lioness who dares to rouse them?
> May those who bless you be blessed and those who curse you be cursed!'
> Numbers 24:5-9 (NIV).

And to those who meet the Angel of the Lord, stand ready to speak for our God as His witness with the power of the Holy Spirit as it falls upon your hearts, your ears, and your lips bringing blessings on the name of your Lord God.

CHAPTER SEVEN

The Choices in a Decision

"Your ears shall hear a word behind you, saying, "This
is the way walk ye in it," Whenever you turn
to the right hand, or whenever you turn to the left"
Isaiah 30:21 (KJV).

"I don't think I am going snowmobiling tomorrow." Mr. Smith announced after he arrived home Friday evening. Mrs. Smith was already in bed and half asleep. "It's up to you, but I am going to be gone all day and evening, remember?" She mumbled sleepily, but he continued "I just don't feel like going," as if he were arguing with himself! "Whatever," Mrs. Smith responded still groggy and a little irritated that he wasn't more sensitive to her trying to sleep! She didn't try to control her husband's choices especially when she had made plans that were not going to be changed. She was spending the day with her best friend, and they had a big day planned. First was church, then they had to pick up some things from Mr. Stacey's that he was donating to the church from his wife's belongings. He had the grievous job of sorting through her things since she passed away. Mrs. Smith felt it was important to support him in his efforts. From there they would be meeting another church member and leaving for the State Prison.

They were convicted to follow the Biblical instruction, "I was a stranger, and you did not take Me in, naked and you did not clothe Me, sick and in prison and you did not visit Me" Matthew 25:43 (NKJV). Beyond this solemn verse, Mrs. Smith was about to meet a man she had not seen in twenty-five years! She never dreamed she would lay eyes on him again but through the prison outreach, she had surprisingly come across this man through her friend's correspondence. It seemed that he was living a converted life behind prison walls, and she was anxious to reconnect with him. She had no intentions of changing her plans.

Mr. Smith usually occupied himself while she was at church so now, he would just have to find something else to do till late evening since visiting hours didn't begin until 6:30 p.m. at the prison. It was a two-hour drive with a two-hour visiting schedule. She wouldn't be home until late. She perked up to relate the scene of events to Mr. Smith as she anticipated what was to take place that next day.

She had been a little ticked at him for being late this evening and not leaving her a note to let her know his whereabouts. She had arrived home at 8:20 p.m. and went to bed at 9:00. Here it was 9:30 and he had quite a matter-of-fact attitude as to where he had been as if she should have known! All these thoughts were reenacting in her mind while he was deciding whether he should go snowmobiling in a conversation that only vaguely involved her. Then he decided he was not going and called his friend, Leon. "I don't think I will be going tomorrow." "No," he continued, "it is supposed to be pretty warm like today and snowmobiling won't be much fun without snow!" Evidently Leon was trying to be persuasive on his end with Mr. Smith responding, "Yeah, you think so?" Hesitantly he continued, "Well, maybe so but I think I'll stay home this time and wait till next year," then added as an afterthought, "I can't really afford it anyway." His conversation ended and the lights went out.

At 4:00 a.m. the alarm sounded. 'How come you set the alarm?" Mrs. Smith was still irritated from last night and now the alarm was going off when he had decided to stay home! "Maybe I should go," as he picked up the argument with himself before he had fallen asleep. In a moment, he had made his decision. "I better call Leon," he was still having his own conversation. After a few minutes had lapsed, he dragged himself out of bed and made the phone call. Leon's hearty laugh could be heard across the room with the phone held to Mr. Smith's ear. "I knew you'd change your mind," Leon bellowed with confidence.

It was 6:00 a.m. when she waved goodbye to them as they pulled out of the driveway heading north to their destination. They actually went twenty or thirty miles beyond their stopping point since they had to make a stop at the Polaris Dealer to pick up Leon's son's sled, Leon's fourteen-year-old son had a sled in for repairs and it wasn't ready, but they were given a brandnew sled to use free of charge. They acquired directions to continue to their point of drop off at the first trail they came to. It was now 9:15 a.m.

Leon liked to be in control, so he was the one who made the decisions. He had changed his mind and said, "Hey, I think I wanna go another direction. How about on the other side of the mountain where the ponds are?" Leon only asked out of a sort of courtesy as his mind was already made up. "I don't know, Leon," Mr. Smith was skeptical. "Don't you think it's a little warm to be heading that way?" Leon disregarded his friend's caution, "Nah, come on it's gonna be an adventure." Leon laughed at Mr. Smith's uneasiness. So, the three some drove their sleds around a large lake and headed further north. It was about halfway to their destination when they came up to a river with about four inches of water flowing over the top of the wooden bridge.

A warning flag flashed in Mr. Smith's mind, "Leon, I don't think we should chance it. It looks pretty scary." Leon was agitated with Mr. Smith's cautious attitude, "Come on man, don't be a wimp. You are being way too cautious. We're out for a good time." Mr. Smith still wasn't convinced and pressed Leon further, "You know it's pretty warm and if we cross, the river could rise and ruin our chances to return."

Now Leon was losing control, "Geez Man, I didn't come all this way to turn back now." Mr. Smith reluctantly conceded to Leon's wishes, "Okay, okay, I just don't want to be hasty." and with that and Leon's deep laugh they skimmed across the water to the other side.

The next thirty-five miles were crazy. Mr. Smith was going right along at a good clip when he missed the upcoming turn. The trail had formed a V and instead of going straight Mr. Smith veered to the right. He hadn't gone far when he realized his mistake and made a U-turn to get back on the right trail. Leon thought something might be wrong so had turned back to find his friend. Leon's sled plunged off the trail and sunk into the soft snow. "Oh no!" Leon shrieked. "Hey man, you gotta help me," when he caught sight of Mr. Smith Embarrassed at his predicament, but not enough to admit any wrong. "Where's the boy?" was Mr. Smith's concern as he called back to Leon. "Oh, he's way ahead, you know kids." Leon called back.

A half hour later, Mr. Smith and Leon were back riding the trail again after using a pull rope on hand to get Leon's sled free. Another half hour on the trail and they found Leon's son, Reggie hung up on some alders with branches sticking out of his sled track like porcupine quills. "What the heck happened?" Mr. Smith was angry at the scene he was looking at, knowing that it could have only happened from being careless. Reggie shrugged his shoulders and gave a wide grin, "Stop with the mouth works man, and help me," he teased.

At last arriving in a small town, they stopped at the diner to eat. They were so hungry they practically inhaled their food. Soon they realized that so much time had been wasted by all their mishaps, they better be heading back before they couldn't get back. The weather was really getting warm. The forestry warden had called the diner and told the owner that they were closing Trail 89 and to alert his customers that were snowmobiles that they could no longer take that trail. That was the only way back for Mr. Smith, Leon and his son. "If we hurry up, we might beat the odds." Leon sounded worried for the first time. It was about eight miles before the bridge, and a section of the trail had flooded over that looked about three feet deep and at least three hundred feet long. "Holy cow!" Leon was devastated. "Yeah, what did I tell you," Mr. Smith's heart started pounding as he spoke." He surveyed the area and ordered, "We don't have any choice, we have to make an attempt to cross."

Leon went first, then his son followed, and Mr. Smith picked up the rear. Reggie made it, but when Mr. Smith came through, there was Leon standing on the seat of his sled with the rest of his sled under water up to the windshield. This was no time to stop so making a quick decision Mr. Smith leaned exactly right on his sled, maneuvering between Leon and a tree, he whizzed through, spraying water that washed over Leon. Mr. Smith and Reggie were safely past the danger zone, but there was Leon, with water dripping off his nose, still teetering on the seat of his sled. No one dared to laugh but it would have been good for a comic strip! Leon threw his tow rope to Mr. Smith as Mr. Smith shouted, "You've got to get off and hook that on your sled, Leon." Leon was not in a good mood and sarcastically answered, "No kidding." He got off his sled, crotch deep in ice water. "Ee-e gads it's cold." Leon was suffering the shock of ice water. He hooked up his sled while Mr. Smith and Reggie slowly pulled Leon out. It wasn't an easy haul, but they managed. Leon took off his boots and poured the water out. In silent disgust, he yanked the liners out of his boots and angrily wadded them up, hurling them into the woods. "What did you do that for Dad?" his son quizzed? "Shad up, will ya?" came the angry reply.

Heading now for the bridge that earlier in the day already had about four inches of water over the top, the threesome met up with four other snowmobilers, who stopped to warn them, "You can't keep going that way." Leon was not ready for anymore detours, "Why?" he quizzed in his gruff voice. The worst fear was being realized by Mr. Smith as the return answer came, "The river has risen considerably," as one of the four continued speaking, "and washed out the bridge. There is no way to cross. It is about fifteen feet deep and fifty feet across." Adding impact to their warning, Mr. Smith added "Well, isn't that great? Now we are *really* in trouble." He was remembering that he really had not wanted to come in the first place. While they were sitting there contemplating their next move, two ice fishermen came along and informed them of an alternate route. It was beginning to get dark so it would be difficult to see where they were going especially since they were in unfamiliar territory.

The alternate route wasn't marked. It took them around the water that ended up back at the diner that they had previously been at, and knowing there was no time to lose, they got started taking the alternate route. It was about 10:30 that night when they came in wet and tired. The cook at the restaurant had a diesel truck with a boxed in bed attached. "I can help you all out by giving you a ride back to where you came on the trail, in the back of my truck," he offered. "Sounds great at this point in time," one of the snowmobilers seemed relieved. Four sleds were able to fit into the back of his truck and two fit on the trailer that was being pulled, leaving one sled behind. There were about twelve people that piled into the back of the box truck.

They had not traveled far when someone said, "Do you smell that?" Someone else began complaining about the fumes that seemed to be coming into the box of the truck, as they headed down the road. "Yeah, it's diesel fumes." Someone else responded. "Boy I hope it doesn't get any worse" came another remark. "I can't breathe." It was Mr. Smith's voice. Someone began pounding on the walls of the metal box of the truck while screaming, "Hey! Hey!" they yelled louder. Soon everyone was pounding on the walls, "Hey, stop, man! Stop. Stop. We can't breathe back here. Stop!" The driver seemed to be oblivious to any commotion, but by God's grace someone had a flashlight and began shining it out the side of the truck. Two and a half miles, the longest two and a half miles they ever traveled came to a halt. Fresh air at last. "I thought I was going to die in there," Leon's son confided in Mr. Smith. I thought I was too he reflected to Reggie.

Four members of the group went on to the next town on foot and assured those who were left to walk back to where they had gotten in the truck at the diner that they would return in the morning and help them out. Sometimes trusting complete strangers is the only hope to cling to in the dark of night and being so far from home certainly left one to the mercy of strangers. The long walk back to the diner was quiet except for Leon scuffing his feet, breaking the silence as a reminder of his boot liners being tossed into the woods'

Meanwhile

It was 11:22 p.m. and Mrs. Smith walked in her house after a long, wonderful day with her church family. "Hmm, he's not home yet," she thought to herself. "He should be home soon," she mused talking to her dogs as she let them out briefly and prepared for bed. The cat immediately curled beside her on the bed and before she fell asleep with the outside light on, and the kitchen light still blaring, she prayed, "Lord, bring my husband home safely and soon." It was 3:30 in the morning when she awoke abruptly from a strange dream, and the lights were still on and no sign of Mr. Smith.

The owner of the diner, himself helped the wretched threesome. He had rooms but they were all rented out, but he had a trailer available in his trailer park nearby. "That's twenty bucks a piece for the night," he quoted to his new customers. Leon paid for Mr. Smith as he had not brought any extra money with him since it was just one day of snowmobiling fun! Mr. Smith wore contact lenses, and his eyes were burning from being in for so long. "Thank God," he thought silently, "my wife had put my heart pill in a baggie in my pocket, and to think I wasn't going to bother to bring it." He continued to muse to himself.

Mr. Smith found two white bowls to keep his contact lenses separate. He took them out, carefully putting each one in a separate bowl to soak in water for the night. There was no phone, and he knew his wife would be worried and he hoped to be able to reach her before this. He knew she wouldn't rest until she knew he was okay. When Leon was snoring, and Reggie was fast asleep Mr. Smith knelt by his cot and prayed, "Dear God if you can hear me, help me to get out of here safely and back home. Please watch over my wife and keep her safe."

This wasn't the usual for Mr. Smith, but after the day's events and all the close calls, he came to realize that someone had been praying for him and home was important. *"Give ear and hear my voice, listen and hear my speech." Isaiah 28:23 (NKJV) Mr.* Smith had once been a part of the church life. He had been baptized and attended regularly. But somehow the things of the world became more important than attending church and slowly and methodically, he was lured away by other things. *"The great deceiver has prepared his wiles for every soul that is not braced for trial and guarded by constant prayer and living faith" (Selected Messages Book 1, pg. 123 by EG White}.*

He had just fallen asleep when suddenly, "Yeehaw," shrieked outside with gales of laughter mixed with vulgar curses, echoing country music loud enough to wake the dead. Leon must have been close to that because he never woke up. The laughter changed to anger. Fights and brawls could be heard with the grunts and groans of fists connecting with jaws, Mr. Smith listened in the darkness and wishing to be home more than ever. It was 6:30 in the morning when sun made daybreak.

The day after the nightmare that hadn't ended.

Waiting

It was 5:00 a.m. and Mrs. Smith only had a few hours of sleep. She decided she couldn't wait any longer. Something was desperately wrong. She kept looking at the answering machine thinking she might have missed a call and wondered if it were broken. She called her son and woke him up. After explaining the situation and ready for tears she waited for his advice. He was as frantic as she was and in panic-stricken words, he exclaimed." Mom, this isn't like Dad, I think you better call the police." She hung up feeling more scared than ever.

With a heavy heart she called the local police. They called the State Police and within a few minutes, the State Police returned her call. "I know you usually wait 24 hours to report someone missing, but I am telling you, this is not like my husband. He wears hard contact lenses, and his eyes must be burning holes in his head right now. He takes medication for Tachycardia, and he doesn't have his medication with him or his contact cleaning aides. Something is wrong." She was near tears and the adamant demand in her voice proved convincing enough for the officer to concede that he would contact the Warden's Dept. and get back to her. They asked questions about who he was with and where they put in with descriptions that she was unsure of but promised to find out so that when the Warden called, she would have the answers.

First, she called Leon's ex-wife and got a busy signal at 5:30 in the morning! "Who are they talking to?" She fretted aloud to herself. The line continued to be busy 15 minutes later and there was no time to waste, so she called her son's best friend who lived in the same building "Hello?" It was Junior and he sounded like he had been sleeping. "Junior, it's Mrs. Smith. Without waiting for a comment, she rambled, "Mr. Smith went snowmobiling with Leon and Reggie. They haven't gotten home yet. Something is wrong. I called the State Police, but they need more information about Leon, so I need to get in touch with his ex-wife, but their line keeps ringing busy. Can you go knock on their door?" she gasped in her emotional frenzy explaining everything all in one breath. Calmly Junior answered, "Sure. I'll call you back." A few minutes later, he did call back, "I can't get through to them. They must really be sleeping," he explained. Mrs. Smith was feeling defeated and alone, but she quietly responded, "Thanks, Junior," and hung up.

The warden called and they reviewed all the events that she had previously relayed to the State Police. He was kind and tried to calm her fears giving reasons where and why Mr. Smith might not have been able to call. Pressing near to her heart was the thought, "Lord, send the angels, send the angels." The warden mentioned that a bridge was out, and he had heard some people were stranded. Mr. Smith might be among them. They were sending out wardens on the trails right away. He said he would get back to her and he hung up.

Mr Smith

Mr. Smith didn't have cleaner for his contact lenses so tried to wash a lens with Ivory liquid, he found by the sink in the trailer. He couldn't get it rinsed clear so wore one lens in foggy condition all day. The trio had a good breakfast at the diner they had been at the day before Mr. Smith set out walking to find a phone to call home. It was now 8:30 a.m.: "Hello?" Mrs. Smith was sitting by the phone waiting for the return call from the warden. They were getting ready to send out the helicopters. The response from her answering came through, "Will you accept a collect call from Eddie?" the electronic operator was programmed, and her husband's voice came in clear. It continued "Press one or say yes, after the tone." Mrs. Smith pressed one and said "yes" several times. "I'm okay." Eddie's voice was shaky and sounded tired. "Where are you? Are you okay? I've called the State Police and the Wardens." She blurted without waiting for an answer after each question. "I knew you'd do that." He quietly responded sounding depressed and very weary.

She defended her actions as the tears were spilling over into her voice. "I know, I know," he answered softly. "I'm okay. We have been through a lot. The bridge has gone out and we are waiting for some people to come back and help us. You can call the search off; I'm going to be okay, and I'll be home soon." He consoled her. "I have been praying for you." She wanted to give him hope and he answered with "I know you have."

Mr. Smith turned to Leon and said, "My wife called the State Police and wardens are looking for us." Leon exploded, "Your wife is erratic! I can't believe she did that." He kept shaking his head in disbelief. "What do you mean?" Mr. Smith confronted him in shock at his reaction. "I am one lucky man to have a wife that loves me and cares about where I am." Leon was silent.

Mr. Smith was disgusted with Leon's attitude, and now fear crept in as he thought about these people that they did not know. He and Leon were trusting them with their sleds as well as their lives. They were complete strangers taking them in a Chevy Blazer for a one-and-a-half-hour drive continuing toward their incoming route. Mr. Smith and Leon's son were cramped in a small compartment behind the rear seat of the Blazer for the duration of their ride while Leon was able to sit up front comfortably. Sometimes it pays to be big! When they arrived, the sleds were loaded on the truck and taken to the next town. This was their parting point. They started up their sleds and began making their way on the trail. They were about four miles out of town when they came to a river running rapidly. It seemed like another dead end.

Back home Mrs. Smith was not convinced that all was okay so continued to pray continuously, "Lord send Your angels." "*Bless the Lord, you His angels who excel in strength, who do His Word, heeding the voice of His Word" Psalms 103:20 (NKJV).*

Back On the Trail

"Now what?" Leon's voice was gruff and coarse. "Some adventure, huh Leon?" Mr. Smith 's voice resonated with sarcasm as he recapped the events before this all took place and was realizing he had not listened to the voice of reason but just decided to go on the adventure. He was not happy with himself just as much as he was disgusted with Leon and still tired from little sleep, a fogged-up contact lens and praying his heart wouldn't act up throughout the day. "I guess we turn around," he replied matter of fact to the situation. The service station in the small town they just left was the first place they went asking if there was another trail. The station attendant hopped on his sled and led them to another part of the river that had thawed leaving open water about fifty feet across.

Their guide was just a kid but seemed to know what he was doing. "Don't worry, I'm familiar with the territory around here and I have had to get myself out of some tight spots." He was positive and encouraging. "Just do as I tell you and you'll do fine." he continued. "Open your sleds up for all they are worth, and you will make it across" he smiled at them with confidence.

"He's out of his mind." Leon's negativity was discouraging. "I don't see much choice," Mr. Smith retorted calmly. He knew inside it was going to be okay even though it looked impossible. Reggie went first. "I did it!" he beamed! "I made it! I can't believe it! Totally awesome! Come on Dad, you can do it," his son cheered him on. Leon put all he had into it. His sled track hit an ice rut sending him airborne, and when he landed, he came down hard piercing his tail bone into the seat. Mr.

Smith brought up the rear with a smooth skim across the open water. It seemed like clear riding ahead so maybe their troubles were over. Those thoughts disappeared quickly when they approached a beaver dam where a bridge had been washed out.

After that impressive hydroplaning experience across open water, Reggie was sure that this was a piece of cake so went for the gusto across the top of the dam. The sticks caught in the tracks of his sled and right before Mr. Smith's eyes, Reggie went hurtling through the air doing somersaults with his sled. His sky sledding came to a halt when his sled came crashing down was on top of him. Mr. Smith leaped from his sled, adrenaline pumping, he raced to the rescue, lifting the sled off from him, expecting the worst, but instead of seeing a mangled boy, he was greeted with sparkling blue eyes and a wide grin. With his glib manner, he quipped, "Pretty neat, huh?" The snow was soft and cushioned his fall which kept him from any serious injury. While Mr. Smith was rescuing Reggie, Leon was standing off to the side watching his son in seething rage. His main concern seemed to be the sled that wasn't theirs. He began hysterically bellowing at him. "I am going to kill you for being so stupid and not paying attention, as he continued cursing his son with clenched fists mingled with frustration and probably worry even though he would never admit it.

As soon as Reggie was back on the trail, Mr. Smith found an area of about twenty-five feet of open water. He was confident after crossing the previous river opening, that they could make this pond with no problem. Leaning on a prayer under his breath, "Lord, help me," he got up his courage, and made the decision to cross. It was a successful leap of faith. Leon followed through the washed-out area just making it by the skin of his teeth.

Calling for Prayer

It was now 2:30 p.m. and Mrs. Smith called a church brother to pray. She explained the circumstances and the promise to pray was in action. A few hours later, he called back. "Is he home yet?" Mrs. Smith feeling very weary-worn answered, "No, not yet. I haven't heard anything since he called this morning." This brother in the church spoke with confidence, "He'll be okay, I just got off my knees from praying for him. He'll be fine." With that certainty, he added, "Call me when he gets home," and he hung up. "Lord," Mrs. Smith clenched her husband's tee shirt to her breast, "take care of him and Leon and his son. Bring them home safe, please." She couldn't hold back the tears. She felt a new fear gripping her heart. She didn't feel as certain as her brother in the church seemed to be. But all she had was her faith that God heard and would answer. She had to wait.

The threesome was still making their way home. It was but a little way further when they came on to yet another stream. They had no choice but to cross open water once again. Leon was right, his son hadn't learned anything from all these near mishaps. He was driving crazier than ever, passing them, and holding back and then passing again. Each time he would pass, he threw snow and dirt in Mr. Smith's face. All his horsing around and again he went sideways flipping his sled, ski tracks pointing toward the sky and Leon was more furious than ever. Mr. Smith's patience had worn thin now. It had been a long two days and it hadn't ended yet with having little sleep, tempers exploding easily. Fortunately, their dare-devil rider was okay and so was his dad and Mr. Smith. They were even better when they saw the sign seventeen miles and they would be at their destination. Anticipation for the end of their nightmare was materializing.

Not far beyond that point was another sign, "Gas—7 miles." Mr. Smith was relieved as he called out, "Leon, I need gas, I'm on empty." Leon was not concerned with his need. Son like father, the attitude was the same. Leon called out, "You are always worrying about something. Relax you'll make it. We are almost there." He just didn't want to take any more time to do anything but get out of there. "Leon, I'm telling you, I need gas. What will we do if I run out on the trail?" Mr. Smith persisted. "Look Buddy, trust me, you are going to make it. You worry too much. Don't sweat the small stuff." Leon waved him off as if it was of no concern and Mr. Smith was just making up a problem that didn't really exist. Nine miles later, Mr. Smith ran out of gas.

Leon began to sputter and curse. Mr. Smith wanted to say, "I told you so," but held back as it would have only made matters worse. "I'll go on ahead and get some fuel." Leon offered with resentment dripping off his lips. He was the only choice so there was no other alternative and he knew it. He was probably mad at himself for not listening to Mr. Smith in the first place. When Leon was out of sight, Mr. Smith suggested to Reggie, now his comrade, "Let's turn your sled on its side and maybe we can get enough gas out of your machine to get mine started. I have an empty oil can in my pack and I can use my key to open up the top wide enough to fill it from your sled." Reggie thought this was an ingenious idea complimenting with, "Cool." He was ready to help. "It's no use, Mr. Smith determined. "You just don't have enough gas to get any out."

"Wait," Reggie sounded excited. "I have this emergency start rope. Maybe I can tow you with it." Mr. Smith looked at Reggie with a skeptical eye. "Listen son, Mr. Smith tried to be gentle, I don't think that little rope is going to do much." Reggie, the adventurer, was persistent, "But it's worth a try, isn't it?" Obediently, Mr. Smith hooked it to his sled and to Reggie's. "Okay, I'm going to let you pull and I'll run alongside of it until you get some momentum going." Instructions were followed as Mr. Smith trotted a long side the sled. The sled began going along fast, when Mr. Smith grabbed hold of the handlebars and hopped on. The boy pulled him the remaining eight miles to their destination! Just as they made it to the side of the open roadway on Route 16, the rope snapped!

Reggie took off to find his father so he could come back to where they were with the trailer to load the sled. The gas station was closed! That meant they had to load the sled by hand onto Leon's trailer. A sled weighing 550 pounds was a tough pull. It was now about 4:30 p.m. The sleds were finally loaded, and they were heading home. Thank God they were heading home, Mr. Smith sighed a silent sigh of relief. It was 7:30 that evening when they pulled into the Smith's driveway. The Smith's embraced as Mrs. Smith gave way to tears of relief and thankfulness to her heavenly Father who was there throughout all their episodes and brought them to safety. It was the demise of Satan to destroy them and cause great grief, but God in His mercy spared their lives by giving them, especially Mr. Smith, a former church member another chance to serve Him and give Him glory.

"Bless the Lord, O my soul, and forget not His benefits:
Who redeems your life from destruction?
Who crowns you with loving kindness and tender mercies"
Psalms 103: 2, 4 (NKJV).

CHAPTER EIGHT

Preparing to Meet God at the Mountain

"I AM the Lord, that is My Name and my glory I will not give to another, nor my praise to carved images"
Isaiah 42:8 (NKJV).

There it stood the majestic 6,288-foot mountain considered the most dangerous small mountain hike in the world! Wind velocity has reached up to 231 miles per hour there. You can reach the top of this mountain by driving up the roadway to the summit viewing all the spectacular scenes along the way as you comfortably make your way to the top. There are other avenues of attaining the top of this mountain on pathways that aren't comfortable or convenient for the adventuresome and perhaps the fool hardy, so that they can say, "I climbed Mt. Washington." It was the Sabbath Day, and it was a pre-planned event as a church group to climb this mountain together. The challenge of the hike was to be as an accomplishment as well as a time of fellowship.

The only brave souls to take on this feat were my two daughters, my husband, and a friend also a member of the

Unleashed Promises of Merciful Love

church, his son and myself. It was about an hour and a half ride to the base of the mountain where our climb was to begin. We began our journey with a short prayer, just the six of us. Eric & my daughter, Judy were athletic and nimble, and headed out on the trek ahead of everyone. My husband, and church comrade were paced and steady as they went. They assumed their place in the middle of the procession. My youngest, Kathy was disinterested in any exertion and was only part of the procession because she didn't have a choice in the matter. I was overweight and out of shape even though I was always on some sort of diet plan.

At the base of the mountain before the climb began was a sign that read, "Anyone who is not physically fit, should not attempt this climb." I wondered to myself, "why on earth was I attempting this in the first place?" but I ignored the sign and decided this was an adventure and I'd take it one step at a time.

Centuries ago, a man, an old man by today's standards, but physically fit with a steady pace, concentrated with deep meditation and thought when he began his trek up another mountain in another country. He climbed the rugged path leading up to Mt. Sinai (7,497 feet just a tad over 1200 feet more than Mt. Washington) to meet with God. That man was Moses. It has been the educated guess by theologians that Moses was between 90 and 110 years old when he made his trek.

I can picture in my mind how his long walking stick served as a crutch to bring leverage to each step on that rocky path. I did not have a walking stick, but I certainly would have appreciated one. Even though he may have been physically fit (and I am sure he was) as he didn't just climb that mountain once, but several times! Yet it seems to me that his bones must have ached just a little bit and perhaps he had a few weary moments trudging that majestic mountain one step after another. His step was persevering and determined for he was on a mission to meet with God. He even fasted before he began his journey. I didn't fast before going up the mountain. I had a good breakfast, and my husband had a backpack full of things to sustain us along the way for energy. Moses was the go-between, the spokesman for the Children of Israel and relaying messages from God. They were about to enter a pledge, a sacred, solemn promise committing their lives fully and only to God, the Lord Jehovah. Every step of their walk with God, they would first seek His Divine guidance and assurance of what direction they should take.

He had already shown His Divine protection over them by miraculously freeing them from their bondage in slavery with the Egyptians. God, Himself proclaimed to them, "*Now therefore, if you will indeed obey my voice and keep My covenant, then you shall be a special treasure to Me above all people; for all the earth is Mine; and you shall be to Me a kingdom of priests and a holy nation*" Exodus 19:5 & 6 (NKJV).

It was an extremely exhausting climb and I call it that because I can relate to it by my own climb. Of course, I was not on a mission to meet God and that was definitely the excitement of his journey. In his every step God was ever present. The Psalmist exclaims this in detail in *Psalms 139:1-12* that God's presence is everywhere. I was on a journey of physical perseverance and endurance that I did not comprehend when I entered my journey. Moses, however, had an agenda from God. He returned to the people and called all the leaders and elders together repeating the divine message given to him by the Great I AM, Himself.

The response of the people as they stood ready to sign the contract pledging a vow of loyalty, and accepting Jehovah as their One and only God, their supreme Ruler with a ready and willing heart to adhere to all the requirements of obedience with the word that echoed down through the pages of Scripture, *"All that the Lord has spoken, that we will do" Exodus 19:8 (NKJV).*

When have you stood prepared to give your vow to the Lord and then found yourself wandering away from the very vow you took in sacred earnestness? I watched my children take the vows that they accepted the death of Christ by going into the watery grave in baptism signifying they too would follow Him. Being raised up from the watery grave into newness of life they accepted the blood of Christ as the cleansing of their sins. I heard the words of my son as they continue to speak within my thoughts when he was a babe in Christ, say, "My only desire is to follow God." To a Christian mother this was music to my ears. For a time, he took a step away from his faith but like his mother God has never left him nor did He forsake him, and he is stronger now than the day he made that statement.

The majestic, jagged, rocky stairway leading to the top of Mt. Sinai must have been an impressive scene for the Children of Israel. The summit was buried within a dense cloud that covered the mountain. Mount Washington most of the time sits within cloud cover. Due to its height, you cannot always be assured a clear view at the top, but when it is clear you can view Maine, New Hampshire, Vermont, Massachusetts, and New York! You could encounter fierce winds, bolting rain, thunder and lightning or dense cloud cover at the summit when at the base it may seem like a nice day. But at Mt. Sinai the climb was different because Moses was encountering God face to face, close enough to touch, so close that His voice vibrated the whole mountain. Moses described it like this in his blessing on the Children of Israel, *"The Lord came from Sinai, and dawned on them from Seir; He shown forth from Mt. Paran,*

And He came with ten thousands of saints; from His right hand came a fiery law for them. Yes, He loves the people; All His saints are in His hand; they sit down at Your feet; Everyone receives Your words" Deuteronomy 33:2–3 (NKJV).

Everything about God had to be performed in such grandeur that the people would have these scenes embedded deeply in their minds. They would not forget and this service, this covenant and reverence would be passed from generation to generation in awesome, sacred holiness.

In our climb, we became separated from each other. My youngest & I held our own at the rear. The others were set in their course and didn't think of the difficulties that we had in our struggle to climb. They had the water, the back packs with food, so we wouldn't have anything extra to carry, but we lost sight of them. We were not prepared either physically or materially for this climb.

In preparation to meet with God there was a three-day ritual of cleansing before the Children of Israel could meet with God. They were to devote themselves to fasting and prayer with a spirit of humility to be cleansed of sin. This is described in detail in *Exodus 19:10-15*. A barrier was placed around the base of the mountain so no one could touch it during this time of consecration, or they would die. Then the morning of the third day arrived. Everyone gathered at the base of the mountain while God came and ascended upon the Mountain. *"...in the morning, that there were thundering's and lightning's, and a thick cloud on the mountain; and the sound of the trumpet was very loud, so the people who were in the camp trembled."* (V.18) *"...Its smoke ascended like the smoke of a furnace, and the whole mountain quaked greatly"* (V.19). *"And when the blast of the trumpet sounded long and became louder and louder, Moses spoke, and God answered him by Voice"* Exodus 19:16-19 (NKJV).

He gave His introduction not just as Lawgiver and Judge, but also Compassionate Guardian and then He began His Divine instructions with what we know today as the Ten Commandments. *"The law was not spoken at this time exclusively for the benefit of the Hebrews. God honored them by making them the guardians and keepers of His law, but it was to be held as sacred trust for the whole world"* (Patriarchs and Prophets, page 305).

He began the precepts of the Decalogue with, *"Thou shalt have no other gods before Me" Exodus 20:3 (KJV)*. Now let's think of what other gods might be. Back then other gods were golden images, hewn out of stone, wood, or gold and still today in other countries and even in some churches in America these same gods are worshiped. Rah was the sun god and there were numerous different images which represented that god which people worshiped. Later on in Greek Mythology there were the Greek gods that took away worship to the rightful God of the Mountain. As we make our way down through the aisles of time, there are hundreds of gods, if heaped together would make a mountain, such as money, cars, jewelry, television, material possessions, a job, Internet, self-righteousness and the list is endless. Let's not forget the gods of hatred, bitterness, anger, and deceit. Yes, these are also gods because anger and hatred are a power that pumps us up and we lose sight of humility. Sometimes it feels good to be angry or wallow in your self-pity because you have a right to feel sorry for yourself with all the injustices that have been dealt to you. It comes down to *"Whatever we cherish that tends to lessen our love for God or to interfere with the service due Him, of that do we make a god"* (Patriarch's and Prophets pg. 305 Ph. 3 by EG White).

God is first, even before family. I had become so wrapped up in worry about my family, I had put God after my family.

I was frenzied about their lack of worship for God, and I was at them all the time. I prayed for them incessantly, first and foremost—before I gave God any credit for anything, I was concerned about them and brought them and their sorry condition before God in frustration. Then clearly, God opened my understanding that I was worshiping them and not Him. They consumed my mind and He had not. I was startled at this as I began to realize that I was obsessed with them and God was not the object of my worship and reverence, my family was my main and only concern. I had to repent and ask for forgiveness and turn my family and their condition over to Him.

I have found that He handles situations much better than I do. You see, "God is a jealous God." He wants all our affections and does not want to share us because His love is intimate. He created us. *"They provoked Him to jealousy with foreign gods..." Deuteronomy 32:16 (NKJV).*

The love of God is based on the same sacredness as marriage. *"Idolatry being spiritual adultery, the displeasure of God against it is fitly called jealousy"* (Patriarchs and Prophets pg. 306, Ph. 2 by EG White). Putting God first leads to obedience. *"To obey is better than sacrifice..." I Samuel 15:22 (NKJV).* For you see, we receive salvation through the mental process, of choice prompted by faith which in turn brings obedience to the Will of God. What sacrifice could be a substitute for obedience? Giving up a cherished object is a sacrifice, but it doesn't buy obedience. Obedience is doing what God has asked regardless of what it takes to accomplish that act. Obedience is following the Laws of God. Obedience is loving God with all your heart and soul while letting that love show by your actions as an obedient servant of God. It is keeping the lines of communication open with the Compassionate Guardian as well as keeping the Divine Laws of the Law Giver.

When you become a lover of self and self wants and self needs, you close the door of communication shutting out the voice of God so that you can lull yourself into that self-righteous state of serving the vast array of strange gods that give you the right to continue as you are. It is only as we pray the humble prayer of humility and fast and pray for cleansing as the Israelites did before meeting God can we daily keep God first and serve Him without any other gods in the way. When our strange gods are laid at the feet of the mighty God, only then we are prepared to meet the God of the mountain and serve Him and Him only.

Kathy & I were halfway up the mountain and along the way we grew thirsty. We had no water with us, so we laid on our bellies and drank from the stream of water trickling down the rocks beside the path. A little further up was another sign that said, "Don't drink the water. There is bacteria in it." Too late, we already did, and it tasted pretty good to us because we were thirsty. We became entangled with a group of foreigners and watched them snack on raisins and peanut butter cups. They were speaking a language we didn't understand. We were so hungry and as we watched them devour their snacks, we ate as if our eyes were snatching the very food from their lips. We wondered if the others missed us. There were no cell phones then, but we had God and the Holy Spirit as our communicator, so we prayed.

We reached the halfway mark of the mountain and were uncertain which trail to take. We decided to look around and maybe the others had missed us and were waiting. We discovered a lake in the middle of the mountain. It was quiet and serene. It offered a place of contentment and shade. We drew an inner peace from it but we knew we should find the others and so we decided to continue the familiar trail called, Tuckerman's Ravine. Years later I learned that Tuckerman's

Ravine is known as second to the five most treacherous trails to climb. This ravine is famous in the winter as a ski slope because the ravine has an endless crevice within the earth that fills up with snow and is a ski jump for the experienced skier, but when the snow is out of it, it has served as a death trap for the inexperienced hiker who has gone too close. There were little plaques embedded in the rock in places giving the names of those who had died. It seems according to Google 150 people have died on this hiking trail adventure.

I was so tired, and Kathy hated the climb as much as I did at this point, but now she was encouraging me. "Mom, see that yellow paint mark, we'll just go to that one and then we will rest." I would look at it and think, "Well, I can make it to there," as we continued to crawl over the rocks. We would pull ourselves a few more feet upward on the rocks that were straight up with only a slightly slanted incline. The jagged rocks, the smooth rocks, and the hot sun were a combination of battling perseverance as she encouraged me to each yellow painted mark that pointed the trail upward toward our goal.

We finally made it past the rocky openness of the ravine to a narrow pathway winding in dirt and briers also straight up. We had to lean to the side to allow travelers to pass by us. It came to me as some hikers were making their way downward on a trail just above us, when I overheard a conversation about the trail called Lions Head. It was then I was reminded that we were on the wrong trail! I then remembered hearing our church brother say, "We will take Lion's Head. It not as difficult." Kathy & I had no idea now if our group was looking for us on the Lion's Head Trail or if they were already at the top and heading down! We knew now we were on the wrong trail. We asked the people we met, "How much further?" They told us that we were less than a quarter of a mile from the top, but "you won't be able to see anything when you got there as a storm is moving in." We decided we better turn back.

We were separated from our source of communication. We felt like our prayers for them to wait for us had not been answered and we felt deserted, alone, hungry, tired and scared. When we walk away from obedience of the Will of God, when we forget to put Him first and get lost in our own selves, we can become as alone and tired and scared and deserted within our minds as Kathy & I felt that day.

We wandered in a struggle that others were unaware of that day. How often in our daily life do we wander in struggles that others know nothing about, or we perhaps miss-judge another because we do not know the struggle someone else may be facing in their inner soul? We had tried to communicate through fervent prayer that seemed to be to no avail, but God is a covenant keeping God, and He makes no mistakes. He does fulfill His promises. He did stir my husband's heart to "stop and wait," but he listened to another voice that said, "they're okay." We often ignore the "still small voice" speaking to our heart and try to reason that everything is alright when God puts the danger signs in front of us and then soon, we can no longer discern between what is right and what is not.

Kathy & I were unprepared to meet the long day without food or water in heat and exertion, but God provided water even though the warning was posted of the bacteria present in it, we were never affected by it. Even though we were hungry and totally without food except for the sweet clover we found along the trail to chew on, we were sustained. God gave us direction when we were lost and set in our path the voice that told us we were on the wrong trail and turned us around. He provided answers before we called.

In turning back when we did, we were the first back. It was only a moment when Judy & Eric appeared. They said,

"Didn't you guys climb any of the mountain?" They were totally oblivious to the difficulties we had endured. They had been physically prepared to meet the feat of the mountain but were unskilled in recognizing the struggle of those around them. Since that day, their lives have been a life of service to God and man. I am proud of them.

The protectors of the group, the ones that did not listen were caught in the most horrific thunder and lightning storm one could encounter on a mountain. My husband later confessed to me that he trembled as they made their way down. Probably much like Moses and the Children of Israel trembled at the base of the mountain when the glory of God was making the mountain tremble. Kathy & I although hungry had not starved to death; although tired, weary and worn and a little angry because we felt unimportant to our companions who didn't wait for us, but we were dry and safe.

> *"Now all the people witnessed the thundering, the lightning flashes, the sound of the trumpet, and the mountain smoking; and when the people saw it, they trembled and stood afar off. Then they said to Moses, "You speak with us, and we will hear; but let not God speak with us lest we die." And Moses said to the people, "Do not fear, for God has come to test you, and that His fear may be before you, so that you may not sin." So, the people stood afar off, but Moses drew near to the thick darkness where God was" (Exodus 20:19-21 NKJV).*

By putting God first—by not having any other god before the God Who encompassed Mt. Sinai and the same God Who protected us as we climbed Mt. Washington will continue to protect you as you face mountains of circumstances whether literal or imagined. You can face whatever trials in any aspect by observing the commandments of God and placing the yoke of God around your neck. He has promised that "His yoke is easy, and His burden is light" (Matthew 11:30 NKJV), and it is one size fits all. There are no loopholes, no adjustments, no strings attached other than obedience to the God Who created us that by obedience to Him in having "no other gods before Him" (Exodus 20:3). He covers you and prepares you to meet Him at the mountain.

"PREPARE TO MEET GOD AT THE MOUNTAIN"

Here I am Lord.
For these moments, we are of one accord
My soul alone with Thee.
My soul opens for You to see.
I long to know Thy Will,
So, I kneel here quiet and still.
Waiting for all that You should speak, I will do,

I long to know Thy Will,
So, I kneel here quiet and still.
Waiting for all that You should speak, I will do,
Following obedience and humility too.
At the foot of the mountain, I began my wait,
To hear the vibrant Voice of Jehovah Great,
With instruction from on High as my elected fate.
I desire to know O Lord, please hear my humble cry.
My garments have been washed in Thy precious blood,
Thou shed, on the cross where Thou did die.
I wear them with tears of love in repentant heart,
For I want to meet You at the mountain top.

But along the way I have stumbled and fallen a lot.
I lost my way and then I could not hear Your
Voice. I ran this way and that...
I felt I had no choice.
Then, I knew You must be waiting for me all along
With outstretched hand to hold me and keep me strong
And bring me back to where I belong.
I had hurried to put on righteousness and found it
covered with Self!
I didn't kneel in repentance right away,
but deftly fell to my ruin,
as some would say.
But now I understand, and I have set Self aside.
I am waiting for Thee.
I have no other gods before me as low before Thee I bend.
Only the great I AM as my Guide, my
Judge and Compassionate
Friend, ready to give it all another try.
Oh, hear my pleading and do not pass me by-~
For I desire to commune with Thee forevermore.
And I promise that all You command I will do as before.
I will wait, my Savior for Thee to speak
Words of life and love as I stand humble and meek.
So, prepare me now to meet Thee at the mountain base,
So, I may walk the rugged path in a strong and steady pace.
By Joyce A. Leonard—March 6, 1999

CHAPTER NINE

The Silence of the Ticking Clock

"To everything there is a season, a time
for every purpose under heaven:
A time to keep silence, a time to speak.
A time to love, a time to hate.
A time of war, and a time of peace"
Ecclesiastes 3:1, 7b-8 (NKJV).

*I*t sounded like a clock factory with battery operated clocks clicking the minutes by—"Tick-tock, tick-tock." Then each hour was reminded with the cuckoo jumping out of its port hole in serenade of his "cuckoo" to the emptiness that was accompanied by the bird clock in the kitchen with each hour singing its hourly performance.

Tonight's silence reminded her of those hours past and the torment of those endless hours of wait. The churning in the pit of the stomach, the hurt that can only be defined as cruel, helplessly cruel with the burning sensation penetrating the being like an unquenchable fire within the soul.

She would know each time the unfaithfulness occurred because the stomach never lied. The weakness in her arms and the emptied strength forced the silence of her heartbeat so defined that she always knew when there was someone else involved with her husband—the first time and now again and countless other affairs. She knew the choice of lies that bore no evidence of proof to back the words.

She knew by the deceit that had been spewed from his mouth and echoed from his eyes. She knew by the nasty ways that became intolerable with disrespect. She just knew and she was never wrong.

Tonight, especially reminded her of past nights…. her forgiveness and then the repeat, leaving its haunting memory to come back to hurt her again. The waiting games. The endless wait. Then it was a threat of what mood he would be in and would she be beaten for saying the wrong words, voicing the wrong opinion, or worse—to actually tell him the truth of her own thoughts. Would she be able to endure the night, and would she be alive the next day to see the sunshine?

Then the blessing of love became the weight of love turned inside out and made valueless crushing the soul in a silence that only the ticking clock and the ears of God can hear.

> *"And the husband listened to the adulteress tale, she spread her bed with linen and perfume. She caused him to yield with flattering lips…and by her speech, she seduced her lover to slaughter. He did not know it would cost his life. (Paraphrased Proverbs 7:6-27)*

"Or what will a man give for exchange for his own soul?" Matthew 16:26 (NKJV last part).

Internet Affairs

"I haven't done anything!" He defended himself with clenched teeth and green steely eyes penetrating her accusations with his self-assured grimace. "Yes, you did." She retaliated with sobs. The Internet was the cause of this heartache that existed. He couldn't see where he had caused anything. He claimed he hadn't been with a woman the past six hours he was not home, and his wife had no idea where he had been. Within the past two weeks, he had told his wife that he was taking his vacation without her this year and going off with the "boys" which was totally out of character for him. His wife had found chat conversations with Internet women of sexual perversion that were tagged as Cyber Sex. Her husband had explicit conversations with women on the Internet exchanging vows of "I love you" and promising to meet them in the future and even marriage according to the written letter from one of his lovers. Yet, he became evasive and out and out brutal with his snappy retaliation that he had done "nothing" for his wife to continuously sob, to the point of feeling as if she were going into a full-fledged emotional breakdown.

"What the **** are you crying about now?" he sat glaring at her in disgust as if she had just been sitting there and sobbing for no reason. He continued to defend his use of the Internet making her out to be the one who was making up scenes that he continuously denied. "The Internet comes before your marriage," she cried. She felt like screeching the word hoping that it would penetrate his clouded brain and then tearing him from limb to limb for hurting her so deeply. She prayed for control and for the Spirit to squelch the anger that was overwhelming her. "You are a cold hearted, SOB." She finished in despair in a futile attempt of vulgarity to jolt his realization to the degree his actions had soared. "I am not." He roared in denial. "You are allowing the devil to make you think negative thoughts," knowing that to bring the devil in on the conversation would control her by reason of guilt because she wouldn't want to offend God even if he were the culprit of her emotional tirade. "I see nothing wrong with the Internet." He continued reasoning his usage that kept his addiction fed. "I do other things besides the Chat rooms. I like to look up stuff."

Oh yes, she knew the important stuff he looked up. It was very educational and mind enhancing Viagra, not that he needed it but maybe in multiple affairs, the private chats, the deviously changed passwords so she couldn't locate where he had been on the Internet, along with the impromptu meetings that kept him searching his e-mail for free Lotto's and dirty jokes. Not to mention keeping the volume turned down on the computer so not to alert anyone that he had just "got mail" and it was alerting him. There was also the quick shut down of the computer when she entered the room with his excuse, "Oh I forgot to shut it down properly!" Then of course to keep it all on the up and up, he scanned the latest automobiles and checked out Uncle Henry's ads, but the main interests were private pics of unknown women who were searching for lustful conversations that could end up in a motel somewhere off I-90 on some other God forsaken highway to complete the secret rendezvous station with his fling while fulfilling their selfish motives and exposing their loved ones to some possible sexual virus or disease linked with the possibility of death.

But these lovers were "nice" people. They were only out for innocent fun! If only she had minded her own business, she would never know the difference. He could have his freedom to play and still be a husband and have his home life. With each encounter the face might be different and the body shape, the color, but no it wasn't really any different. The sad truth, which she hated admitting to herself was that he had a behavioral pattern that was in severe need of professional help—Jesus, the Life Changer, the Healer, the Transformer. But he wanted no part of losing his privileges to sin.

"If you aren't doing anything, then help me to feel secure." she screamed. "What is it you want me to do?" he screamed back. "How can you be so sensitive to other women and how they feel and totally ignore the feelings of your own wife?" She cried out to him through blurred eyes and her heart wide open with its gouged wounds exposed. Did he once put his arms around and comfort her fears? Or did he once say, he was sorry for making her feel this way with his actions and he would do anything to make up to her for his deceitfulness? No, he did not. He couldn't. His game was still a toss-up of what or whom he wanted, and right now, she was in his way of having his desire—his lustful fantasies fulfilled, and he just sat back in a matter-of-fact way and said, "You are doing this to yourself, and you are turning me off."

There goes the guilt trip pushing the blame at her for her actions, to take away from the responsibility he didn't want to own. She could read the nasty hateful look that spoke the silent message, "I'll teach you not to control me." One of his Internet lovers e-mailed her and said how they had made love for the last three months and how much she loved him, and he loved her and she would have him and the rest of the explicit conversations just kept eating at her soul like a cancerous sore that made her ache to the bone with emotional pain. But she had no right to feel this way because he proved in the last six hours he had not been where he shouldn't be so there should have been no cause for her concern. This was his tainted reasoning.

I don't like being controlled." He bellowed at her. What a joke. If it hadn't been so deceitfully used and in such a manipulated way, it would have been funny. "Controlled? Controlled?" she thought. He is controlling her fears, manipulating her love, and tormenting her state of mind while he had the audacity of telling her she was controlling him! If he loved her—if he genuinely loved her, if he had respect for her, if he treated her with honor she deserved, he would not be saying or doing the things he has done for the last three months. Now that he has been confronted with the proof of the conversations printed out from the Internet, then his insistent denials began that it was "just in fun." He figured if he admitted to a little, then all can be forgotten and go on. After all, this time he hadn't made the bodily contact as he had in the past, but the words on the paper were perverted, sickening, and filled with infidelity, which made her thoughts go wild.

Perhaps he was thinking when the dust settles, he will just pick up the addiction because after all she will return to church, and he will have Friday evenings while she is at Vespers and then at church for three hours to go on to play the Internet Chats. He could plan while she is gone and finagle the next lie. Just perhaps…when you are desperate for answers, you search every nook and cranny of conceivable thoughts for the addiction to continue because now he was good at his game and not even, she would be able to find out what he did on the "privacy" of his Internet interludes.

In desperation she searched her heart and offered him divorce if it was what he wanted. She offered him his freedom. He refused it. He still wore the wedding band, but still carried deceit in his heart. He was in denial, and she could see in his eyes he wanted it all; the romance of what other women said to him and the security of his home. He wanted what all the world wants—both ends and the middle without committing to anything totally and then trying to find happiness somewhere else when happiness is not in this world. Happiness is what God has for them that love Him and trust Him.

This was Internet addiction. Love can make you crazy. It can drive a person to doing insane things. It can destroy you.

Faithfulness is such an important part of love, commitment, and honor. Taking it lightly is a futile and a damnable curse on the one who holds it sacred. She wanted to disappear into the earth as if she never existed, hoping he would wake up and wonder, where she went. But would he even care? It seemed highly doubtful. Where could she escape? He was so busy on the Internet; he could care less, as long as she would just leave him alone. She went out the door and in the heat of the day climbed the stairway in the garage and lay down on the hard floor with her pillow and blanket. The tears wouldn't stop. The ache just wouldn't go away and the prayers she prayed seemed empty and God seemed so far away.

She lay sobbing when it felt like a big hand patted her on the head. It startled her. She looked up and realized a breeze had rushed in through the window opening and brushed through her hair like the assuring hand of God that He was there, and He would supply her needs. "Her needs," she thought, "what are they?" Quickly the answer popped into her head, "to be able to live a profitable life in Christ with or without her husband." But without him stung at the very core of her soul. That wasn't the way it was supposed to be, for you see, "once upon a time" as the story goes—he was converted. That was forever ago and now his goals have changed. They lived for different things. He seemed to be living for himself and she was trying to live for God filled with relationships of love and witnessing. They were serving two different masters and it kept them in constant conflict. He seemed to play with God's affection just like he played with hers. One minute he would use his lovely voice to sing praises to God and in the next breath he could slap God in the face with profanity and infidelity by flirting with the world.

Now when he would sing to God, she ignored it because she felt he only did it as a decoy to throw her off guard and just tease her with a glimpse of hope and to keep her heart hoping, but she didn't hope anymore. She wondered to herself if God still had hope when she had given up? As she cried, she thought, "if my tears are this plentiful and cannot stop, how much greater God's tears must be." If she felt this emotional pain, then God must be in agony. Yes, agony. Christ died in agony, and He gave His life for her when she felt hope was gone and wanted to disappear in a hole and give up on life. He died so she would have a reason to live, a reason to hope. Hope can continue and so she continued to pray for those she loves.

> *"Why are you cast down, O my soul? And*
> *why are you disquieted within me?*
> *Hope in God…"*
> *Psalms 42:5 (NKJV).*

HOSEA

Centuries ago, there was a godly man, named Hosea. There were no ticking clocks or Internet, but the concept is still the same. The Bible tells us in the Book of Hosea all about his love story. It is one of amazing love. He fell in love with Gomer, but before this happened, God told Hosea to take a wife of harlotry—a wife of prostitution in today's terms. Go ahead and have children with her. Their first child was a boy and after that they had three more. Each name was especially given by God as a significant measure of His mercies on Israel as well as the destruction. He would allow on the people who had turned their backs on Him and served other gods.

Hosea was undoubtedly ridiculed for his love for Gomer because she was not content with being his wife and living for God. She was more in tune with finery and Hosea was a poor man of God and could not give her the desires of her heart as she wanted, yet he loved her even though he knew of her secret affairs.

When she had been used up and her beauty was waning and the desire for her and for what she had to offer her conquests was not what it had been, she was then placed on an action block and was to be sold as a slave. It seemed no one was interested in her even as the auctioneer tried to entice men to buy her with her attributes of being able to bear them children. Yet, they took no interest in her. The refinery was gone, and her beauty was lost under scars of abuse and the dirt of living in the slums of that age.

But wait! Here comes Hosea and he had silver to pay for her ransom far more than the auctioneer called for. What? Are you crazy Hosea? She has slept with other lovers and is used up. She walked away from you and left you desolate and a laughingstock among your peers and you want her? You raised your children alone. You could do much better than her. But Hosea walked past the jeers of those who had even been the very ones who had used her and reached down and picked her up into his arms and carried her home. What love! What forgiveness! (The story is paraphrased and can be read in any version in the Book of Hosea).

And didn't God pay a price for you and me? As we read these two encounters and the great love that is shown within these two stories, the clock ticks by and God, Who has not a thought of time as we do, for a day is a year n Bible prophesy and God is eternal for He never gives up on the worst of the worst until the doors of probation have closed, but until that time the clock is ticking silently within all of us to make the decision to follow Him or walk away. And I wonder is God silent within?

"SILENT WITHIN"

The silence deafens within my soul,
When anger lashes out; my mind takes its toll, And
I cannot feel the physical wreaking,
But the emotional pain torments with screeching.
And I am silent within.
There is no reason to give an excuse,
For the content of thought is of no use—
Failure nips at my heels.
I feel the bite as it quietly steals.
And I am silent within.
It is as if my heart lost its throbbing power.
As if moments stand still within the hour.
Everything loses the value of life.
Fear strikes the burden with added strife.
And I am silent within.
I cannot face the cursed lips,
Unforgiveness overtakes my heart and rips
It into shreds mangled and bleeding.
Nothing changes its fury, no method of pleading.
And I am silent within.
So, Lord.... here I stand,
Ashamed, forsaken it seems by Your Hand.
There seems to be no hope as I stand alone.
Silence makes my heart heavy as stone.
There is no need to plead my case—
For dear Jesus I scarred your precious face,

With selfish ways and sins concealed,
The black upon my heart has been revealed.
And I am silent within.
By Joyce A. Leonard ~ November 26, 1997

CHAPTER TEN

"Search for Me with all Your Heart"

*"Put a wall of protection around our hearts that
we may stay pure and true to Him."
~Brenda Walsh~*

Sometimes we are placed in situations that are not caused by our own doing. Yet, we feel like we are either being blamed or drawn into something that affects us that we didn't create, and everything is out of our control to do anything about the situation. This type of situation is a co-dependency on the part of those involved to have someone side with their feelings and often those of us who are drawn in have a more a challenging time to keep from giving wrong advice or projecting opinions that can often sway thoughts and actions of another.

The velocity of the emotions that sweep us into a situation when we analyze and try to find a solution to a problem that was not ours to begin with has now become our burden. How did this happen? This is a left-brain condition. Our left brain controls our verbal skills. It keeps track of time and sequence. It is the rational, scientific, and logical side. I have been accused of not always being logical.

Theology, sermons, Bible study that led to conclusions of defining and reasoning are all part of the left-brain activity. The right brain, however, is the intuitive part that brings out a knowing that has no rational basis for our conclusions. It is the side with the sudden leap of insight that allows us to see the invisible and accept a miracle.

We balance a check book with our left brain, but we visualize the face of a friend with our right side. We learn facts about people from our left side, but we gain a warm relationship from our right side, but it takes both sides to have a complete understanding of life's situations. In taking this a step further we need to learn to pray with both sides of our brain.

Jesus opened right brain thinking when he presented messages in parables. Most often when I write poetry, my right brain takes over and my word skills that come from the left-brain side are prompted by the "mind's eye" picture from my right brain side, but when we logically try to "reason why" to something that has no definite reasoning to it, this is where we should learn to "let go and let God."

One time I was so angry over a circumstance that frustrated me that I screamed at God. I was totally, utterly angry at God and I voiced my anger aloud, within the hearing of my son at the time. He was appalled that I should be "mad" at God. I reasoned with him that it was far better to be angry at God and tell Him so than not to talk to God at all. When we stop talking to Him even in anger, we lose out on communication with Him.

So, when we are faced with an anger that has no immediate solution, we need to face what has caused the anger to begin with for a healing process to take place. We often fail to use both sides of our brain to understand situations that we seem to be thrust into without our consent.

I have found myself in positions that I didn't want to be in looking at the situation of those who caused the action in a jaw-dropped disbelief that they couldn't seem to see beyond their own selfishness that caused the conflict in one way or another and were using others and in this case me as the pawn for their own benefit.

Usually when I am angry, I bake or I do some physical form of labor that helps to dissipate my frustration, or at least make me so tired that I cannot think about it then anyway. This time the lawn mower was my device of hard work to let go of my frustration. When I finished mowing, I decided to walk down into the woods which is a major part of my property. I had a little over twelve acres of woody, swampy land that at times has been a haven for some of my heart cries. It is also a refuge for wildlife. I guess you could say, I was going to go find God and talk to Him. I wanted to be alone, and I wanted to be able to say what I wanted without being heard by human ears and I wanted Him to give me some answers *now*.

In the process of many tearful footsteps, angry reasoning, unfocused wandering, I came to an area that was a mass of branches, brambles, briars, shrubs, and trees that created a wall on all sides. The marshy moss was wet, and my feet were soaked. There was a tree stump I stood up on and cried, "Lord, make a way out of this mess." I was not just referring to the mess of dead branches and thick brambles that formed a hedge around me. I stood there in silence. I heard the birds, and their song was soothing. I heard the squirrels, and their antics were humorous. I heard the brushing of the branches of the tall trees and their presence was majestic. I heard the humming of the mosquitoes, and they were irritating.

I wasn't sure where I was. I could hear distant traffic, faint buzzing of a chain saw, and the occasional barking of a dog far off but most of all I could hear loneliness. It was then in the quietness of the breeze that the words came through, "Search for Me with all your heart."

"What are You talking about God?" This is not the answer I wanted or was even expecting, I shouted back to Him, "Isn't that what I have been doing?" I questioned. "Here I am every day depending on You, calling out to You, Lord, studying about You, giving Bible studies, witnessing and now You have the nerve to say this to me?" I stood like a statue shot in the gut but with internal bleeding, not knowing what was next. "Lord, what do You mean?" Now I could no longer shout. I changed my attitude. "Help me to find You and help me out of this mess emotionally as well as this tangled mass that I am surrounded by." I meant that two-fold and He knew it for I found my way to the wide path that came directly to the backside of my garden. I came out of that tangled mess full of scratches, and soaked feet to the perfect path waiting that brought me to the familiar area.

God had spoken a direct command to me. I decided I needed to look at what the scriptures had to say about "search" to gain a better understanding of what God was trying to tell me (Numbers 10:33 NKJV).—is an explanation of the three-day journey of the ark of the covenant in "searching out a resting place."

We all need a "resting place" where we can find release of the situations that pulls us in and there is no solution that gives us peace. Within this resting place, it is then we can hear God and can be directed. I was brought to a resting place in the midst of a place that both physically and emotionally challenged, and I didn't want to be in it, but until I stopped screaming, I couldn't hear the answer.

"Would not God search this out? For He knows the secrets of the heart" (Psalms 44:21). God already knew what my heart was going through, and He let me go through all the anger and put myself in a position of total dependence before I could hear Him plainly. He was searching for me as eagerly as I was searching for Him. He knew the situation and because He is a righteous and fair God, He searches out all sides. "I call to remembrance my song in the night; I meditate within my heart, and my spirit makes diligent search" (Psalms 77:6 NKJV). This brought to my remembrances at another time when I had just gone through a major surgery. While sleeping I was awakened by a Mockingbird singing his various tunes. It is a Mockingbird that sings in the night and mimics the songs of other birds. His song did not just awaken my sleep, but my heart and I meditated on the wonderful things of God. Had my heart momentarily forgotten God's generous mercy while I was searching in angry pursuit?

"Search me, O God, and know my heart; try me and know my anxieties" (Psalms 139:23 NKJV). That was just what God was doing. He was searching for my heart while I was wandering aimlessly and not using both sides of my brain to function properly. He knew my anxieties and was waiting for me to stop and "be still and know that He is God." (Psalms 46:10 NKJV) "I applied my heart to know, to search and seek out wisdom and the reason of things, to know the wickedness of folly, even of foolishness and madness" Ecclesiastes 7:25 (NKJV).

I thought about all the foolishness I seemed to be going through to come to a simple conclusion. Some might even think it was madness. Our thoughts are not God's thoughts, and neither are our solutions His. We need to search the motives of our own hearts and seek God's wisdom to apply it so that we will not be caught up in such folly. "I, the Lord search the heart, I *test* the mind, even to give every man according to his ways, according to the fruit of his doings" Jeremiah 17:10 (NKJV). My reasoning is pure foolishness when God has everything already under control.

While I was walking in the woods, I plucked a small intricate white flower from the carpet of pine spills and mossy green. It reminded me of a strawberry blossom but that wasn't its purpose. The soft petals and the loveliness stayed within the clasp of my fingers as I had irrationally rambled through broken down branches, twisted and gnarled briars to reach what was a muddled mess. I had dropped the flower along the way. In our folly do we drop the flower of Grace and forget Who is in control? Do we lose sight of the beauty at our fingertips and look always at the mangled mess before us?

Finally, I was brought to what He wanted to tell me. "For I know the thoughts that I think toward you, says the Lord, thoughts of peace and not of evil, to give you a future and a hope. Then you will call upon Me and go and pray to Me, and I will listen to you. And you will seek Me and find Me when you search for Me with all your heart. I will be found by you, says the Lord, and I will bring you back from your captivity" Jeremiah 29: 11-14 (NKJV).

SEARCHING WITH ALL MY HEART

Sometimes it is difficult to make heads or
tails out of what life has to give.
We reason the pros and cons and weigh
the balance of the life we live.
We forget to inhale the breath of life.
Because we are filled up with anger which aides to our strife. Calm is needed for the raging answers of my mind,

Where intense criticisms are all, I find.
I need Thy precious assurance of peace.
That Thy precious promises will never cease.
I beg that evil will not have its way with me.
Rebuke the echoes of its curse and set me free.
Child, "Search for me with all your heart"
I will calm the fears and thwart the flying dart.
Don't let go of the loveliness within your fingertips.
Don't cast aside the blessings from My lips.
I have spoken your name, when you searched for Me.
Beside the tangled mass beside the mossy stump of a tree.
I was there when you could not see.
I heard your cries; the flower you dropped was Me.
Forgive me Lord for the anger I dispelled.
For the doubt and fears that I held.
I thought I had already searched Thee out.
But in a few moments, I let my faith turn to doubt.
Thank you, Lord, for being in control when I was lost:
For buying me back at ransom's cost.
Remind me again when the mistrusting begins to start
To search for Thee once more "with all my heart." And when I released it all to Him;
He spoke again.
"I have loved thee with an everlasting love."
Written by Joyce A. Leonard

"A HOUSE OF TEARS"

Come into my abode, such as it is.
There is no carpet on the kitchen floor,
And tape covers the cracks in the door.
The floor is tilted, it certainly is.
The leaking roof has needs of repair,
And boards creak under your feet going up the stair.
But my little house is gentle
And it came by a miracle along the way,
So, I only lovingly complain about where I stay.
Come into my abode and warm your heart.
The walls are uneven and only half done.
The windows show fingerprints in the sun.
The furnace is noisy but warms the chill.
Just painted shelves is where my dishes sit still.
In my tiny kitchen that has become a part
Of my gentle house where the miracle did start.
So, come into my abode and share with me,
The laughter of today
And the tears of yesterday,
Where only a friend can enter and see
In the gentle house that came to be.

CHAPTER ELEVEN

A House of Tears

If the walls could speak—what would they say? In this little house where four children lived with their mother, was there a father? Maybe once in a while, and it was their father and then another one took his place. Tears flowed heavily when the divorce came and soon after the father sold his children to another name. And that father after years of abuse—converted but then returned to the actions of infidelity and the more tears flowed.

The laughter was expressed by pets that kept them going. The dog and cats, the ducks and chickens were their solace; the good moments of playing flashlight tag, the comfort of school, sports and friends that came by to play. Also, the neighbor who raised turkeys and talking about silly actions of things like weeding the garden and laughing about how one carried on as if weeding the carrots hurt the weeds that were being pulled. Just little silly things kept the laughter alive and when all was quiet tears flowed quietly in their beds. When more problems arose, and the mother fell into depression that took its toll, a neighbor said, "Put the problems on a shelf for a while and someday it will change."

Alone the mother tried to nurture the children God had given her to care for, and she sent her son to a Christian camp. He did not stay long. His thoughts were for his mother, who was working to support and care for his siblings and his mind was infused with getting back home to help. He began his trek to go home and save her from her problems. At 8 years old he began his walk over fifty miles toward home when a minister came by and picked him up and brought him home. God is always watching over His children everywhere and that was the lesson she wanted instilled in her children. The often-quoted scripture "All things work together for good to them who love God and are called according to His purpose" (Romans 8:28 NKJV).

There have been other homes filled with tears; Tears that God had collected in a bottle and what happens to those tears? (Psalms 56:8 NKJV) "You number my wanderings; Put my tears in Your bottle. Are they not in Your Book?" The Book of Life—This is where everything is recorded. And it is my belief that whoever caused those tears will be held accountable if those who caused them did not repent for their act in making those tears happen.

Those who have riches are still vulnerable for tears and heart ache. Riches do not keep you exempt from happiness. In I Samuel 25 the story of Nabal and Abigail unfolds. Beginning in verse 2—They were from the wilderness of Maon and his business was in Carmal, probably the next town over since it was just about a mile north of Maon. Carmel was fertile with green fields and plenty of water for his herds of sheep and goats. The Bible reveals that there were three thousand sheep and a thousand goats. Nabal was a very wealthy man. But because he was wealthy, and he could afford anything he wanted he was greedy as well. His wife, Abigail is described in verse three "as a woman of good understanding and beautiful in appearance," but her husband Nabal was "harsh and evil in his doings."

That tells the story right away that there were many tears in Abigail's home. All the wealth in the world cannot make up for lack of love and respect for each other. Nabal was from the House of Caleb as Caleb was a good friend of Joshua's and that was the connection of their friendship. It was sheep shearing time and David heard about Nabal in the wilderness shearing sheep. David sent ten young men to go greet Nabal in his name announcing that he is the son of Jesse.

The message was sincere with an offer to protect the herds during this time of shearing saying how the Lord had blessed him and he wanted to return the favor. Since Nabal was busy, the servants patiently waited for his answer. He came through harsh and unthankful for any protection. He didn't need it! His reply in verse 10 (paraphrased) "I don't know this David son of Jesse. Who is he and who does he think he is anyway? I am able to care for myself so why should I give any of my food to him and why should I trust them anyway?" The servants of David left and went back and gave the message to David.

David was angry. He was ready to do battle with the insults of this man. He took four hundred men with him and left two hundred to care for their supplies and off he went to pay Nabal a visit. One of the servants went to Abigail and told her the story of what had just taken place.

Abigail listened and with great understanding—she moved quickly. She gathered "two hundred loaves of bread, two skins of wine, five sheep already dressed, five seals of roasted grain, one hundred clusters of grapes, two hundred cakes of figs and loaded them up on donkeys" (Verse 18). She was out to undo what her husband had done and ask for mercy.

She met David on his way to do battle with her husband. She did some pretty fast talking and every bit of it was directed by God to meet David's ears and stop him from bloodshed. His reply to her in verse thirty-two, "Then David said to Abigail, blessed is the Lord God of Israel, who sent you this day to meet me." He respected her wishes and she returned home after their encounter. She found Nabal had returned home and was feasting and was filled with drunkenness. The name Nabal means "foolish." She waited until morning after he had regained some of his senses and told him in part what transpired. He turned to stone which meant he became paralyzed and in verse 38 the Bible says that "after about ten days, the Lord struck Nabal and he died."

Nabal was a harsh and evil man and cared only for himself. I believe that Abigail cried many tears and lived in a house of tears. All that wealth held nothing without the love for others. From ancient times to modern day, events still have the same outcome if you do not live for God. If you live only to satisfy yourself, there will always be a house of tears.

"For Behold, I will create a new heaven and a new earth,
And the former shall not be remembered or come to mind.:
:...the voice of weeping shall no longer be heard...
Nor the voice of crying"
(Isaiah 65:17,19 second part—NKJV).

CHAPTER TWELVE

"Whistling Girls and Crowing Hens"

"What is wise and understanding among you?
Let him show by good conduct that his works are done
In the meekness of wisdom"
James 3:13 (NKJV).

"There she goes again, whistling," was Daddy's remark to his youngest daughter. "Don't you know that whistling girls and crowing hens always come to some bad end?" "Oh daddy" Joyce replied," you are so funny." And with that she went merrily whistling as she continued her day.

The background of this saying developed from an observation of several origins which may have developed in the 17th or 18th century. The definition comes with one thought that old ladies often tell tales and hens don't usually crow unless they have some altering disease! It comes about as being some sort of warning signal and was quipped to warn the listener to be wary.

Unleashed Promises of Merciful Love

I have seen cartoon characters after they have done something quite mischievous walk off whistling as if they knew nothing of what had just transpired! In following along this story line let us take a peek back into Bible times.

In II Samuel chapter 13, we will see who was whistling and how the crowing hens were an evil influence that came about in the lives of some important people. Starting in verse twenty-three in chapter 13, Absalom, King David's son was preparing for sheep shearing that was to be a time of festive rejoicing. This was located near Ephraim which was about fifteen miles from Jerusalem where his father King David reigned.

Absalom had invited all the princes which were his brothers and half-brothers. Absalom was third born. He also invited Annon who was in line for the throne. There were some odds with the two, but all was well in this festive event or seemed well on the surface of the event that was to take place. Even King David, his father was invited. It was important to Absalom to have his father present, but David declined. At least Annon was going to be there, and he would represent his father. That all seems like good intentional reasoning, doesn't it?

But Absaom was crafty maybe like some "whistling girls." He had an intense hatred for his brother Annon that had been festering for two years. It seems to run in the family because Annon was as crafty as his brother. It was a battle that raged inside both of them. It seems that Annon disgraced their beautiful sister Tamar. Annon desired his half-sister Tamar to the point of making himself sick over her.

Well, here comes the "crowing hen" Jonadab, a friend in the palace. He was aware of Annon's desire for his sister and so planted the seed of deceit in his mind and Annon followed through with his evil plot. He used his father, King David to supply his whim. Now King David was not naive to the situation that Annon was looking at his sister in ways that he shouldn't, but he had no idea of his son's intent. If he had, he never would have allowed the plot to take place as it had been forbidden that his sister go to his apartment alone.

Annon used the same crafty game that a child uses with their parents. The child goes to the mother and asks if they can do something. They know it may be denied but they ask anyway. And the mother will say, not really wanting to be the "bad guy," "ask your father." So, the child goes with the same request to Dad. Dad not wanting to disappoint the child says about the same thing and then the child now has the control and says, "Well, mom said it is okay with her if it is with you." And so, the dad says "okay" because evidently it is okay with mom! This is the same scenario in a greater form with Annon. He probably didn't have a mom to get permission from, but he did need the permission of his father. If his father would allow his sister to enter into his room under the guise of illness, his plot would be a success.

Tamar was a royal virgin and her attire showed respect for her purity as well as the aura of her beauty. She did not expect any foul play when she was called to Annon's room, after all her father would not place her in jeopardy. If David had for a minute thought his son had evil intentions toward Tamar, he never would have allowed her to go there alone. King David was always filled with guilt from his own sins committing adultery with Bathsheba. God had forgiven him, but David was not confident in forgiving himself and that was always in the back of his mind. David had not been emotionally stable since that incident.

Have you heard people say, "Look what David did? And God called him the apple of His eye." They seem to think that because David did such a transgression that it is okay and an excuse for their own transgression. The Bible says, "all have sinned and fallen short of the glory of God" Romans 3:23 (NKJV). And the part they forget is that David had a contrite and repentant heart to the point of never committing that sin again. It was his sensitivity and his humble attitude that was pleasing to God. But he paid a price for his gentleness toward his sons because it allowed his sons to go "whistling" in their own folly creating "crowing hens" in their lives. They even lost respect for their own father.

It is a tough call when you remember your own sins and become lenient toward those who need discipline. Then comes the saying "do as I say not as I do." God forgives the heart that is truly repentant, but the healing comes when you are able to forgive yourself and show your reputation to those around you as honorable.

It was difficult for David to be able to have the authority of a father with his sons when he himself had fallen under the same temptations. He should not have condoned the sins of his sons. Young people know their parents pretty well and know just how far they can push the envelope. Annon and Absalom were no exception. They took advantage of their father's sensitivity and his love for them.

Back to Annon and how he powerfully overtook Tamar when she entered his room alone. She desperately tried to reason with him. His senses were dulled with lust, and he could not even connect with a reasoning mind and so he overtook her without regard to the humiliation she would endure or recognizing that this was a shame and disgrace not only to her but to the family. He did not listen. Then adding insult to injury for what he had just done to her—literal rape, he demanded that she leave. Verse fifteen says "He hated her exceedingly and that hatred was greater than the love for which he loved her." Tamar openly tore her clothes, her majestic robe of many colors and put ashes on her head wailing in bitter grief of the horrible sin that had been committed against her.

Absalom was livid with his brother, and it says that David was "wroth." Instead of taking care of the matter legally and punishing Annon for his crime, Absalom just let his anger fester and become like a cancer. He seethed in anger and plotted his revenge for two years! And dear old Dad... what did he do? He was still caught up in his own guilt. He felt his hands were tied because of his own sin. So Annon was left unpunished for his sin or so it seemed.

Annon and Absalom were not out to make peace with one another. Their lives were lacking in discipline. They were selfish and rampant in evil, one evil deed leading to another. It was a classic case of corruption and controversy of who would be first, best and most powerful.

The party began and while the feasting was in full swing, the order was given by Absalom to his servants to murder his brother Annon. Like his father he contracted the murder. It was as if because he didn't do it himself, his hands were not dirtied. That was the attitude of David when he had Uriah killed so he could have Bathsheba. Sin added to sin and sin to cover sin.

All the brothers fled including Absalom. They all went to a place of safety figuring that there may be a mass murder, so they took off. And then the news media announced to King David that his son Absalom had murdered all his sons (Verse 30). David in his grief-stricken heart tore his clothes and lay on the ground with his servants surrounding him.

Wait, here comes the "crowing hen" Jonadab. "No, no King David, don't take this to heart, it was only revenge from Absalom for the sin against Tamar, for only Annon is dead." David knew in his heart that this was the outcome of his own failure to address that which had happened two years ago. I am sure he looked back on his own life and was filled with anxiety of his own past sins and how history had repeated itself.

How many times in our own lives have we walked outside of the path of righteousness and felt the guilt and the deep remorse for our sins. Maybe we have thought "if I had only followed the path of the Lord in the first place." But God often allows detours. He says in Revelation 3:19 NKJV "As many as I love, I rebuke and chasten. Therefore, be zealous and repent." I am thankful that repentance brings us back to our rightful place and that God doesn't just let us wallow in our sins.

It was three years before Absalom tried to get back in the good graces of his father. When he returned to Jerusalem, it took a while before his father, King David permitted his son to even be in his presence. During the time of not being able to be treated as royalty, Absalom began to have the sympathies of the people. They felt it was unfair for Absalom to be treated this way. II Samuel 14:25(NKJV) portrays Absalom in this way—"…there was no one who was praised as much as Absalom for his good looks. From the sole of his foot to the crown of his head, there was no blemish on him." His hair was long and heavy, and it flowed beautifully. His beauty became a deceiver of the people.

Lucifer, the fallen angel, also had great beauty and he was called "son of the morning." He was the highest angel in heaven, an angel of light and great beauty. Isaiah 14:13-14 (NKJV) Lucifer said, "I will ascend into the heaven, I will exalt my throne above the stars of God, I will sit upon the mount of the congregation, in the sides of the north: I will ascend above the heights of the clouds; I will be like the Most High."

Absalom had the same desire for attainment to be like the highest in his father's position. His scheming was crafty, dishonest, and unfair. He was practicing the flattery of the "crowing hens." Absalom was a follower of Satan. He had been permitted to do his own selfish acts and be rewarded for them for so long that he could now attain whatever he wanted and now he was ready to attack the throne and overthrow his father. That is the same story as Satan himself. He attacked the Thone of God and connived to overthrow the Most High.

Absalom had exonerated himself from the death of his brother. After all he was justified after what Annon had done to their sister Tamar. But as the saying goes—"two wrongs do not make a right." It seemed that the people were mesmerized by Absalom. At long last he was reinstated by the "kiss" of acceptance from his father. He gained control over his father and went head-long "whistling" into his scheme displaying the profile of the dutiful son. He gained allegiance and power from influential men with position that said "GO" in his last-ditch effort to overthrow his father from the throne. He forgot that he was not dealing with just his father, he was dealing with God. "If God is for us who can be against us?" Romans 8:31 (NKJV).

II Samuel 18:9 climaxes the story with Absalom's death. He was caught in an Oak tree by the neck when his mule went into the thicket. Joah had instigated the parable given by a woman to persuade David to have Absalom reunite with his son, finished Absalom off "with three darts and royalty was thrown into a pit and covered with stones." King David reflected the sorrow of a grieving father but also for the responsibility of his sins that were the catalyst to his sons' sins. David cried, with heart wrenching grief that echoes down through the ages for any parent who loses a child, 'My son, my son Absalom." His desolation of losing this son reeked grief throughout the courtyard with his loss. No whistling girls or crowing hens can cover the sins of the fathers upon the children.

"WHISTLING GIRLS AND CROWING HENS"

Oh, whistling girls, with mischief eyes,
Spinning your tale of woes and whys.
Oh crowing hens…
With immoral friends
Learn that the gentle spirit is better yet,
Covered under the Almighty wings as a safety net.
Little Girls have changed their whistling tune
To Jesus loves me, He is coming soon.
Old hens have stopped crowing with flatter,
Clucking gossip with back biting that doesn't matter.
The "bad ends" have turned into a victory feast.
What once meant the most is now the least?
The created lies
Have turned to repentant cries.
The crafty ways spelling envy and deceit,
Are now sins laid at Jesus feet.
The tangled web of confusion
Is the folly of a fool's conclusion?
For God is God and sin is sin.
He can give victory; He is the win.
For little girls changed their whistling tune,
Humming Jesus loves me, He is coming soon.
And crowing hens now cluck a new tale.
Jesus is first, He does not fail.
Written by Joyce A. Leonard December 5, 1998
"…reject profane and old wives' fables
and Exercise yourself toward godliness"
I Timothy 4:7 (NKJV).

CHAPTER THIRTEEN

A Bittersweet Love Story

"He brought me to the banqueting house,
And His banner over me was love"
Song of Solomon 2:4 (NKJV).

*A*lta you cannot lay on the couch sobbing everyday of your life away. It was time for Walter to go out on his own. He is twenty-three you know." Between sobs, Alta lamented, "I know Mama, but I miss him so much and he was always going to milk the cows, so I didn't have to and now he is gone. I have to help Pa with the milking, I hate it." She continued sobbing while expressing her desire to find a help mate that would love her throughout her life. "I am getting old, and I want to have children and my own home." In the Wetmore home of nine children living on a farm selling eggs and milk in the buggy from door to door was not always a profitable life, but Pa Wetmore always paid a faithful tithe and God supplied all their needs. They were rich in love and trusted the Almighty with every part of their life.

Ma made delicious molasses popcorn balls and brought them to all the church socials and Christmas school programs. Everyone wanted to be first in line to get their share. Mama couldn't make those delicious popcorn balls for long as she had her first stroke just before she and Pa were leaving to go Christmas shopping, Mama went to the hospital, but Pa went on alone to shop for us girls. He got my sister and I sweaters. Mine was brown and hers was fuchsia. We wore them for a long time. My first boyfriend was Harry at school, and we had to be separated because we spent so much time writing notes to each other. Those wonderful meals and all the canning Mama did came to a halt. She made the best chicken dinners from the canned white meat chicken. She worked hard to make sure we had good meals. And the cookie jar was always full of white. thick cookies. We never went without.

Pa would hitch up his team of horses "Prince and Frank" and off he would go in the buggy to take chickens to the meat market and peddled eggs around Salamanca, which was near Bucktooth Run in Upper New York State. Ma was my example, and I was impressed with her gentleness. She always made her bed before leaving the bedroom and combed her hair. And Pa always got up singing in his melodious voice. He worked hard on the farm and drove school bus as well. But he took time to beautify his home as he loved flowers and they were displayed throughout the rock garden by our home. There was a bleeding-heart plant that was planted in memory of my brother Victor who died not long after his appendectomy. I watched Ma break down in church in tears while she and Pa were singing after Victor's death "There's No Disappointment in Heaven."

As tragic as these times were—there was always love manifested in our home from the time we got up until we went to bed. God was first and foremost in our minds and we were brought up to keep the Sabbath holy and go to church every week. Our family filled the pews. We sang the loudest and were fervent in prayer. Pa was emotional and often tears trickled down his cheeks while he prayed.

Then the day came—"Alta, I would like you to meet our friend Howard," Phyllis was beaming as she introduced us. Sheepishly I took his hand and made some remark, but in my heart—I knew this was the one I would marry, Howard Sampson. It wasn't long after meeting Howard that I had a proposal. "Alta," Pa questioned in his deep voice, why I was carrying on so "What is the matter?" I sobbed, "Clinton asked me to marry him, and I don't want to." Pa immediately consoled me with, "You don't have to marry anyone you don't want to." What a relief! Since I had longed to be married and Howard had not asked me yet, I just thought that was my fate.

I had dropped out of high school after I had a tonsillectomy. I always wanted to finish and so returned and was in the same grade as my younger sister. We finished together. I had gone to a 4-H party that had square dancing. When Ma found out, she hollered at me, but later apologized for doing so. I really had done a lot worse in my life. I recounted worse things in my life, some of which if Pa had known about, he would have let me go see "Gone with The Wind" with my friend instead of ending up at Sawmill Run necking!

My journey took me to Washington, D.C. to finish my course in secretarial credits. During that time, I had become so undernourished that I came down with diphtheria and was put in intensive care. Later after my recovery and marrying Howard, we lived in Ohio for a time. He was an ordained Baptist minister. He had been previously married with three children. He found his wife was being unfaithful to him and he got a divorce. I actually paid for the divorce with money I had saved for college.

I attended Atlantic Union College in Massachusetts and acquired my LPN degree. That was one of the happiest days of my life. Howard went to church on Sunday, and I went to Sabbath. There was contention during those years, but I continued to pray for him. We had seven beautiful children. Howard was a hunter and our home was decorated with all the taxidermist kills he had made in different states. Gene, our precious baby was killed in the process of making a pond by our home. Gene had crawled out in the tall grass,. Howard had a bucket loader and not seeing baby Gene scooped him up in the shovel! By the time he recognized what happened, Gene had died.

My family was all there with my little girls picking buttercups and daisies to put on the top of his glass topped coffin. I remember screaming, "I must hold him one more time" as I flipped the cover off and my brothers raced to hold me. Howard was a harsh man and always had to be tough. He never let his emotions show. It was considered a weakness. I knew he was in the valley of despair even though he didn't show it to anyone.

The years passed by with my children and all the challenges that come with bringing up such a large family. I was determined to make it work regardless of the disputes and sometimes the frustrations and heartache. He asked me to join his church band since I played guitar and so I took lessons to play the twelve-string guitar and played in the church band where he attended. He had changed his vocation after a brief time of pastoral work and began to work for Ford Motor Company. He was a good provider.

It was after many years of marriage I continued to attend church with him on Sunday and he went to church with me on Saturday, the Bible Sabbath. I felt my prayers were being answered. After fifty-two years of marriage, I had come down with breast cancer and passed away in 2004. It was four months later that Howard died.

I, Joyce A. Leonard, her niece am privileged to know her story from her own words. She always told me how proud she was that I took my first steps as a toddler. I am writing this tribute of her life from the pages she wrote that is in my keeping showing her courageous life through much adversity; a woman that was strong in her faith with a tremendous love for God and family.. Although there is much that is unsaid in these few pages, the greatest and most valuable part of this bittersweet love story is that her love for God never waned. Her marriage was not perfect, but it was a witness to those who knew her and watched her life. She was a light that reflected Jesus and His banner over her was love.

IF THE LOVE OF A DEAD BABY COULD SPEAK

Mommy, hold God's hand
And you will be holding me.
Obey His command
And you will be loving me. Never give up your dream,
Never let your hopes go.
Watch for your answers in moonbeams,
And when they come, you'll know.
Mommy, never cry for me,
For one day when heartaches are gone,
In your arms I will be
When we have the new Dawn.
With your faith we can't go wrong-
So please don't let me down.
Lift up your chin and sing a song.
Keep lookin' up and we'll be foun.'
Hang on to that dream
And follow that star
Someday we will ride on that heavenly beam,
And we will go far

For into those pearly gates,
Where the loving Jesus awaits
I am sleeping in the arms of the earth,
Ready to awaken for the new birth,
Until then He sends the assurance of His word.
"Blessed are they who have not seen but have believed"
With each promise that is heard a blessing is received.
So, have faith, Mommy, till the day when we will know
When we have reached the end of our rainbow.
Written by Joyce A. Wetmore age 16
In remembrance of Gene Ellis Sampson
March 27, 1964

Linda Sampson beside Joyce Leonard holding Gene Sampson & Alicia Sampson sitting next to her on right

CHAPTER FOURTEEN

What Can A Dream Mean?

"In all your ways acknowledge Him
And He will direct your path"
Proverbs 3:6 (NKJV).

*I*t was 1953 and the Kuykendall's were burning all their bridges behind them and heading for Honolulu, Hawaii. The invitation was more than they could have possibly hoped for, impeccable weather and people of so many nationalities and an active church with much work to be done for the Lord. Josephine and Milton Kuykendall were workers for the Lord and used their many talents to be a witness for those they encountered. Milton was a carpenter and a contractor. And Josephine fondly known as Jo was a highly educated secretary and well advanced in Bible studies. There were two new areas for the Hawaiian Mission Academy, a church in Kailua across from the island of Honolulu and a school on the island of Maui.

Milton's work with building and designing was only part of their work there along with the Bible studies with the islanders in their homes, they also enjoyed the incredible expeditions that proved to be an exhilarating experience of underwater exploring the reefs. Milton did his work for the Conference concerning the school and church, he was concentrating on starting his business. He had begun an extensive shell collection and they had bought a house. Their roots were being grounded in this paradise as they worked for the Lord. Life was good and there was nothing better instore for them, or so they thought.

Jo had cousins who were active in the Bath, Maine Church and they had talked about Bath being a mission field early on before Jo and Milton left for Hawaii. Then the letter came from her cousin Marion with the questions, "Isn't it time, haven't you finished your work in Hawaii? We need you in Bath, too." Jo was annoyed with the letter and wrote back, "Surely you can find someone closer to do your work for you?" Some time went by, and another letter came. "Plans are being made for a new hospital and Milton needs to be in charge of the construction." On the heels of that the offer came from one of the doctors they knew offering Jo as the receptionist for his office since she was well equipped as a medical secretary. Jo promptly sent back another letter, "Milton had plenty of work in Honolulu and I am not interested in sitting at a desk all day!" The response to that was "As soon as you have enough Bible studies, I will relieve you of your desk job." Irritation was growing and Jo answered back quite curtly, "Thanks, but no thanks." The letters continued and then the light went on—Jo asked Milton, "Do you suppose the Lord wants us to go to Maine? They discussed the thought since they had always relied on the Lord to lead them, and they began to pray for conviction.

Then it happened. Jo had a vivid dream. It was so vivid it was well remembered, every detail. She was remembering her dream that next morning. She and Milton were seated with two of their friends on a sloping hillside. On her right was a road by a river and a bridge. To the left the world was on fire which seemed to be sweeping toward her. She knew that this was the end of the world, and Jesus was coming. Her heart was happy. Immediately a group of young people came up to her and asked, "Do you have a picnic basket?" She asked "Why do you want a picnic basket? They answered, "We thought we would pack a basket and go on the other side of the river until the fire went out." In her dream, she told them," That will not do any good, for this is the end of the world and Jesus is coming." She did not hear a reply and they faded from sight. She turned to her friends who were with them on the hillside, and she asked, "Shouldn't we cross the river as the fire is getting really close?" They answered, "No the fire will not touch us." The dream ended.

As Jo stood by her kitchen sink reviewing the dream, she had the impression that this was her answer. "The answer to what?" she asked out loud. She then suddenly realized that in this dream there were no palm trees, and the scenery was New England scenery. She knew that this was where the Lord wanted them to go. When Milton returned home that evening, she related the dream and without giving him any personal observations, she asked what he thought. His answer was immediate. "Write and tell them we will come to Maine."

Once settled back in Maine, Jo went looking for the bridge she saw in her dream back in Hawaii. Then it happened. She was driving from Wonderance General Store in Bath back via Washington Street and there before her eyes was the bridge, and the river with the sloping hillside. This can only be seen in a few places along the river. This was confirmation that she was in the exact spot that God wanted her to be. Milton was the overseer of the erection of Parkview Hospital in Brunswick, Maine and later he was instrumental in the beginnings of Pine Tree Academy in Freeport, Maine. Jo sat at a desk as medical secretary for over 20 years. She also held nutrition classes, Bible studies and was active in many ways as she and Milton continued their work for the Lord. They began their own bread bakery business and fed many people along with providing for young people to attend a Christian school during their ministry for God. Their death was a loss on this earth, but their rewards will be many in the heavenly kingdom for those they so sacrificially worked for both in Hawaii and Maine.

Joseph's Dreams

Everyone knows the story of Joseph and his coat of many colors. He seemed to be the favored child for the Bible says, "Israel loved Joseph more than all his children because he was the son of his old age" Genesis 37:3 (NKJV). His brothers began to hate Joseph because they saw this favoritism. Joseph dreamed dreams and then he told them to his brothers and that incited their hatred even more. Verse 7—"There we were binding sheaves in the field, then behold, my sheaf arose and also stood upright; and indeed, your sheaves stood all around and bowed down to my sheaf." That didn't set well among the brothers.

It seemed like Joseph couldn't keep his mouth shut about his dreams. He didn't realize the hatred that was brewing in his brothers' hearts, so he had another dream and pleaded with them to listen to his dream. He told this dream in verse 9—"Look, I have dreamed another dream. And this time, the sun, moon and the eleven stars bowed down to me."

The day came that Joseph's brothers were tending the flocks in Shechem, and Joseph was sent by his father to make sure all was well. On his journey to find his brothers, he found out from a certain man that his brothers had moved on to Dothan. Joseph continued to look for them. They spotted

Joseph coming and decided among themselves to conspire against him (Verse 19). "Look, this dreamer is coming! (Verse 20) "Come let us now kill him and cast him into the pit and we shall say 'Some wild beast has devoured him.' We shall see what becomes of his dreams."

The elder brother Reuben spoke up and said they should not shed any blood but to cast him in the pit and leave him. It was Reuben's intention to come back later and pull him out, but that isn't what happened. Can you imagine such a conniving treatment of their brother because of jealousy? It seems that Joseph should have been more careful about telling his dreams but at seventeen he didn't seem to think much about it and was just sharing what he had dreamt.

They stripped his coat of many colors from him and threw him into the pit with no water then sat down to eat a meal! They had hardened hearts that had not thought of the outcome of these circumstances or compassion on the welfare of their brother. They thought they had covered themselves quite nicely. While eating, they looked up to see a band of Ishmaelites bearing goods that they could get money for on their way to Egypt.

It was Judah who decided they should sell him. They lifted their brother out of the pit and sold him for twenty shekels of silver which would have been about $200 in today's increments. In the meantime, Reuben returned to find Joseph missing and tore his clothes in grief. He went to his brothers frantic. They took Joseph's coat of many colors, killed a baby goat and dipped his coat in it then took it to their father saying a wild beast had killed Joseph.

There must have been a pact between them never to reveal what really happened as their father refused to be comforted and wept bitterly. Joseph was sold to Potiphar, captain of the guards, an officer of Pharaoh. Joseph gained recognition for his loyalty to Potiphar and worked hard for him until Potiphar's wife noticed Joseph and how handsome and strong he was. She determined that she wanted Joseph and propositioned him. The Lord had His hand on Joseph, and He had plans that no one could imagine.

The day came when Joseph came in to work for Potiphar's wife and there were not any other men there. She was alone. She took hold of his garment, but he left his garment in her hand and fled outside. She was humiliated that he refused her and screamed so other men came to her and her web of lies began. It went from them to her husband, then Joseph was thrown into prison. The Bible says, in Genesis 39:19 "the Lord was with Joseph and showed him mercy and gave him favor in the sight of the keeper of the prison."

Within the prison were a butler and baker from the palace of Pharaoh were under the confinement of the prison keeper. They were cell mates with Joseph. Both of them had a dream. They were confused about the dream and Joseph told them that the interpretation of dreams belongs to God and only God can reveal the meaning of them. The Chief Butler told his dream to Joseph. His dream was about a vine that had three branches coming from it and there were grapes in great clusters on it. He pressed the grapes and wine went into the Pharoah's cup. Joseph told him the three branches represented three days and then Pharaoh would restore him to his place in the palace. Joseph asked the Chief Butler to remember him when he was well accepted to speak to Pharaoh concerning him as he had been thrown into prison for a crime he did not commit.

When the Chief Baker saw that the interpretation was true, he told Joseph that he also had a dream, and he told his dream to Joseph; his dream was of three white baskets on his head. The upper most basket had baked goods for the Pharaoh, and birds came and ate the baked goods out of the basket on his head. Joseph told the Chief Baker what it meant. The three baskets represented three days and within those three days Pharaoh would lift off the baker's head and hang him from a tree and the birds would eat his flesh. I don't think I would like hearing that. These dreams did come to pass but the Chief Butler forgot all about Joseph.

It was two more years that Joseph spent in that dungeon. Do you often wonder why he had to spend such a long time for a crime he never committed? He was sold as a slave by his brothers and treated unfairly and here he was in a dungeon. It wasn't like he was in Hawaii! Then the Pharaoh himself had a dream and it troubled him. He called his magicians to tell him what it meant, and they didn't have a clue. Then the Butler remembered how Joseph interpreted his dream and he told the Pharaoh, and Joseph was sent for immediately. Again, Joseph did not take any credit for himself but told the Pharaoh in Chapter forty-one—verse sixteen, "It is not me; God will give Pharaoh an answer of peace." So, the dream was unfolded to Joseph, Pharaoh saw himself standing on the bank of the river, cows came up out of the river looking fat and they fed in the meadow. Then seven other cows came up came up after them and they were ugly and undernourished as if just bones and no flesh. The horrible looking cows ate up the first nice fat cows that had come up first. No one would have known they had eaten the good cows because they still looked ugly.

The second dream that Pharoah described was seven heads came up on one stalk full and good. Then the seven stalks withered and thin were blighted by an east wind that came up. Then those heads that were thin devoured the good ones. Joseph explained that both dreams the second dream that Pharoah described was seven heads came up on one stalk full meant the same. Seven represented seven years of plenty throughout the land of Egypt but after that would be seven years of famine. The famine will be very severe. Pharoah had the dream again two more times before he decided as to what he should do. After consideration of the most wise and discerning man that could advise and oversee this grave situation, Joseph found favor with the Pharoah and had rule over the land becoming the top man in the land second in command to Pharoah himself.

The dreams that came into play early in Joseph's life with the sheaves bowing down came to pass when his whole family came to Egypt for food. They bowed before Joseph and honored him. God's plan was devised long before it took place. He had a plan, and it was for good and not for evil. He united Joseph with his family and his brothers were truly repentant of what they had done to their brother long before they knew the power that their brother now held.

Some dream dreamless insignificant dreams that hold no meaning only replayed in the night after something they have seen that affected them. Some dreams are hilariously funny while others are called nightmares and you don't want a rerun of those. The Bible tells us in Joel 2:28-29 (NKJV)—

> "And it shall come to pass afterward that I
> will pour out My Spirit on all flesh.
> Your sons and daughters shall prophesy,
> Your old men shall dream dreams,
> Your young men shall see visions,
> and also on My menservants and on My maidservants
> I will pour out My Spirit in those days."

CHAPTER FIFTEEN

Love Him Now, Love Him Again

*"So, they come before You as people do, they sit before
You as My people, and they hear Your
word, but they do not do them,
for with their mouth they show much love, but their
hearts pursue their own gain"*
Ezekiel 33:31 (NKJV).

It was Monday five days before the presentation of her sermon., and her husband asked, "Have you ever given a sermon before? Quietly she answered with a lump in her throat, "No." He pursued, "Aren't you nervous?" Again, she answered softly, "Very." Getting a bit frustrated with her, he continued to quiz," Then why didn't you say no?" Before she could answer that, he pushed with another question. "Why do you put yourself through these things?" She looked him in the face and explained, "I didn't feel like I had a choice." Now sarcasm dripped from his lips, "Oh, you considered it an honor." The conversation continued with her explanation, "Not everyone is asked to preach. I didn't think of it as the pastor asking me, but as God using the pastor to ask me. I have asked the Lord to use me in whatever way He felt I could be effective for His service." She continued to confide, "I have been asking God to give me the message that I must give." There was no more discussion.

She related with Ezekiel when he was given a message to give to the Children of Israel, particularly the remnant of the tribe of Judah. It seems that Ezekiel was afraid too. He didn't consider himself to be a prophet, but he called himself "the priest of the son of Buzi." Evidently, he was proud to be the "son of Buzi" even though not much is known about him, at least nothing so important that it was worth mentioning in Scripture. Just knowing that Ezekiel was his son, was enough. It was customary for God to call Ezekiel "son of man" which indicated that he was called the ministry of sharing messages that God called him to give. Usually, a prophet is called to a ministry that is uncomfortable to give. Prophesy is one of the gifts of the Spirit (I Corinthians 12:28). This is not a choice; It is a divine appointment. While in vision Ezekiel fell prostrate at the vision of God's glory. He had been raised up from among the captives of Babylon to confirm the word of God hat had been given through the prophet Jeremiah. (Prophets & Kings by EG White pg. 448). Daniel had also been under vision, and he pronounced "That there is no strength in me," (Daniel 10: 16–17) after his vision.

So how did this correlate to this woman about to preach. This was the thought brought to her. She is the daughter of upright Sabbath-keeping parents that never wavered from their faith. She came from a Christian lineage that traced the background of her heritage to a family that never deviated from the Bible standards and neither did they take on the traditions of man, but held the Bible and it authority above any man. It was on this she stood firm as one God called to speak with the assurance that He would speak through her.

Today those who think they are rich in truth and have need of nothing are the Laodiceans. Even though they have the truth within them and can quote scripture and verse, some have also become lukewarm and feel as if they are alright. Maybe they are alright as the world sees them but how does God see them? He says in Revelation 3:15-17 paraphrased) "If you don't change your ways, I will vomit you out of My mouth and you will not enter into the kingdom." He goes on to say in verse 19 "As many as I love, I rebuke and chasten therefore be zealous and repent." This is talking about modern Israel. God sees us as He would like us to be, yet He accepts us as we are. So, because we understand this, are we lulled into a false thinking, "Oh God understands me, and he forgives so I am okay." Another thought process is, "Be patient (when we happened to have over-stepped His boundaries), God isn't finished with me yet:" There are some expectations that follow what His conditions stand for in Psalms 138:8 that says, He will "perfect that which concerns us." BUT it is necessary to ask Him to show us what needs to be perfected and how it does affect our well-being, that what we do is acceptable unto Him.

Ezekiel's name means "whom God will strengthen." It is God Who strengthens each of us. When God gives us a message to share whether from the pulpit or in our everyday lives or on the pages of a book, it can only be given as He gives us strength from the Holy Spirit. That strength becomes greater as we keep a daily prayer life.

Ezekiel was a young man in his mid-to late twenties when the doom of captivity fell on him. He was married but his wife died suddenly during the ninth year of his captivity. She was the 'desire of his eyes" (Ezekiel 24:16).

The intensity of his captivity could be compared with the Holocaust of 1941. God often allows dreadful times of trial and crisis that may bring about great oppression, but these circumstances allow lessons that may not have been learned otherwise. Adversity can bring about repentance that during times of prosperity would never have surfaced. When you have all you need and lack nothing, you become lazy and indifferent losing the gift to have compassion on those who fall on hard times.

Ten of the twelve tribes of Israel had been previously under captivity by the Assyrians, and now they were all reunited under a foreign yoke. Who were the twelve tribes? God's chosen people just as modern Israel is today. God's chosen people who had literally become heathen and totally rebelled. They willfully departed from God. They worshiped idols within the very temple built for God. They burned incense to a false god in the court of the Lord's temple. They were obstinate, stubborn, and rebellious. They became "hard-faced." Have you ever approached someone that set their face as stone against you and whatever you said, there was no softness? You just couldn't seem to penetrate their defiance. Only the Lord can break hard, cold hearts. "Is not My word like fire? says the Lord, and like a hammer that breaks the rock in pieces?" Jeremiah 23:29 (NKJV).

The charge that the Lord gave Ezekiel was a divine commission and that same commission echoes down through the ages to every teacher and expositor of sacred truth. Opinions do not matter, either yours or mine. God's truth is straight and what you or I have to say only counts if we have a "thus saith the Lord" to back it up! Regardless of the abominations that were being done, God wanted to save these people because they were made in His image, and He loved them even though He hated what they were doing. They were being offered another chance.

God's salvation embraces all, that means our enemies, those we may criticize, those we may judge and those we don't happen to like those who talk differently than we do, those who are crude and haughty. "He is not willing that any should perish but that all would come to repentance" (II Peter 3:9).

Ezekiel was commissioned to "Go tell the children of captivity" whether they "listen or whether they refuse" (Ezekiel 3:11). He would be meeting opposition on all fronts from within the church and without. He would be meeting head on with opposition, ridicule, scorn and a resounding "who do you think you are, Ezekiel? Jonah ran from that and ended up paying quite a price for his abandoning his commission, but he came to repentance. And many were saved because of his calling those in Nineveh to repentance so now Ezekiel is faced with a similar responsibility. God said don't let them intimidate you or be afraid of them.

There is a danger in looking at those around you who have not committed to serve God and continue in a manner of self-serving, looking for a pat on the back showing how good they are. The new Christian that walks in the church thinks everyone is perfect and they are the only imperfect one until they look around and see another member doing the same thing they gave up or worse and then their eyes have been taken off Jesus and focused on self. They take their eyes off the very One that can transform them and make them the loving, caring person they should be. And they lick their wounds as they walk out the door. Ezekiel had the task of telling God's chosen people to stop their actions against God, return to Him and love Him again.

"There is a subtle poison in the atmosphere of society." It is difficult for one to be faithful amid faithlessness. Therefore, the greatest danger comes from within the church. So why bother the question is asked. Because—those who desire to do what is right need to come together to strengthen each other and have a greater force for good. We are to "confess our faults one to another, repent and be healed" (James 5:16). A repentant heart moves the arm of God to move for them through the power of prayer.

Ezekiel's message to the rebellious house of the remnant of Judah, the children of Israel was a call to repent. A call for obedience. A call to love God. God used Ezekiel to give the message because he was committed. He didn't feel adequate or honored or exalted above anyone one else to give this unpopular message. God asked and there was no choice. Not fear, or persuasion could make Ezekiel waver from giving the message that God gave him to deliver. And that is the commission of each one who loves God to give the message to put God above everything in your life and serve Him with all your heart. "Seek first the kingdom of God and His righteousness and all these things will be added unto you." (Matthew 6:33) If you loved Him once and walked away, call out to Him now and love Him again.

The apple never seems to fall far from the tree.
My pointed fingers were pointing right back at me.
I stood on the edge and rebelled.
I defied, and my look was haughty when I yelled.
Look at the people of God, look at their sins.
Pretending righteousness with their silly grins.
Nodding their heads with their pitiful look,
Judging my actions recorded in their book.
So, I walked in my own willful way,
And I regret that time of rebellion to this day.
For I robbed God and the message He gave me to give.
I called His name in vain and I chose how I would live.
Yes, God saw me how I was and how He wanted me to be,

And it was the intercessory prayer that no eye cold see
That moved the power of His love over me.
Even as I resisted the earnest plea.
His long-suffering love worked to set me free.
When I let go of the obstinate hard-faced sneers,
Then repentance gave way to tears.
I came out of. the House of Rebellion with a new heart.
The armor of God caught the brunt of the tempter's dart.
No longer do I need to be enslaved by sin and be lost,
For I have been freed with a priceless cost,
And so have you, my friend,
So why not love Him now and love Him again.
Written by Joyce A. Leonard
12-26-1996

CHAPTER SIXTEEN

The Lamb Was Slain

*"Worthy is the Lamb Who was slain to
receive power and riches and w
isdom, and strength, and honor and glory and blessing"
Revelation 5:12 (NKJV).*

Jesus was betrayed by one of His very own disciples in the Garden of Gethsemane. Oh, He knew this was going to happen. It wasn't a surprise. He had told the twelve that one of them was going to betray Him before the night was over. That was Tuesday in the Upper Room during the Passover. He asked Peter and the two sons of Zebedee, James and John to go with Him to "watch and pray." It was during that time that Judas went to the priests which wasn't his first encounter with them, but was now the finalization of the betrayal of Jesus—selling him out for 30 pieces of silver.

It was under demonic suggestion that the leaders of the Sanhedrin felt that their authority was jeopardized if Jesus was allowed to live. He must be put to death, but they had to be careful not to incite the people against them considering Lazarus' recent resurrection. They found a sympathizer in Judas to put their plot in action. Judas was the keeper of the money bags. He was willing to bargain to fill the pouch that he controlled and that by his act, Jesus would set up His kingdom here. It was worth betraying the Son of God to make his own selfish motives come to fruition.

It was beyond comprehension while Jesus was in the Garden to hear the guards coming and among them was Judas to give the kiss of betrayal. Upon Judas' entrance in the garden he approached Jesus who knew what Judas was about to do yet He said to Judas, "Friend, why have you come?" (Matthew 26:50). Jesus called His betrayer, "Friend." How quickly do we call a lifelong friend, "friend" who has become our enemy once they spread false accusations or do some malicious act against us? Do we then consider them or even speak of them as a "friend?"

The Courtyard

"What is going on in the courtyard?" A young peasant girl was curious. The commotion had drawn her out of her home to go look and find out what was happening. "Oh, it is Jesus and His disciples who are causing all the stir," she thought out loud. There is the fisherman Peter hiding in the corner. Continuing her train of thought she approached Peter, "Aren't you one the followers of Jesus?" He answered her as he brushed her off and waving his hands as if to shake off her question, "I don't know what you are talking about, of course not!"

As he raced away from her, her friend saw him as well and she exclaimed that he was a follower of Jesus of Galilee. Now angry that he had been dentified a second time Peter cursed and said, "I do not know the Man" (Matthew 26:72). He scrambled to get away from them when a little bit later a group that had been speaking with him, said, "Hey, aren't you one of His followers, we can tell by your accent." Still in denial, Peter cursed again denying Jesus for the third time. And then the rooster crowed. Peter was heartbroken by his own actions. How could he have denied the Son of God? He was broken and he "wept bitterly" (verse 75).

How many times have we cursed and denied the Son of God, walked in denial of our actions and taken up for ourselves because we didn't want to be identified with purity? The world seems to hold more of an attraction than the kingdom of heaven. We don't want to give up what? Playing games on the computer, watching TV, gambling, smoking, drinking, drugs, sex and whatever else the world offers for instant gratification which seems to have become our heaven. Have you heard the saying, "It's my life and I am going to live it the way I want to, or I worked hard, and I am going to use my money for what I want?" How about, "No one is going to tell me what to do." My friend, you are a slave to sin. You are under Satan's control, and he has you where he wants you. "…Choose for yourselves this day whom you will serve'" (Joshua 24:15).

Crucify Him

"I can't believe what they are saying" the peasant girl was murmuring. This Man did nothing but good and yet here they are causing all sorts of commotion and screaming in the streets to "crucify Him." This has got to be a nightmare. Upon entrance into the city on the platform of the City Hall stood two men, Jesus and Barabbas. Barabbas was a known criminal and Jesus was a known healer. The Governor stood between them and asking which one they wanted set free as it was customary to set a prisoner free during the time of the Passover Feast. It was obvious that Pilate was having difficulty with the process, and it seemed like a no brainer as I watched in disbelief the scene as it unfolded before me.

The chanting began "Crucify Him, Crucify Him." Who are they calling for to be crucified? One man looked unsavory with his eyes darting back and forth and profanities spewing out of his mouth, and there stood Jesus, beside him, the healer with kind eyes, quietly standing before His accusers without any malice of any kind. His head was bowed, then for a moment, I just know He looked at me. I turned around to see if there was someone else behind me that He may have been directing His gaze at. No, it was me! He was looking at me! I was sure in my heart that He had not done anything wrong, it was those eyes...and I had to hurry on and get errands done. This wasn't my business, and I felt that surely, they would make the right choice. They just can't crucify Jesus of Galilee. It was evident that even the Governor made that clear!

The next day I had to go back to the city, and I noticed that there were three men carrying crosses and a parade of people following. Two of them were well known thieves and wait a minute, isn't that the Man I saw yesterday standing on the Governor's porch of the City Hall? I can't believe they think He is a thief. It was difficult to believe that this was happening right here in my city—such an injustice. This can't be happening.

He looked so weak. I could tell He had been beaten. Blood was dripping off his back and down His arms. It trickled down to His legs. A crown of thorns was on His head that appeared to be driven into His skull and blood dripped on His face. The lacerations from the whipping left wounds that gouged deep into His skin. How could the Governor have allowed this to happen? I thought yesterday he made it clear that He was "washing his hands of the verdict of this just Man?"

Yet here He was having difficulty to carry the cross they had laid on His shoulders. I crept up as close as I dared, and my heart was alarmed, and fear gripped inside me for Him with all that He was going through. People were taunting Him and laughing and jeering as He staggered. They were calling Him the "King of Jews." Their ridicule was sickening and demonic with not one thought of compassion. At last, someone realized He just was unable to carry that huge wooden cross. The man was a visitor to the city and yet he seemed to know this Jesus and quickly lifted the cross off Jesus' shoulders and carried it for Him.

My heart ached and I cried inside for Him, then the tears flowed down my cheeks. I couldn't contain them. I had never witnessed such cruelty. They cruelly nailed His hands and feet to the cross. The other two were tied on the cross but they showed no compassion or remorse for their actions of such hideous violence. I watched one of the soldiers pierce His side with his sword. The rage exploded by the priests and all those religious men all around showing openly sneers of violence. Those who should be comforting the innocent and caring for the needs of the widows and the poor turned into outrageous bigots. I couldn't cower any longer as if I were untouched by this scene and my tears became bitter and I head Him say, "Daughters of Jerusalem, do not weep for Me, but weep for yourselves and for your children" Luke 23:28 (NKJV). I felt so helpless, but His eyes were consoling me as I looked into His face filled with love. That was all I saw…love.

I heard one of the thieves ask Him if he could be saved when He came into His kingdom. It was immediate even with all the mockery going on and the reviling of those around the cross that His answer comforted the dying thief with "I tell you today, you will be with Me in Paradise." Only a Man of Divine character could possibly endure the beating, the reviling, the mockery and still have love for those who nailed Him to a cross. He must be the Messiah. My heart was convicted. I couldn't walk away the same as I had been before this experience..

It was the sixth hour when the sky grew dark. The soldiers that were casting lots for His clothing and they stopped what they were doing for the ground rumbled and an earthquake shook the earth opening graves of saints being resurrected from the dead. Those who had previously strutted about the cross in mockery now were trembling. I heard Him commit His mother into the keeping of His disciple named John and then He cried out with a loud voice, "Eli, Eli lama sabachtani? that is My God, My God why have You forsaken Me?" Matthew 27:46 (NKJV).

I heard Him cry out in a loud voice again before He gave up His spirit and died on that huge, wooden cross filled with splinters on a Hill called Golgotha which meant "Place of a Skull." The lightening flashed the darkness into daylight. It was not long after that I heard the priests shriek in horror, "The veil in the temple has been torn from top to bottom with unseen hands." There was fear in their voices and the centurion standing at the foot of the cross exclaimed "Truly this was the Son of God" Matthew 27:54 (NKJV).

THE TOMB WAS EMPTY

Rumors came from all directions, that it was Joseph of Arimathea who was quite wealthy, and he provided the tomb for Jesus, the Great Healer to be laid. I wondered where he had been before all of this took place. Why didn't this man of influence come forward to stop this hideous death of such a wonderful Man. Questions, questions, questions. I was full of them so after the Sabbath I scurried during the early morning hours on Sunday to where the tomb was, and I wanted to show my respect for Him as He laid in he tomb. I held back as I saw two women ahead of me. I could hear them talking about Him and I could tell they knew Him quite well.

I wasn't ready for what I was about to see, and neither were they. The huge rock that was used to seal the tomb was moved. It was an immovable rock, how did it possibly get moved? The guards were on the ground like dead men in front of the tomb. They were passed out cold—maybe they were dead, I didn't really want to find out. Maybe they collapsed from exhaustion trying to move the rock. The two women had more courage than I did as they went to look in the tomb and turned and frantically ran crying, "He is gone!"

I decided I better get out of there as quickly as possible before I got blamed for something I didn't do. I began to run as fast as I could and tripped on a small rock that loosened up in the gravel and fell at the feet of the Man. He was radiant. I could see the scars on His feet, and I looked up into those eyes again. The ones that had penetrated mine before at the City Courtyard and again at the Cross. I knew when I looked at Him, He was the Lamb that was slain. "The Lamb of God Who takes away the sins of the world."

This was a paraphrased account—The actual
Biblical account can be found in
Matthew 27, Mark 15 & 16, Luke 23, John 18 & 19

CHAPTER SEVENTEEN

We All Loved Lucy

> "She opens her mouth with wisdom, and her
> tongue is the law of kindness
> She watches over the ways of her household,
> And does not eat the bread of idleness."
> Proverbs 31: 26-27 (NKJV)

Maria was two and a half years old when those red spots appeared on her body and turned into holes. It was smallpox. Her twin sister Lucia did not get them, and it was not very long before Maria died. There were six siblings, five sisters and one brother. Kyle was closest to Lucia. It was during Hitler's reign which began in 1933. Maria and Lucia were born August 23, 1918. Lucia, fondly called "Lucy" and known as that far and wide personally told me the story of when the guards barged into their home when she and Kyle were little.

Maria had already died. Her mother wore heavy long skirts for it was during the cold months. She hid them under her skirts just before they came in and cautioned them to stay very still. I can only imagine those heavy woolen skirts covering her children and the fear that must have gripped her heart of the possibility of them being discovered and taken away by the guards for manual labor in refugee camps. Lucy laughed as she remembered her brother coming out from under the heavy covering of secrecy and his first words were, "It stinks under there!"

It was years later Lucia Jessan married Ezra Miller and their first born was Gerhart. They lived in Flinchburg, Germany until 1952. Gerhart was born in 1939 and three years later a daughter, Rotraud was born. During this time Lucy had discovered the Bible truths of the Sabbath since during the reign of Hitler was the persecution of the Jews who kept the Sabbath. She was baptized into the Seventh-day Adventist church in 1946. Somewhere along this time frame, Ezra became unfaithful to Lucy, and they divorced in 1949, leaving her to care for her two small children. She lived alone for two years. Ezra remarried and during his marriage to his second wife, he soon realized how he had disgraced God. Just as he had been unfaithful to Lucia, so his second wife was unfaithful to him. He had turned from a faithful wife and the truths of the church and being unable to handle his guilt, he committed suicide.

Lucia met Ernest Stahl in the church. He had a great desire to go to America. His girlfriend before Lucy did not share his desire to move to another country but when he asked Lucia if she would go with him, she said she would, and it was then he asked her to marry him. They were married in 1951. They traveled across the waters in an Army ship through the English Channel. The waters were so turbulent that everyone became terribly seasick. Only dry bread bought them any relief. If that wasn't bad enough, they endured a hurricane that was so raging that they closed off one side of the ship.

They arrived in Portland, Maine and were met at the dock by Erlin and Marjorie Bridgham from Auburn, Maine in

1952. From there they traveled by train to Auburn and lived with the Bridgham family who were Seventh-day Adventist church members in Auburn. Lucia and Ernest had been sponsored by the Council of Churches and this was how the Bridgham's found them.

It was a climate shock for Lucia and Ernest as they had lived by the Gulf stream in Germany, which keeps the climate quite pleasant. Erlin had two old sheds with trailers attached that were used to house Ernest, Lucia and their two children. Ernest had adopted Gerhart and Rotraud. They lived there for two years adjusting to their new life in America.

By 1954 they had saved enough money to buy the old schoolhouse up the road from the Bridgham family for $250. The schoolhouse had been built in 1802 and was in desperate need of repairs. It was set to be demolished and the land had been donated for the schoolhouse was to go back to the original owners, but Ernest and Lucia set to work to make this a home for their children.

Marjorie Bridgham's sister-in-law, Viola and Lucia became best friends. It was with Viola's help that Ernest and Lucia went to the Registry of Deeds and had the land transferred to them. Ernest and Gerhart, now thirteen, began to work together to repair the old schoolhouse and make it a livable home.

The Stahl's continued to work for the Bridgham's until one day when Ernest was in the woods cutting trees, he fell, and a tree landed on him. He was severely hurt. He was laid up for many months flat on his back on a hard board. Gerhart worked for the Brigham's caring for them, milking cows and doing whatever chores were necessary while Ernest was laid up.

During the time that Ernest couldn't work—Lucia worked at a job cleaning for the Whitings'—who owned land for gardening and selling produce and later incorporated flowers with several greenhouses.

Lucy and Viola decided to go job-hunting together. Lucy found another job, but Viola didn't. She started work at a business called Hogan Spray in Auburn where she packed children's shoes. She worked for them for two and a half years before they closed permanently. From there she found another job at Wallingford's apple orchard and Viola was hired as well and worked with Lucy packing apples. Viola's friend Thelma who lived with her, had a boyfriend that notified them of a job opening at Bates College in Lewiston (the next town over from Auburn) that Ernest might be able to get. Ernest went there right away and was hired for maintenance work both inside the building and outside on the campus. He worked there for 12 years.

Lucy and Ernest never had a car, so they walked to and from work which was an average of 12 miles a day. They would leave their home from Center Minot Hill Road in Auburn to begin their journey to work at five in the morning so they would be there on time. They didn't feel there was any excuse for them to be late. Occasionally someone would give them a ride. There was one kind gentleman who picked them up quite often. They were finally able to buy a car which was a Dodge and they paid $100 for it.

Mrs. Whiting was a kind soul, and she was the one who helped Ernest to get his license. Church school was held in the basement of the Auburn church and Marjorie Bridgham would pick up Gerhart and Rotraud and take them to school along with her children in the back of an old panel truck. In 1958, Pastor Remick felt that the older children should go to Woodstock to church school so they would be separated from the younger ones. Every Friday, Ernest would go right from work to Woodstock, about an hour drive from Auburn, and brought the children to their homes. Gerhart and Rotraud worked for Brother Thurlow in Woodstock on a farm for their room and board to be able to attend church school.

The Accident

It was a weekday, and the young people were in a car driven by Brother Thurlow's nephew who was also a student at Woodstock. They were on their way to school going up an old dirt road that was built up extending on an uphill grade. It was so narrow that two cars could barely pass each other. That morning Rotraud and Edith Hall were in the back and decided to climb in the front with the boys. There were children playing and they wouldn't move out of the way so they could not pass by. Each time they tried the children deliberately blocked the way. Brother Thurlow's nephew was frustrated with these children so decided to turn the car around and go another way. In his attempt to turn around on this narrow roadway, the car overturned and rolled over several times landing upside down.

The Rescue

Everyone that was nearby who witnessed the accident came running to pull the girls out of the car. Gerhart was sitting by the driver and got injured by the steering wheel on the left side of his head. Gasoline was spilling out everywhere and gas was all over the girls' dresses. Rotraud lost her glasses. They were all transported to the nearest hospital in So. Paris to have their bruises checked. Fortunately, the car did not burst into flames as that was a fear. Gerhart had been so traumatized by the accident that he feared anytime they were all in a car together. He would cry out to Ernest when he drove, "Daddy be careful, don't drive fast."

Gerhart's Life

Gerhart graduated from high school and then went right to work with Ernest at Bates College. He did not work there long when he began to hallucinate and began running down the street. Lucy and Ernest took him to Augusta to the state hospital to determine the extent of his injuries. He was in and out of there for a couple years. The staff at that time were very inconsiderate toward Lucia and Ernest and showed no compassion to the injuries of Gerhart. He received no help that was healing in any respect. They medicated him to keep him lethargic. A nurse confided in Lucy that he never should have been medicated. Ernest had to pay half of his salary of $58 every two weeks to pay off the debt to the hospital. Gerhart led a very sad life where people misunderstood him because his injuries were not fully known or understood. He was brought faithfully to church each week and even church members would make faces when no one was around, or they stayed clear of Gerhart. He developed a tendency to want to drink too much water which disturbed the electrolytes in his brain. In later years Lucy had to take the handles off the water faucets so he would not over drink water. Gerhart finished his life in Ledgeview Nursing Home in West Paris, Maine. He died in 2004. He is buried in the little cemetery in West Minot, Maine near his "daddy' Ernest who adopted him and loved him, cared for him during those tragic years.

We have a "daddy" in heaven, "Abba." He cares for us as tenderly and has paid the price for us during our time on this earth with all the injustices that have come to us. We will one day be resurrected to be with Him forever and Gerhart will be made new, and you will find him at Jesus feet.

Ernest

Ernest was a hard worker and filled with determination and fortitude. He was a faithful servant of God. He took leadership as Head Deacon in the Auburn, Maine Seventh-day Adventist Church for many years. His dedication to God and the church was a virtuous commitment that he honored faithfully. When he did not have a vehicle to make the trip to the church about five miles away, he walked even in the winter months to be sure to turn the heat on so it would be warm enough for the service. Even though Ernest never had children of his own blood, he loved the two he adopted with the love of a true father. He claimed them as his very own and worked for their well being. When tragedy struck, he was there to console, to provide and to spiritually nurture. Truly he made his mark on this earth and in heaven as a "man of God." Ernest was laid to rest in the West Minot Cemetery in 1989.

Rotraud

Rotraud was energetic and filled with determination but could be easily swayed in matters of love especially under financial duress. After graduation from high school, Rotraud traveled with her best friend Esther Pendleton to Madison, Tennessee. This is where she met Richard Kohler and fell in love. His mother owned a nursing home and Rotraud worked for her while he attended college to become a teacher. Rotraud worked in the laundromat at the college where they met.

They married and traveled to California where her first child, a little girl was born. In 1967 when her little girl was two and a half, they returned to Maine. She had two more children within the next seven years, two sons. To help with finances Rotraud went to work at Hillcrest chicken factory. It was here she met a charming man who flirted with her and promised her a life of prosperity. He was much older than she was and quite well off. He was married with a son but continued to place advances on Rotraud promising her everything she could ever want. t wasn't long before Richard returned to Madison for College and to his mother's. It was then they divorced.

Promises Turned to Tears

Tom Christians was not a Christian. He belonged to the Masons and his life was wrapped up in their secret lodge. He loved Rotraud. However even though he built her a home that looked like a dollhouse, he hated children. The children were young when she married Tom. They had no way of defending themselves against his hatred. They were made to live in the cellar and endured many beating under his cruel hand.

Rotraud fell while ice skating and it was later that a bone stood out in her neck and the nervous system was cut off. She was paralyzed. The oldest boy could not bear the beatings and ran away. He took his bicycle in the night and rode it from Winthrop to Auburn about a 50 mile distance to his grandparents, Ernest and Lucy. He went to work in a local grocery store. He was a good worker and held the job to help with the finances of his grandparents. The youngest boy endured the beatings and after school cared for his mother as she had deteriorated to the point that she could no longer lift her arms. As soon as it was possible, the youngest boy and Rotraud went to Auburn where Lucy cared for her daughter for the next five years of her life until she struggled for her last breath and died at the home of her mother in 1991. Tom had died from a painless cancer that took him quietly.

ALICE

Alice was a little mentally challenged lady who lived in Lucy's home under her care. She attended church regularly with Lucy and she loved to play the piano. She was not by any means fluent, but you could recognize the hymns she plunked out as she sat tirelessly before the piano. Church members would often visit at Lucy's on Sabbath afternoons. It was the place to go. A place where you were accepted, fed and most of all loved. She was Grammie Lucy not just to her grandchildren but to many in the church she was called "Gram." After the meal had been served and the table cleared, there followed spiritual conversations and she loved to talk about what it would be like to see Jesus and how we must be ready for His return.

Lucy was a natural healer. She had a remedy for every known ailment and chewed garlic cloves as a medical necessity. She had an herb that could heal every cut, sore or bruise. Alice was a little pudgy lady with faded red hair tied up in braids. She played continuously at the piano while we were in our discussions of great need. My family was in particularly trying circumstances at the time. We all prayed as a group about what we all faced. The day was fast coming to an end, and we were about to leave. As we were saying our good-byes, Alice got up from the piano stool and called out to my husband. We were in astonishment. He turned to her and with a radiance that was glowing on her face, she firmly gave him this commission, "No matter what, don't give up on God." The few words and the sincerity of her countenance left a marked impression.

Lucia—"Lucy"—"Gram"

Lucy also raised her great grandson from the time of six-months old. There was much adversity in her oldest granddaughter's life and when her son was born, the father paid for his support for a while until he found out that she was seeing someone. He had no right to hold anything over her as he was married with five other children. She was young and seemingly incapable of caring for a baby. Lucy took charge and brought up her only great grandchild. There was no child she did not love. There was no church family member that she did not reach out to and call them into her home. Even if you were a friend of one of her grandchildren and you came into her home, you were family. There was nothing that could separate anyone one from Lucy's love regardless of circumstances. She never missed an opportunity to tell people about Jesus and His soon return. She was relentless in her pursuit to give others the love of Jesus.

Some of her known quips that she would often say would make me laugh. One was "You have to turn your pennies around." I would pick her up and take her grocery shopping. One day I thought I would help her out and so I said, "Lucy why don't you give me your shopping list and I will get things for you?" She passed me her slip of paper and I could not read a word of it. You see Lucy said, "The Holy Spirit taught me to read English," but she never learned to write it. Obviously I was not as big a help like I thought I would be and she just grinned.

Instead of the using the commonly known saying, as "get it off your chest"—Lucy's version was "get it off your liver." I never corrected her because it was just too funny. If she was upset with someone she would say, "I hope he gets his nose full!" How can anyone be upset over that? Then two others that always made me smile—is she always had to "swip the floor." She made known her disgust with the actions of young girls around men and would say, "girls today, just put their legs up to get a man!" There was only one Lucy that I have ever known, and she was a joy to be around in all sorts of circumstances. She could change the worst to be either funny or heart-warming. She was Lucy and we all loved her.

She spent a couple months of the last days of her life in Russell Park Manor. Many visited her and her youngest grandson was there faithfully each week. She was his strength during many adversities. And now he finds a greater strength in the Jesus that she talked to him about daily. Another saying that Lucy would say, "we have no time to dilly-dally, Jesus is coming soon."

Lucia D Stahl put down her work on this earth and awaits her Savior next to her husband Ernest, her son Gerhart and her daughter Rotraud in the little West Minot, Maine cemetery at 92 years of age. She never took any medication for anything. She worked hard and loved God.

Her death—November 28, 2010

Lucia as a young woman—Lucia at age 90

CHAPTER EIGHTEEN

Condemn One, Condemn All

*'Judge not and you shall not be judged,
condemn not and you shall not be
condemned. Forgive and you will be forgiven."*
Luke 6:37

Blonde hair and small framed for a twelve-year-old boy, he condemned himself with voice that was loud and aggressive. His thin face and small features showed signs of softness that did not match the vulgar words that would blurt out of his mouth. He never seemed to take thought that he might be offending someone, but instead assumed that everyone knew he was joking, even the recipient of his offensive words. We will call him Jeff and he had such an obnoxious way about him that it was as if he had a knack to get under your skin and become an irritant.

When Jeff was quiet, it was somewhat peaceful on the bus. You see I was the bus driver and Jeff was one of the children I picked up every day. When he was loud the whole bus became chaotic. Because Jeff's voice was always on high volume and made this penetrating, shrieking, irritating sound,

I often found myself saying, "Jeff please lower the volume on your voice."

Then there was the other side of Jeff (and we all have another side). If a small child needed a seat and couldn't find one in the sea of faces, Jeff would be first to stand up and take that child under his care. One time when the bus wouldn't make it up over an especially steep and slippery hill on a winter day to pick up students waiting, Jeff volunteered to run up the hill and round up the waiting students to walk down to the bus. Jeff had a hot-shot attitude among his peers, so many offered their warning that Jeff wouldn't return, but I knew under the conditions of the situation, I could trust him to do what I sent him to do.

I waited for him at the bottom of the hill that extended from the one I had previously been at to pick up other waiting students. It was only a matter of minutes, I saw Jeff running for all he was worth with the band of students racing behind him to get on the bus. He breathlessly got on the bus and sank into his seat with the calmness and sense of good behavior that glowed on his face.

Jeff had received his third major warning from me for his unacceptable behavior. It was the first day back after Christmas break. I heard the shrill voice as he told another student that his haircut made him look like a whale. I chose to ignore the statement as the child he insulted happened to be an irritating insulter himself. I guess if one had to choose who was the most sneaky and underhanded of the two, you would have to say it was Kevin. Kevin was always ratting someone out for their actions when truth be known, he was the one who instigated the action to begin with. I could see that, Jeff's insult was borderline joking and immediately Kevin looked away to see if I had caught the episode.

I didn't say anything. I kept quiet and was secretly thinking that he deserved the insult to make up for all the past insults he had gotten away with. It was one of those circumstances that you felt justified to let it slip. "After all," I reasoned with myself, "Jeff wasn't serious, and this is only kid's stuff."

My conscience tugged at me that possibly this child might have had his feelings hurt and I even gave thought to soothing the blow by giving him a compliment about his hair cut. But I never said a word.

The next day I received a note from Kevin's mother telling me about the insult that her child received. I knew the inevitable had happened. Jeff had to receive a third and final major warning. I should have been relieved that I was giving this obnoxious kid his third warning, but part of me couldn't keep that sense of happiness as I listened to Jeff defend his actions and point to the injustices of Kevin. The missing component in Kevin's defense was he didn't get caught. Jeff did!

I held the white warning sheet that held the fatal decision for Jeff meaning he would have to present it to a greater authority than mine—his mom! Jeff wasn't the product of a broken home, but he was what is known as a latch-key kid. Both parents held jobs and worked, but when Jeff got home from school, no one was there. Mom worked second shift and Dad got home late so Jeff and his sister took care of themselves. They became the uninvited guests around the neighborhood.

They watched what they wanted on television without any censure and kept company with whoever they chose. Basically, they were bringing themselves up and I held a deep compassion for Jeff.

I tried to soothe the blow with words that went similar to this: "Jeff I believe all you have said about Kevin, but it doesn't change the fact that I did hear what you said about him, and it was wrong. This is your third warning. I do want you to know that when things seem unjust, they do have a way of turning themselves around eventually. I am sorry, Jeff. I didn't want to do this, but I have no choice."

*Even if I were innocent, my mouth would condemn me.
If I were blameless, it would pronounce me guilty"
Job 9:20 (NIV).*

This is what Jeff's mouth had done for him.

It didn't matter that Kevin was guilty of similar actions at one time or another, it didn't even matter that even I had my own sense of justification that was wrong. What mattered is that Jeff was caught, and he was paying the price for it.

Did Jeff understand the impact of my words or were they just words? He had been ratted out by his peer to his mother and tables had been turned on Jeff. Kevin had deserved the same punishment, but Jeff was the only one being condemned.

*It is unthinkable that the Almighty would be wrong.
That the Almighty would pervert justice"
Job 34:12 (NIV).*

Even I was wrong.

It is man who perverts justice. We can only see things from our own perspective and injustices that look unfair and perhaps are not fair. We feel we need to avenge ourselves, but by doing so we condemn ourselves

SPEEDING

There was another incident I was involved in. It was a Friday night, and I was on my way home from church. I had been to a Vespers program, and it was getting late. I came to the route that was clear open roadway and I put the pedal to the metal exceeding 70 mph. I skidded into my driveway and parked my car. It was only seconds, and my son came skidding into the driveway the same way I did and jumped out of his car before I even shut my car door. It was only long enough for me to walk to the end of my car when a cruiser skidded into my driveway with an officer I had known since he was a kid. And he was irate and demanding for my son's credentials, license and registration. Behind the cruiser was my husband who also skidded in behind the cruiser, coming to an abrupt stop.

My mother authority kicked in and I snarled, "What's the problem?" He didn't answer. He checked the paperwork that my son passed to him while I entered the house. The realization that my son was about to get a speeding ticket, and my sense of justice was in sync with my son's guilt, and I marched out the door to defend him and throwing myself in the way of setting the record straight. My son met me before I could say anything as I made my thoughts clear to him, he silenced me with, "Mother be quiet."

> *His eyes are on the way of men: He sees their every step"*
> *Job 34:21 (NIV).*

Because we both had been speeding, the officer couldn't get an accurate reading logged into his radar. He didn't get me, but he got my son for improper pass. So, was justice served? If my son was going to be condemned, then we all should have been. My husband decided it was in his right to admonish me as he began to scold, "You were going 70 in a 50? My son had seen me and was trying to catch up to me. So, who was the most to blame here?

I was disgusted and angry with the reprimand given me since he has been stopped several times for speeding, and I retorted, "Don't pretend innocence with me, I have seen you drive." When someone points the finger to set straight your mistakes and you know what their faults are in the same issue, don't you become a little indignant at their measures to correct you? Wouldn't that fall under removing the plank from your own eye before removing the speck in your brother's eye? (Matthew 7).

> *"Suppose a man says to God, I am guilty,*
> *but I will offend no more.*
> *Teach me what I cannot see; if I have done*
> *wrong, I will not do so again.*
> *Should God then reward*
> *you on your terms when you refuse to repent"*
> *Job 43:31 (NIV)?*

If each one of us had repented at that moment, would the law have shown leniency? Would we have truly repented if two weeks later we were speeding again or even the next day?
I John 3:20-22 (NKJV) brings the point home.

> "For if our heart condemns us, God is greater than our heart.
> And knows all things. Beloved, if our heart does not condemn us,
> We have confidence toward God, and whatever we ask we receive
> of Him because we keep His commandments' and do those
> things that are pleasing in His sight.".

BACK TO JEFF

Mercy for Jeff's circumstances overwhelmed me. "Blessed are the merciful for they shall obtain mercy" Matthew 5:7 (NKJV). Isn't that what each of us desires? Mercy—yet we are hesitant to give it out when circumstances arise in our lives, for we desire it for ourselves.

I went to my boss and pleaded Jeff"s case. I showed both sides of Jeff and gave my consent to willingly work with Jeff if his mother appealed the decision of being kicked off the bus for the rest of the school year. There would be a lesser sentence for Jeff allowing him to again have "one more chance."

My boss looked at me and pointedly asked with a serious look that required a commitment from me. "Are you willing to work with Jeff?" I answered immediately, "Yes." I knew this meant I would be committing my time to help Jeff help himself. I was willing if his mother would intercede on his behalf. She had to appeal the decision. I was cautioned not to interfere, but to allow things to go as they would. Jeff needed to walk to school for a while to think about what caused his troubles to begin with. I promised I would not interfere, but I did pray for Jeff.

We all stand in Jeff"s place at one time or another in our life. We can all point the finger at the accuser and say, "but look at his sins." But we are all held accountable for our own actions, if not here and now, our judgment time will come for Romans 2:6 tells us that we are judged according to our deeds. It may seem that the Kevins' of the world get away with their malicious actions. There are always the Jeffs that get caught. We may think our actions are harmless no matter what we may have said or done. Some of us like to point to the other guy's mistakes to take eyes off ourselves and focus on their sins. It is an instinct of survival ingrained from childhood. Jeff and Kevin just serve as that example.

> *"Judge not, and you shall not be judged. Condemn not, and you shall not be condemned.*
> *Forgive and you will be forgiven.*
> *Give and it will be given back to you; good measure, pressed down and shaken together, running over will be put in your bosom.*
> *For with the same measure that you use, it will be measured back to you"*
> Luke 6:37-38 (NKJV).

When we condemn ourselves by our own words or actions that have been revealed by another pointed finger, our vision becomes blurred by our anger if we do not repent of our deeds. And even if we have repented, somewhere down the road there is an enemy waiting to jump out and accuse us of our past sins. We as Christians must be certain that our walk with Christ is genuine for there is always an opponent waiting to point the finger. "…sound speech that cannot be condemned, that one who is an opponent, may be ashamed having nothing evil to say of you" Titus 2:8 (NKJV).

In our anger we have turned and pointed the finger at God, placing the blame on Him for allowing this to happen. We may reason that He could have changed the circumstances. But if he had and we had not had our sins revealed, would we have been better off? Would we have realized what we were becoming and just continued in our own mire? The simple truth is that we have to learn to "keep our mouths shut." That was what Jeff had to learn. If anything, productive was going to come out of it, then he had to learn to keep quiet.

> *"For by your words you will be*
> *justified, and by your words,*
> *you will be condemned"*
> Matthew 12:37 (NKJV).

Many adults have been a waft of criticism with vulgar insults and cursed joking, followed by the applause of laughter that has been accepted. Even I have been guilty of curtsying to its approval by joining in the confirmation of the activity which is just as self-condemning as if I spoke the words myself. When the lullaby of time has erased the act from your vision, when the death angel has marked our door post with judgment, when we have failed to repent or even to feel the guilt of what that judgment might be, when the probation door of time has slammed shut and there is no way to re-enter under the shadow of grace and obtain mercy—we are caught. The decision has been made. The executioner of our peril hands us the white sheet of paper with the final decision marked in detail for the unrepented sin. Jeff is not the only one condemned. We all stand there.

I do not want to leave anyone without hope. Jeff was not left without hope. We all have an Advocate with the Father, Jesus Christ the Righteous (I John 2:1). Those who do not know the Father and have not learned that they can trust Jesus Christ the Righteous to intercede for them and their sinful condition, who profess Christianity can have a relationship with Jesus Christ our Advocate to intercede for them. In this way you become the intercessor for them in leading them to the cross of Christ's Righteousness.

I promised to wait for Jeff"s mother to intercede for him. While waiting, I prayed earnestly, and it was two weeks later that she even acknowledged the situation because Jeff had not told her. Her neighbor did. Her neighbor felt the situation was unfair and asked Jeff"s mother "why" she didn't do anything about it.

Jeff felt the situation was hopeless and final, so he walked without complaining or telling his parents about it. Our situation is also hopeless, and it would be final death for it is written: "The wages of sin is death," (Romans 6:23) "But the gift of God is eternal life in Jesus Christ our Lord."

Jeff's sentence was altered. He was to clean my bus on Wednesday afternoon for an hour for three times. The first week, he washed the ceiling of my bus and did a good job. I shared a granola bar with him, and we had an opportunity to share some of Jeff's home life. The second week he had an obligation at school so couldn't fulfil his commitment. The third week it was especially cold so that week slipped by.

Before the fourth week had arrived, Jeff"s mouth took over again.

This time the offense was worse. This time there could be no leniency, and this time was final. Probation door had slammed shut for Jeff to ride the bus. There was no time for repentance. The opportunity to change was over. This was not by my authority but by the authority I had to abide by.

Time is short, dear reader. We have all sinned and "fallen short of the glory of God." But we have hope for the Intercessor still stands between us and the verdict in our condemned condition. Not just one is condemned but all of us are condemned and we all should have been crucified, but He interceded; He paid the price for me and for you.

MERCY

The sobbing anguishing implore
Of the convicted heart at probation's door,
Desire for the mercy drops were being sought,
For alone and condemned by the "accuser's plot."
The tears of the contrite, repent.
Pitifully, sorrowfully rent.
As words denied
Mercy for the tried.
Too many convictions held the score.
Mercy had closed its door..
Then restoring grace gave it all,
And redeemed the sinner from his fall.
The ransom price was heavily paid,
For on the cross the Savior laid.
His life was held for you and me
In shameful exploit for the world to see.
I looked about for my accusers sneer,
But only saw mercy standing near.
It was because of mercy I was restored by grace.
My blackened sins were cleansed without a stain or trace.
Written by Joyce A. Leonard—May 31, 1997

CHAPTER NINETEEN

Where is the Healing Balm of Gilead?

*"Is there no balm in Gilead, Is there no physician there?
Why then is there no recovery…?
Jeremiah 8:22 (NKJV).*

September 23, 1978 was a horrific day and it all started taking the trash out. Robert was born March 21, 1947, just 13 months before me, his half first cousin. My mother used to be very close to her half-sister Eva and spent much time with her particularly when she had children and since I was born closest to Bobby's age, they spent hours together while we were in our formative years of sitting up and leaning to walk along with all the things that babies learn to do. I was always ahead of Bobby in the areas of progression in many ways, even though he was older. I guess you might say Bobby was a little slower than normal. I have a picture of Bobby and I in Concord, New Hampshire by White's Park feeding the ducks and the swans. when we were older. That is about all that I really know about him other than his later years. His sister, Connie who was closer to my sister's age became like a sister to me. I loved her dearly and we spoke so many times on the phone. She was always worrying about me. We shared secrets and discussed family issues and Bobby. Bobby lived with her a little later in life along with her husband and her four boys.

They lived in Malden, Massachusetts. My Aunt Eva who I would call her Aunt Eve was a beautiful woman, just as her sister Vesta was. They were Swedish. Their father was Swedish along with their mother, my grandmother. Their father was a Johansson, and my mother's father was a Hutchinson, English descent. Connie's father was Conrad Nelson and Bobby's was William Lunde.

I cannot tell you much about his dad, but his mother was a brilliant woman with many talents. She was a nurse, a singer, a mother and had an adventurous spirit. My mother often said I was the epitome of her as if I was her daughter and not Mama's! I would go to Aunt Eve when Mama and I didn't get along and she always seemed to have some sort of advice that I accepted, and it helped to keep my overactive adventuresome spirit in check sometimes.

Connie became the extension of her mother for me, for when my mother was killed in the shockingly unbelievable car accident it was only six months later that Aunt Eve died. Everyone felt she died from a broken heart as there seemed to be no other explanation for her death to happen as quickly as it did. Connie, her daughter took Aunt Eve's place in my life.

It was a sunny fall day and still very warm out. The days were beginning to get shorter, and it was just before the dinner hour. Connie was preparing dinner and Bobby began taking out the trash. Connie stopped him from continuing as she said, "Bobby, don't put the trash out today, the pick-up is not scheduled for several more days." The family had dinner together and when the table had been cleared, Connie set out to do some shopping taking her twelve-year-old son with her. The oldest one went back to the kitchen to feed the dog. The two youngest ones went to the living room to watch television with their father.

The younger ones saw Bobby take two or three bags of trash back out to the sidewalk and reported what he was doing to their father. At this point I am going to interject a possibility of what may have been said. Phil may have been perturbed that Bobby had gone back to take trash out since he had already been told not to and the reason explained. He went to the doorway and called out to Bobby, possibly perturbed, "Hey Bob, didn't your sister tell you the trash isn't being collected for a few days?" And I am sure he didn't patiently wait for an explanation from Bobby, and possibly some vulgarities were added, but he pressed the point, perhaps angrily now, since he had been called away from the program he had been watching, "Bring those bags back, NOW!" Bobby was heard to answer him with calm demeanor, "Alright." He then was bringing the bags up the porch stairs, at least halfway then left them and continued to his bedroom.

Phil went back to his program on the television with his two younger boys and then Bobby came out of his bedroom and went to the bathroom. He was there for two or three minutes then came out and walked to the doorway of the living room and pointed a gun (a semi-automatic pistol and a magazine that held 108 bullets) at Phil and began shooting. After five or six shots, he started to reload the gun when the youngest child went to his uncle and pleaded with him to stop. Bobby's response to him was "You better get out of here before I kill you. As the child turned and ran, he heard more shots being fired.

When the police arrived, Bobby directed them into the house to the living room and claimed that the victim had called him a child molester along with obscene names. Bobby was taken into custody. From there while under investigation and officers relating the incident within Bobby's hearing, he began to see colored lights flashing in his brain. It was determined after much psychiatric testing that Bobby was not criminally responsible but suffered from paranoid schizophrenia.

During the autopsy it was found that there were eighteen bullets taken out of Phil's chest and stomach and 20 discharged casings were found on the floor. When Connie arrived home to this scene, she was in shock, and she related to me some thoughts which were senseless and had no particular origin other than being in shock. Traffic was going by her home very slowly and she wondered why, asking herself aloud, "What is happening to slow the traffic down? Then another thought was "Who is going to help me put the groceries away?"

Bobby was found guilty of second-degree murder. He suffered for 21 years with mental illness but that was not presented at the trial since he was calm and seemed coherent when arrested as well as during his trial. There was a second trial since much had been eradicated from the first trial. The finalization was five years later ending August 26, 1983. Bobby was committed to the Bridgewater State Hospital Bridgewater, Massachusetts and to this writing is still there.

DEMONIAC

The story unfolds in the country of Gadarenes, which was across from Galilee. Some of the disciples were with Jesus as they docked on the sands bordering the land from the waters of Galilee. It was most likely Peter who accompanied Him and most likely James and John as well. They had just come from quite a ravenous storm they had encountered, and Jesus quieted it. Now they were met by a man who wore no clothing and was bound in chains but seemed to be able to snap them very easily. No one was able to hold him or control him, so they stayed away as they feared him.

Jesus had no fear for with perfect love, there is no fear. He said, "What is your name?" Now the Bible account does not say how the disciples reacted. Perhaps they were just a little skeptical as to how Jesus was going to handle this. The demon-possessed man answered, "Legion, for many demons have entered into me." The demons were utterly afraid of Jesus and the man fell down to worship Him.

Bobby

Bobby had demons controlling him. With his sister requesting him to return the trash to the house, he didn't become violent. He knew she loved him and there was no reprimand in her voice. She understood her brother's condition and accepted him the way he was. Due to his mental condition, he was violated by his brother-in-law's commanding with obscenities, and I can believe that he surely did speak them out and perhaps quite often and this was the straw that broke the camel's back as the saying goes, coupled with the fact that Phil was not a Christian man. Remembering conversations I had with Connie years later after the incident, her husband always had an irritation with Bobby. He kept it in check when she was around evidently but when she left, the little pebble in the shoe of irritation became too big to just not push the sentiment. Now these are my speculations. No one has validated them. Heaven holds an accurate account.

Legion

Legion "cried out in a loud voice, and said., 'What have I to do with You, Jesus, Son of the Most High God'" Mark 5:7

(NKJV). The demon implored Jesus not to torment him! Jesus commanded "Come out of him unclean spirit!" The unclean spirit begged Jesus not to send him away from the country. About this time there was a herd of swine feeding there in the mountains. The demons cried for Jesus to send them into the swine. Jesus granted them permission and as soon as they had entered the swine, which the Biblical account says was about two thousand, the swine ran violently down a steep cliff and went into the sea and drowned. (Account can be read Mark 5:1-17). The demon possessed man was set free and was told to go back to the city to those people who were afraid of him and tell them what happened.

Healing

There was healing from Gilead for the demon-possessed man, but what about Bobby? How could his outcome have been different? There are many within society that have been taken over by demon possession. This wasn't how God created His children to be. But nevertheless, many have fallen into the trap of Satanic demise and listened to the evil spirits who whisper obscenities which deliver a message of hatred, skepticism. and incite utter disobedience. Unless they come face to face with the Healer, there is no balm to heal their wounds and the recovery stands stagnant.

> *"Gilead is a city of evildoers*
> *And defiled with blood"*
> Hosea 6:8 (NKJV).

Joseph was sold by his brothers to men of Gilead. They were on their way to Egypt with spices and perfumes to sell, because of the wickedness in Gilead it was probably products they had acquired through lewdness, so buying Joseph was a good prospect for them to make some good money for the price of this strong boy in the slavery market. This suggests that Gilead was rich with balms of healing and since they had acquired these rich spices and perfumes, they were sure to get a good price for their wares.

"Go up to Gilead to take balm, O virgin, the daughter of Egypt,
In vain you shall use many medicines.
You shall not be cured"
Jeremiah 46:11 (NKJV).

So, the balm there in Gilead was worth a lot. It was a healing potion that served as a cure all. But the cure all for the Legion, the demon-possessed man was Jesus for He is the Healer, and His balm is lasting. You won't need to buy it, just accept it, and believe in Him and you will be healed.

"But I will heal your wounds and restore your health,
I will care for you and plead your cause.
They have called you an outcast,
But you are still my son"
Jeremiah 30:17 (Message).

LETTER

My last letter from Connie—May 7, 2003

"Dear Joyce,

It was so nice to talk to you today, I am also glad you are doing good. I worry about you believe it or not. You are always on my mind even though I don't call as often as I should. I am glad things are going good for you and you seem to be more sure of yourself and where you are going.

As you can see Bobby (she had included his picture) it just breaks my heart every time I look at his picture, but I just keep praying for him and giving it to God. Going to close and I know this is short, but I already warned you. Just remember I love you no matter what."

Love your Cuz, Connie

Connie Jones died July 21, 2015, after a battle with breast cancer. She is buried at Forestdale cemetery in Malden, Massachusetts next to Phil.

Bobby's Healing Balm

In Connie's words, "I just keep praying for him." Prayer is the healing balm. When someone cannot pray for themselves, there is healing power in prayer for those who cannot pray, don't know how to pray and can't pray. That is the healing balm of Gilead. We are in the wickedness, of a sin-filled world awaiting Christ Jesus' soon return. "Prayer moves the arm of God." This is where we find healing in Gilead.

DWELLING WITHIN

Whitewashed walls,
Cold empty halls,
Dignity stripped,
Self-esteem whipped
Failures enforced with defeat,
Victories scorned in retreat.
The mind haunts the broken heart.
Guilt drives the weak to depart,
In hideous ways the voices demand
Imperiling the heart on command.
Windows encased with bars,
Hide even the moon and the stars.
Child, I see the tears that streak your pillow.
I see your heart bending as deep as the weeping willow
I promise, if you trust Me, it will not break.
I will restore your mind for My sake.
Victory will fling the door open wide,
For freedom to live is the reason I died.
Written by Joyce A. Leonard 2/16/1998

CHAPTER TWENTY

The Legend of a Name

Yahweh—Jehovah
Mighty God—The Great I AM
"God's Name is His Character"

*T*racing the lineage of the notorious Jesse James begins like this. The children of Grace and Will Wetmore were Grace Green Wetmore, my grandmother, born 1887. Her mother was Lucy C. DeGroff Green born in 1866. Her mother was Mary Strang DeGroff born 1843, followed by David and Priscilla Strang, my grandmother's great, great grandmother and following that heritage was Abigail James Strang my grandmother's great, great, great grandmother. This is the lineage of how Jesse James is related to me as sixth cousin!

Much of the following information comes from "The Complete and Authentic Life of Jesse James" by Carl W. Brenham New Edition 1972 Frederick Fell Inc. along with documented history passed down through the family of the Wetmore history. Reverend Robert S. James was the brother to Abigail James Strang, and she was my third great grandmother. Zeralda Elizabeth Cole was born 1825 and died

1911. She married the Reverend Robert Sallee James and they had Frank, who was born 1844 and Jesse was born 1847, their sister Susan Lavenia was born November 1849.

Jesse and Frank were a curious pair. Jesse was happy-go-lucky and tended to be mischievous and active as the town joker. Frank was more selfcomposed and quiet, intelligent, and well read. Jesse dressed flashy and wanted to be noticed while Frank was reserved with a conservative style. Jesse robbed a stagecoach near Lexington, Missouri. The owner of the coach was an Eastern school teacher who came to Missouri to teach. Jesse liked the looks of his clothing and forced him to disrobe and rode off with his prize. He wore the tight-fitting coal black suit until it worn out. He always wore black gloves to cover his disfigured righthand with the missing fingertip. Despite his jokester lifestyle there was a time that he became so depressed that he contemplated and even attempted suicide. His dear sister Susan was going to marry Allen Parmer who was an ex-Quintillion outlaw. She did marry him against Jesse's wishes for his sister.

There are two schools of thought concerning Jesse and Frank as citizens during their days of being an outlaw team, but there is no question regarding their background that came from upright citizens of reputable and respectable people.

They were marked in their religious convictions evidenced by a number of ministers among them. Their ancestors who settled in Goochland County, Virginia were of solid stock that upheld their religious convictions. Even today some of the back woods people of the several Missouri counties speak of Jesse and Frank in tones of reverence.

However, Jesse and his men did perform the first train hold up west of the Mississippi River. This happened near Adair, Iowa where today the citizens have erected a monument to commemorate that historical fact. In the first train robbery of 1873, he had moved a section of the track to derail the train.

QUOTE BY HARRY S. TRUMAN

"Jesse James was not actually a bad man at heart. I studied his life carefully and I come from his part of the country. Jesse James was a modern-day Robin Hood. He stole from the rich and gave to the poor, which in general, is not a bad policy. I am convinced that Jesse would have been an asset to his community, if he had not diverted to a lawless life."
Harry S. Truman March 1949

Special Note: The oldest US citizen of Landale, PA who was born the year Jesse James robbed his first train and President US Grant began his second term.

REVEREND ROBERT S. JAMES

It was during the time of the gold-rush in California when many were going to find their fortune and the hopes to become rich and escape the poverty that dominated their lives. Families that had come from Pennsylvania, Virginia and Kentucky and settled in Missouri now began to follow the lure of the gold rush and took on the challenge as they headed off to Sutter's Fort and other California hamlets. The preacher resisted the temptation to follow the lure of the gold rush, but on April 12, 1951, he could resist no longer. He pulled up stakes, leaving his family until he could make his fortune and return to them bringing with him the comforts, he desired for them. Many felt that he left due to his wife henpecking him constantly as she was the one who seemed to rule the roost. It took him until August 1, 1851, to make his journey to the "promised land" of hope that he dreamed would bring wealth to his family. Within eighteen days after his arrival, he came down with an intense fever and died. His death took place in Hangtown, California now known as Placerville. It was said that Jesse and Frank in their wanderings searched for their father's grave. It was a certainty that other descendants of Robert James made efforts to locate his burial place, but in the anarchy of the western mining camps, it was a fruitless hope that the graves of one lone wanderer searching after the "Golden Fleece" should ever have been marked.

The legacy that was left by Reverend Robert James was his sincerity for the Gospel message. He finished his theological studies between 1842–1843 at the Georgetown Kentucky College which was on the heels of the Great Revival of the 1840's. He divided his time between farming to make a living for his family and preaching. He was as vigorous worker for the Lord just as he was in his farming. He erected a number of Baptist church plants while on horseback carrying his Bible in wooded areas of the frontier. He left as real a monument in the legend of ministry as the lives of his pistol-packing sons.

Zerelda Elizabeth Cole James

After the death of her husband, she cared for her children with a stern hand and an aura of severity about her that was ready for any onslaught. Her eyes showed the unsubdued courage of a hawk for she had been stricken with many bitter moments within her life. She brought up her boys to attend the community church even though she went to a Catholic convent, she adhered to the Protestant community church which served as a place of socialization and community interest. Reverend James had met her while she was attending the convent and fell in love with her. She stayed with his mother

(Abigail Strang} while he finished his training to become a preacher. She was supportive of him until later years when her rearing within the Roman church took precedence and was a point of contention between them. He preferred meekness and abhorred strife.

Zerelda remarried in 1855 to Dr. Rueben Samuel. She idolized her boys and stood against anything that became a threat against them which brought fear from those who would oppose her. It was natural for men to carry a pistol then as it was the way of the back woods. Her instincts could have been carried to an extreme if Dr Samuel had not been there to offer his guidance. It was in later years that Jesse and Frank turned to violence. Along with carrying a pistol they also wore a mask to cover their identity which was well known in those parts. It was well-known that their waywardness was not due to their up bringing.

Zerelda was partial to Frank and called him "Mister" Frank regardless of the circumstances. She supported her sons' loyalties as secessionists. She was a sympathizer of the Confederacy along with her son Jesse. There was a fiery war between the secessionists, and the abolitionists which was the catalyst that put Jesse on the road to lawlessness. Zerelda DOB:01/29/1825 D: 2/10/1911

Dr Reuben Samuel

According to the obituary on the Internet search concerning Dr. Samuel, he died in the insane asylum at the age of 82. He and Zerelda James Samuel had two sons about the close of the war. One son was killed in1875 from a bomb explosion that had been thrown into their home near Kearney, Missouri. Mrs. (Zerelda) Samuel attempted to roll the missile into the fireplace and in the process, it exploded before she could accomplish her mission. Therefore, she lost her arm in the process and her seven-year-old son died. Their second son, John lived in Excelsior Springs, Missouri and became one of the most highly respected residents of the community.

Jesse and Frank

There were four siblings—Robert Reuben James Jr was born 1845 and died 1845. Frank was born in1844, Jesse in 1847 and Susan in 1849. Jesse was the leader of the twosome even though he was the younger. Frank's personality was one that was more poetic, and he was a good listener. He was always concerned for his friends and would listen intently to their woes. He was a compassionate man and held respect for those he came in touch with.

Jesse was not of the same nature. He found his outlets in shooting game for food being out in nature. You could hear him singing hymns while on his horse riding which seemed to bring him comfort. He had steely blue eyes that were compounded by a granulated eye lids that made his gaze more of a threat when he was in intense anger. Those same steely blue eyes were passed down to some of the Wetmore family members. My father had that same gaze about him and so does my brother. It is a penetrating blue that seems to pierce through you.

Jesse was nominated boss and he chose two favorite men to be part of their gang. Bill Ryan and Cole Younger rode with the James boys and they were not good company. They did not possess the same background the James boys did. Jesse married Zerelda Amanda Mimms. They were first cousins. They had seven children, Jesse Edward James Jr., Gould James who died at birth, Montgomery James who died young, Mary Susan 1875-1935, Richard James who also died young, Joseph Henry Clark estimated time frame—1853-

1912, Dollie Rose Simmons died 1902. He had one son, Joseph "Joe" Jesse 1870-1940 by Maggie Wabasta. Jesse Edwards became a well-respected and well-known attorney in Los Angeles, California and raised a wonderful family.

During Jesse's life of criminal escapades, he stole over a half a million dollars but died a poor man. With today's inflation that would be an approximate estimated amount of $16,445,963. In a home in St. Joseph, Missouri Bob Ford shot Jesse James in the head with a .44 caliber rifle. Bob Ford and his brother Charley thought the deed to the house would bring them renown riches. It only brought them misery. The house has been moved from its original site in the 1930's to the Outer Belt of St. Joseph, MO which is now a tourist attraction.

Jesse was thirty-five years old when he was killed. It was April 3,1842. He is buried in Kearney, Missouri. Jesse died but his legend lives on. His brother Frank turned himself in after Jesse's death and was acquitted by the jury in the famous trial at Gallatin, Missouri in 1883. Frank had married Ann Ralston James born January 25, 1853. She was loyal to him and true to her vows, she never revealed anything to anyone concerning his unlawful activities. She died July 6, 1944. They had one son, Robert Franklin James. Frank died in 1915 and many claimed his ashes were strewn over the old farm. This was not true. Both his urn and the urn of his wife Ann were buried in a private cemetery on Rock Creek near Independence, Missouri. Robert Franklin died in 1959 and he had no children.

What is in a Name?

When you reach a certain section of the Bible you begin to read the begats! The Book of Numbers beginning with the first chapter has a section of all those people who had this one and that one. Genesis gives an account of this king and that one who had once reigned. Often it gets tiring to go through all those names of who had who and when unless you are a genealogist. The truth of the matter is knowing this is important for if you study, you find out things like King Solomon was actually King David's son and then who the eight people of Noah's family were who entered the ark and where their heritage took them. But it gets pretty interesting in Matthew for the genealogy of Jesus Christ is there! In the genealogy of Jesus, you come to the part that says in Matthew1:5 "Salmon begat Boaz by Rahab and Boaz begat Obed by Ruth, Obed begat Jesse (v6) and Jesse begat David the king. David the king begat Solomon by her who had been the wife of Uriah" (NKJV). Then skipping down to verse 16 "And Jacob begat Joseph, the husband of Mary of whom was born Jesus who is called Christ." Now among these particularly with Rahab was a very interesting story. Rahab was a harlot. The dictionary characterizes this word as "euphemism whore" (Webster's New World College Dictionary). The word euphemism has the meaning of less offensive or less distasteful. If you put the two meanings together you come up with a less offensive or distasteful whore! Another connection placed on the name through Biblical context is a woman consecrated or devoted to prostitution." or as another place it is found in Judges 11:2 either "another woman" or a "strange woman" depending on the version. I consider it safe to say that no matter how the term is read, Rahab was a woman of "ill repute." And she is right in the midst of the genealogy of Jesus Christ.

So, let's open her story. The account is written in Joshua 2:1-24. I am writing as if I were at least tuned in to the circumstances and had a bird's eye view of the situation.

After the death of Moses, Joshua, son of Nun was called to fill his shoes and continue in leading the Children of Israel. God made clear His promise that he had told Moses carefully and explicitly and made an outline of all that was given to the Children of Israel as long as they followed His commands. Evidently Joshua had some reservations that he might not be able to fill Moses' shoes as adequately as he should, and God reassured him with a significant promise in Joshua 1:9 (NKJV).

> *"Have I not commanded you? Be strong and*
> *of good courage; do not be afraid, or*
> *dismayed, for the Lord your God is with you wherever you go."*

It is then after he had spoken with the Children of Israel and told them of what God had to say, that they responded and would heed his words and were ready to move forward. Joshua sent two men as spies from Acacia Grove to secretly check out the land but particularly Joshua wanted to know what the City of Jericho had to offer. There must have been a snitch among them for the King of Jericho was warned that some men were coming from the camp of the Israelites. The King thought that Rahab would be the one to look out for them, after all she had the reputation who men sought after first, so he instructed her, "When these men arrive at your house, bring them to me because they are here to look at what they can take from our country." When they showed up, she was to send them to him.

Rahab answered, "They already came, and I didn't know where they came from, and they have already left." She continued her ploy to distract the king. "It was getting dark, and the gate was being shut to the city when the men left. Maybe you should go after them quickly before they go very far."

She continued with her plan to care for these men and hide them from the king and the guards who were in search of them. She took the two spies up to the roof and instructed them. "I will cover you with these stalks of flax, but you need to lie very still and make no movement." While she was in the process of preparing their hiding place and securing their safety, the soldiers went on their hunt for these men all the way to Jordan and in the fork. Once they had left, she went to the men she had hidden and said, "I know that the Lord has given you the land, that the terror of has fallen on us, and that the inhabitance of the land are fainthearted because of you" (Verse 9).

She went on to explain to them that they had heard how God had delivered them out of Egypt and dried up the Red Sea for them to cross and then how the Israelites had destroyed the two kings of the Amorites "utterly." Certainly, if I had been in those circumstances and not serving the Creator God, I would be shaking in my sandals. She was pretty gutsy I would say to put her life on the line, but she also had a motive to save her family.

Rahab gave credit to the God of heaven for all that had been done and recognizing the power of His mighty hand, she was going to press in on the spies she had hidden with a plea for the saving of her household, which included her father, mother, her brothers and sisters and all that belonged to them. It is unclear how Rahab knew about Jehovah, and it could be that the stories she heard of the deliverance of the Israelite Children could have been the factor of her knowledge for the spies had not been with her long enough to explain anything to her. The spies recognized her sincerity and her compassion on them and made a vow to her inverse 14, "our lives for yours, if none of you tell this business of ours. And it shall be, when the Lord gives us the land, that we will deal kindly and truly with you".(NKJV).

Rahab lived high up on the city wall and put a scaler rope out her window for them to make their escape. The fact that it seemed that the rope was handy makes one wonder if that rope had been used before for others in circumstances that have never been revealed. Just speculation. With their escape she gave them instruction to go to the mountain and stay three days which would give the pursuers time to return. The Bible has a reason for a specific number of days and having said this—all things numbered have some sort of purpose in Scripture as theoretically there is usually a two-fold meaning behind it. Since the nearest mountain was "situated at the western edge of the valley." (SDA Bible Commentary pg. 184) which was closest to them being only about a mile away, they did as she instructed. But before they left, they also left with her a firm vow that if she did not keep her end of the bargain, they would not be held responsible for what happened to her and her family. If she left "a line of scarlet cord in the window" they would recognize her intentions were honorable. The difference from the rope or cord that she had let them down on was that a "line" was actually scarlet linen of which was a product of her trade. This would not attract attention if it was seen since she often used this as her calling card for visitors.

They continued with their warning that if anyone in her family went out into the street, their blood was on them, and the spies would be guiltless of their act. They also counseled that if their business was revealed, then they were free from the oath she made (Verse 20). The spies made it back to the camp of Joshua and reported all that happened and the arrangements that were made as well as assuring Joshua that the Lord was delivering this land to them. Those in Jericho were "fainthearted."

AND THE WALLS CAME TUMBLING DOWN

The story picks up in Chapter 4 which brings us to the crossing of the Jordan River and God drying up the land for them to pass over it. News traveled fast when the king of the Amorites learned of this, he was probably ready to tear his hair out in frustration knowing that the Israelite children were the God of heaven and earth's chosen and he was no match for the Creator God.

Chapter Six and here comes the army against Jericho. The inhabitants of Jericho locked themselves in because they knew they were no match for the Israelite army. God gave explicit instructions of how the fight was to begin. It wasn't the normal swords and man to man fight. Oh no, God had a much better way, and it took faith to believe it would happen. It was a test of trust and obedience and victory would be the outcome.

The instructions were to march around the city, all the men of war for six days. Seven priests would bear seven trumpets of rams' horns about the ark (Joshua 6:4) *"But the seventh day they shall march around the city seven times and the priest shall blow the trumpets"* (NKJV). Here is the clincher (verse 50 *"It shall come to pass, when they make a long blast with the rams' horn, and when they hear the sound of the trumpet, that all the people shall shout; then the wall of the city shall fall flat. And the people shall go up every man straight before him."* (NKJV) And the walls came tumbling down.

RAHAB AND HER FAMILY

When all was said and done, then Joshua told the two spies to go to Rahab the harlot and bring her and her entire family out to safety. And they did. (verses 22 and 23) According to SDA Commentary pg. 199. (In my words) Rahab was instructed in the service of religious expectations and she and her family had to cleanse themselves of any heathen practices that were not in accordance with the laws of Jehovah before they could be admitted into the camp. They fully complied.

And Today

The expectations is to come to church just as you are and then the Holy Spirit cleans you up and you are accepted fully as part of the family of God. This is a much happier ending than that of Jesse James. Yet in both instances the Legend of a Name is important and how and where we came from and where we are going today is a matter of eternal life or eternal death. As much as Jesse loved to sing hymns and be in nature, he chose a path of destruction, Yet God is his judge. Rahab was living for selfish survival reasons it seems, yet she was willing to make the change to live. In both the lives are gone and waiting for their judgment day and the legend still lives on. I believe this is allowed to live on for our admonition for which path we would choose and how the legend of our name can be a witness for eternal life. "Choose you this day whom you will serve..." Joshua 24:15 (NKJV).

CHAPTER TWENTY-ONE

Cast the First Stone

"Do not be envious of evil men, Nor desire to be with them"
Proverbs 24:1 (NKJV).

Evil-doers are always on the lookout for how to set the next trap. Sometimes you wonder if they stay awake at night trying to determine just how to make it work without making themselves look bad. It wasn't any different Jesus' day than it is today or how it has been throughout history. The Pharisees (those are the leaders in the church) didn't like Jesus. He healed the sick, took in the homeless, worked for the underdog and walked on water! They didn't like it because they didn't want their sins exposed as the upright blessed ones who held hands with the state leaders and used their influence to sway things to their liking.

Caught in the act—who? In the act of what? Mary, the adulterous woman about town, they had been watching her carefully and finding someone who would walk in on the situation and be able to bring a public accusation against her. I am sure they must have had some bolts to lock doors then or some sort of way of privacy. And then again, the one that the act was being done with could have been ~ in on it and left the door ajar. We don't know—we can only assume, and that is probably pretty accurate. The story picks up in Chapter 8 of John. Jesús had just returned from the Mount of Olives, most likely after a time of prayer, and went to the temple to teach.

The Pharisees hurried out to see Him while dragging along a woman found in adultery while in the very act no less. It was the law that adultery be punishable by stoning. So, they placed her in the midst of those crowded around to see what was going to happen next. They approached Jesus, displaying her sin in detail, and reminding Him of the Commandment and what the punishment was. They asked pointedly, and I am sure were tapping their toes and thinking, "Aha, we have Him now." They slyly asked, "So Master, what do you say about this?" They were thinking in their minds, they had Jesus in a trap, because He would have to concede having her stoned, since this was the Law, and the Law was to be obeyed.

If you notice in Scripture, Jesus never argued about anything. He would answer a question with a question or a story or a parable about a circumstance that brought the point home and made people think carefully about their motive. This time however, He stooped down and began to write in the dirt, as if He hadn't heard a word they said. One daring soul came closer to see what He was doing. He was writing something. What was He writing?

He stood up and spoke to the throng of evil-doers and it could most likely have been one of them in the midst that may have molested this woman in her younger years causing her to be promiscuous, contributing to her sense of survival or to come under the act of being their sex slave. The Bible doesn't fully explain that but in today's world it has been proven that these things are fact, as horrible as it may seem—sin leads men and women to do sinful acts.

As Jesus stood up and had not answered them, they pressed Him further (Verse7) "…and He said to them, he who is without sin among you, let him first cast a stone at her" (KJV). The one who had been peeking over Jesus' shoulder to see what He was writing slunk away hoping not to be noticed. Then Jesus stooped down again and began to write some more. It was as if the words that were written in the dirt became bold letters, displaying their very own sins and they looked hideous! The oldest to the youngest saw their own sins written in he dirt, clear as day, and one by one, they felt the hot embarrassment of what they had done and had not been caught at or chastised for because they thought their sins were hidden. "Be sure your sins find you out" Numbers 32:23 (NKJV).

As the woman lay face down on the ground, waiting for the stones to pummel her body, she expected she may die from the hands of the very ones who indoctrinated her into the position she carried as an adulterous woman. They were now going to dig her grave. Then she heard the most musical voice speak kindly, "Woman where are your accusers? Has no one condemned you? (verse10). And she answered Him in verse 11, "No one Lord," then the sweetest words anyone could ever hear today are the following. "Neither do I condemn you and go and sin no more."

Today's Fornication

Young girls deliberately dress provocatively and expect that "look but don't touch" is one size fits all. There she was getting home late again. "Where have you been?" as the demanding voice of mother penetrated the ears of anyone within a 100-yard distance. Mother's voice was loud and not withholding any of her disgruntled scolding. Mother had seen her taking off with a neighborhood boy in a pair of shorts that were so short the inside pockets hung below the frayed edges of the pant leg she had cut off. Mother furiously screamed her rebuke, "If those shorts were any shorter, there would be nothing to wear!" Continuing the demand of her whereabouts, the phone rang and interrupted the confrontation of her rebuke as daughter ran to answer the phone.

Mother stormed up the stairs feeling defeated. She decided to listen in on her daughter's conversation. The male voice on the other end was asking her, "So why did you take off so fast?" She giggled and said, "I was already late, and my mother was taking a fit." He went on to tell her that there were three others beside himself waiting to gang bang her. She giggled again and in a coy voice she replied, "Wait and I will see what I can give for an excuse." They hung up.

Mother was livid. She raced back down the stairs and demanded that her daughter stay put and she would be back without saying anything about where she was going. Mother knew who these boys were and what house they were at. When she arrived there, she was met by he young man who had been on the phone line with her daughter. He said, "My mother isn't here right now, Mrs." Without any further intimidation, mother said to him, "Oh I know she isn't here," and barged her way through the door, facing the rest of the boys head on. "What do you think you are doing?" she demanded. "I heard the conversation," she continued. They threw their hands up in defense and tried to excuse themselves with, "It seems to be the kind of treatment she likes, and we thought we would have some fun. It is not her first time you know." Mother looked them square in the eyes with a voice of authority, "As long as my daughter lives in my house, you will respect me, and my rules and I will deal with you."

When mother returned home, she told her daughter what had just transpired. Daughter went to her room in an angry rage, but before she turned away, she screamed obscenities at her mother in defiance straining every blood vessel in her neck as she angrily yelled, "You will not run my life."

Adultry—Fornication—Lust

What happens to children that are trying to be adults while seeing the outcome of their parents' failures? They think they will get to do as they please and can reverse the transaction at any given moment. Young men and women are brought up in God-fearing homes, (and sometimes those homes are too strict) where there is no room to wiggle or sometimes, they are not strict enough and there is too much wiggle room. There is no right or wrong in a good share of these situations.

Sin as it filters down from the woman caught in adultery to the young girl playing games with flirtation and lust—sin is sin. Jesus came to save the lost, the sinful, the perverted lust of the used and abused. He came to pick up the broken pieces of our lives and transform us to reflect Him and become His children. He came to redeem the very ones who perpetrated the victim. The victim who was caught in the demise of the perpetrator. He came to shed His blood for the evildoer and if you are without sin, "cast the first stone."

CHAPTER TWENTY-TWO

Tongues of Men and Angels

*"Kind words can be easy to speak
but their echoes are endless."*
~Mother Theresa

Every word that is spoken, every motive and intention that has been verbally expressed out loud, and every criticism and judgmental word, every harmful disbursement of a word uttered cannot be taken back once it has left the lips. "All such words lay the groundwork for the harvest of evil."

Have you felt the agitation of someone who presses you with that irritating spirit of being a know-it-all? It seems to press in on you at every side and you find yourself harboring anger toward them and the more it settles within you the more it grows and becomes a thorn in your side that you cannot seem to get rid of. Words start spewing out of your mouth in anger and it makes you even more angry that you have fallen into the devil's trap and now you are under his control or so it seems. The Bible says, "Be angry and do not sin; do not let the sun go down on your wrath, nor give place to the devil" (Ephesians 4:26-27). In other words, do not let your words become physical or cause your anger to become so hurtful that the words themselves become an avenue for emotional or mental harm.

Counsel is given from the Book of Romans Chapter 14:12-13 "So each of us shall give an account of himself to God. Therefore, let us not judge one another, but rather resolve this, not to put a stumbling block or a cause to fall in our brother's way." An agitator or an instigator is someone who frustrates even the saints and becomes a stumbling block to that person or persons. When teasing has gone beyond teasing you have entered aggravation. This is the tongue of man that has not been bridled by the Love of God and the holiness of His Spirit.

MY UNCLE WALTER
January 23, 1925–December 31, 2001

I am going to open with a snapshot of my uncle's life written by his very own words in the book of memories written from his thoughts. I grew up on "a small farm with spruces, rock garden, a spring, a lily pond that was located on Bucktooth Run in Salamanca Township, New York. I never left home until I was 23 years old."

"During my early years, I ate, slept and must have cried a bit because my brother, Stan (11 years older) used to say, when I cried, he pushed the baby carriage just as fast as he could to stop my squalling. Probably scared me to death so I couldn't cry!"

In the second grade I used to walk to school down past Riddle's house (their neighbor) and their rooster would come out and fly at me and land on my head. I would carry a long pole and scare him away. Mildred Riddle used to get a kick out of the size of the pole. I would water the chickens at home and fill the wood box. That was my chore. I had a kiddie car, and I broke the wheel on it. Stan cut a block off a tree and fixed it for me."

"My bother Victor and I played many times together, but one day he became sick, and we were saddened by his death. We missed hearing him sing and speak. He did it so eloquently."

"Finally, the engine on Ma's washing machine quit. My older brother rigged up a belt to the driveshaft of a Model T engine and run it like that until we got electricity in 1938. In the Spring after the snow melted away, my sister's and I used to find checker berries by the Pine grove in the cow pasture." (Side note: Checker berries have many heath benefits. If you can find them, they are good for you and yummy! The leaves make an excellent tea).

"Later in the Spring we would find lady slippers in among the Pines. While walking throughout the grove, partridges would fly up from hidden spot, and scare us with the whir of their wings. There were trout in the brook and when I caught one Ma would fry it for me. It tasted good! Days were long and full of hard work, plowing and harrowing with tractor and helping Pa repair the barn, milking cows and berry pocking, but it was mixed with good times like swinging on the ropes in the barn and tumbling in the hay, swimming at the creek so we didn't mind. We weren't rich, but we had all we needed, and Ma and Pa provided a Christian home."

My dear Uncle Walter learned lessons that I am still trying to learn just from the hardships he lived as a boy, but he never complained about anything or at least I never heard him and many who knew him can testify to the same attitude. No matter how frustrating circumstances were or inconvenient it may have been to himself, or how bad a situation was, he maintained a calm about him. He never lost his temper or spoke harshly or gave way to criticism. In all the years of my growing up and being around him, he always showed true Christian love.

One time we were canoeing with a group from the church. When we arrived at the island we canoed to, two people got out, then I stood up. It was only Uncle and I left in the canoe so when I stood up, the canoe tipped upside down and Uncle and I fell in the water with church clothes on no less! He lost his wallet and glasses. I went diving after them and fortunately retrieved them. He just chuckled it off without so much as an irritated glance in my direction or any chiding. He just calmly said, "I guess you shouldn't have stood up so quick." We laughed and that was it. This was the way his life reflected a serenity and peace no matter what was dealt to him.

I never heard him say a thoughtless, unkind word. It was the Sabbath day, and he was a strict Sabbath keeper but this particular day he came to visit me and my boyfriend at the time who was having car problems. Uncle took off his suit jacket and helped repair the car because he was being a witness. He was a walking testimony to the love of God.

He taught me how to tell what the tree was by the bark and then when he heard a bird call, he knew what the bird was. He loved to take walks in nature and he knew much about the floor of the woodland as far as what had been there and close to when it may have been there. When he was subjected to someone that was antagonistic, there was only one time I heard him raise his voice and he said to this individual that was causing a stir with a person he cared about, "If you want to rag on someone, rag on me." That person said no more.

I have often prayed the counsel in Psalms 32:9 NKJV "Do not be like the horse or like the mule, which have no understanding, which must be harnessed with a bit and bridle else they will not come near you." I asked for God to put a bit and bridle on my tongue so that I would not offend or instigate an argument. He has certainly helped me through the years and there is still much refining to do.

Uncle's Love Story

Earlier I wrote the words from his own writing of leaving home when he was 23 years old. At that time he came to live with my mom and dad in New Hampshire I had not been born yet, but my sister was. He met a woman which was my mother's first cousin, Florence. She wasn't well, being a severe and brittle diabetic from birth. She was very frail and had been told she would not live past her twenties, but Uncle Walter fell in love with her and desired to marry her and be with her no matter how many years she had left. He made it his goal to show her everything she could see as her eyesight was bad from her condition.

    They married and had a little girl and she died at birth. They were devastated but Uncle was certain that if God wanted them to have a child that He would allow them to have one. Everett was born August 7, 1955. Aunt Florence eyesight kept getting worse and there was nothing they could do about it. Together they became avid bird watchers. He wanted her to see all the beauty she could see while her eyesight was still fair. They joined the Audubon Society and traveled all over the United States in an old Chevy station wagon just to see birds, climbing mountains and taking trails to where special birds had been located. They traveled hither and yon. She was able to work as a switch-board operator at New England Memorial Sanitarium and Hospital and he worked as Head of Maintenance there as well. Weekends were spent traveling and enjoying nature. He fulfilled his goal of love for her.

    She lost her legs at the very end, and he was up night and day caring for her to test her blood sugar and minister to her over a year before she died. His unconditional love for her gave her a life she would not have known otherwise, and it was his love and kindness to her that gave her a desire to live. She died November 1989.

The Parallel of this Love

We can parallel this love to the greater love that God has for us—His unconditional love in that He gave His only begotten Son to die for our redemption from sin and to have the choice to live with Him forever. No matter how the world treated Him. He never mistreated anyone not even those who persecuted Him. He didn't fuss about how someone acted or what they said.

He didn't put up with the self-righteous bigots or those who thought they could manipulate Him or catch Him in some sort of trap for the leaders were jealous of Him. No, He was calm and just wrote their errors in the dirt. It wasn't in stone—it could be erased but only if their repented and then it would never be seen again. He just waited patiently to the point of His death. He waited and continued to love by asking for their forgiveness for the way they treated Him. There is no condemnation in love that has the tongue of a man but speaks as an angel.

Joyce A. Leonard

TONGUES OF MEN AND ANGELS

Let words of loving kindness flow like well springs
Overflowing within the depths of life that drought brings,
Discouragement, confusion, and despair.
Tongues of Men and Angels
Let me speak with the tongue of an
angel that speaks with care.
Take away my haughty and proud attire,
The murky words that make one a liar.
I do not want to speak as men of worldly wit.
Get out the bridle and the bit,
And let my understanding be fit.
Carry my words to ears that want to hear,
Truth and love…forgiveness and hope without fear.
Speak as an angel would in my filthy
mouth with words worth saving
Words that fill the empty heart that has been craving.
For the renewal of the love of God to the thirsty soul.
To the brother and the sister in need
of healing is heaven's goal.
Awaken within myself my own hurtful words formed of men

And listen
Let the angels make my words sweet
As I lay my filthiness at Your feet.
Let the words of my mouth and the meditation of my heart
Be acceptable in Your sight"
That I will be empowered to do what is right,
By Your power and Your might.
Written by Joyce A. Leonard August 14, 2010

CHAPTER TWENTY-THREE

It's Time to Fly

*"And are not two sparrows sold for two copper coins?
And not one of them is forgotten before God"
Luke 12:6 (NKJV).*

"Listen." Mother warned for silence from her husband. "It sounds like some birds are taking a fit!" The ruckus of chirping birds interrupted their favorite television program.

They hurried to the living room window to see their twenty-five-pound Maine Coon cat sneaking toward the fir tree that was right on their front lawn. This tree had become a yearly nesting place for robins to nurture their babies until they were ready to fly on their own. A tiny robin had fallen from the nest to the ground and Higgins the Maine coon was making his way steadily toward his victim. "No! Shoo! Shoo! NO!" Mother scolded in her attempt to rescue this ball of fluff and she didn't want it to be from the jaws of her cat. Husband came out and snatched Higgins in his arms and put him in the house away from his prey. It became evident that several baby robins had fallen from the nest. Ever so gently Mother. and Husband scooped up the babies and gently placed them back in the nest while Mother robin watched from the guide wire calling frantically her warning that danger was near.

Retreating to the house after the rescue, it wasn't long before another frenzied squawking started up of not just robins, but other species as well were joining in with their frantic worry. Higgins was in the house and there didn't seem to be any other predator nearby. Within a couple hours two of the babies had fallen one died, and one remained living. A few moments later, a huge hawk swooped down and took the dead birds from the ground as well as Mama robin in midair! It was evident the one that was still alive could not remain alone. The new arrival was brought into the house for safety and Higgins would have to learn to stay away from the new occupant. The safest place of refuge was the bathroom.

A shoe box was found and soft cloth over cotton balls was this little one's new place to stay. Its little heart was beating so fast you could actually see it throbbing. The next thing was to determine how they would feed this little creature. A medicine dropper filled with warm milk was placed near its bill and he would open his mouth wide allowing the droplets to be squeezed into his mouth.

It became a study to figure out what to feed this pink skinned baby with bits of fuzz that covered his baldness. His head was much larger than the rest of his body. Mother and Husband guessed it was a "he" for generalization. They carefully opened and shut the bathroom door each time they entered so other household pets couldn't sneak in and make lunch out of Be-be which became his name translated "Baby" which was baby talk fashioned in a high-pitched coo when they spoke.

Bebe soon learned that when the bathroom door opened that it probably meant feeding time, so he would hop from his shoe box and skid to the edge of the bathroom countertop supporting the sink, flapping his wings to keep from falling over the edge of the slippery surface then welcome whoever entered.

After quite a bit of research, it was decided that Bebe needed to advance to worms as soon as possible. Digging worms and catching night crawlers became a daily activity. Each time one was brought in for Bebe and held over his head, he tipped his head back and opened wide his little beak to accommodate the squirming, wriggling worm into his mouth. His throat would bulge as he held the worm in his gullet until it slithered onto his stomach. It was an amazing performance to watch the process and the number of worms he could take in before he would swallow.

It was time for Bebe to learn the basics of life that he would have normally learned from his parents. As good, adopted parents, Husband and Mother took the necessary steps to provide this knowledge by placing a Rubbermaid kitty litter box filled with rich soil and lots of worms buried in it. Bebe was placed in the box and prodded to help him follow his instincts to pull out his own worms. It became a nightly ritual to the garden and dig worms at night that eventually totaled sixty worms a night to provide for his hungry needs. A tin pie plate served as Bebe's private bathtub. It was filled with water and Bebe was placed in it then water was splashed on him. It didn't take too many times before he learned he should preen his feathers that were beginning to develop from his fuzzy covering.

The dogs soon decided that each time Bebe chirped behind the bathroom door at the crack of dawn, that it was translated into breakfast! They took up the serenade to be sure everyone was awake and come to Bebe's aide while at the same time take care of theirs. It was early June when Bebe developed an appetite of 25 worms a day.

Conflict in the Home

Number one son was last to leave the home nest. It seemed to be a point of contention with Husband, who was the adoptive father of Number One son. There was verbal abusiveness toward Mother concerning her son. Husband had been brought up by an abusive father and it seemsed that if the cycle isn't stopped it continues to grow with each generation. The threats conveyed to Mother were so hurtful and even scary that she often feared for her son's life under Husband's hand. It stirred within her defensive anger, and she was heard to say," If you lay a hand on him, what you start, I promise I will finish." Mother was feisty but often went to bed with the streaks of hot tears staining her pillow.

Number One son and Bebe had some things in common. They both were about to transition from one home to another. Bebe had to leave the home that had been provided and it seemed more than likely Bebe was a girl as female birds are a duller color than males. Males are brilliant while the female has softer coloring. Number One son was going to live in a cockroach filth ridden rundown garage amid the city and start a business of sorts with a friend who was not really a friend, but became one who took advantage, yet Number One had to leave. It was time to fly.

Mother knew he had to do what he had to do regardless of conditions for in her heart she knew it was a better place for him to be. She had determined to provide meals for him so he wouldn't starve to death, after all she wouldn't allow a robin to starve.

Letting Go

Bebe's first flight attempt was a disaster. Husband took her in his hands and gave her a gentle thrust to fly into the world on her own. Bebe flapped her wings and soared upward then spun around returning toward the house, making a crash landing into the side of the building. Husband and Mother came. to the rescue. Husband looked at Mother and said, "She isn't ready yet." Number One was not ready yet either. Yet Husband did not have the same compassion for him that he had for Bebe.

It was a Sunday afternoon when Husband announced that it was time for Bebe to fly. The thought crushed the insides of Mother just thinking about letting Bebe go. Newspapers had been decorating the house as Bebe took sweeping flight from room to room while Higgins and the dogs were out for the day.

She would swoop from one piece of furniture to another as she made her journey. Often, she would follow Mother down the hallway walking on the linoleum and the click, click, click, of her nails on the floor was music to Mother's ears. She knew Husband was right. It was time to let go and let her find her way into the wild. She was taken down by the garden edge where the trees were and once again, Husband let her go, and she flew into the trees with ease.

It had been a long busy day and Mother went to take her shower. Husband was cleaning up and took Bebe's Rubbermaid worm garden out to be dumped. Bebe had been nearby and spotted her worm garden in his hands and swooped down to get her feeding. She hadn't learned yet how to get her own worms from the earth. Just as Mother stepped out of the shower, she heard the wild chirping outside and frantically she screamed at Husband while clad in her towel to save Bebe.

Higgins was ready to have Bebe for lunch and she was once again called and rescued as she came spinning in and landing on Mother's arm. She was brought back to her mansion in the bathroom. She had become the coveted pet. When Mother sat at the kitchen table, Bebe hopped on the table and up on Mother's shoulder, inching her way down her arm and tipping her head from side to side making soothing noises. Bebe and Mother were bonded.

Fall Was Coming

Bebe had to be slowly weaned outside. Number One son and Husband were still at odds and Mother continued to feel the onslaught of Husband's negativity concerning son. Bebe was a great source of comfort. Bebe was out of the house and Husband was at work. A thunder and lightening storm came up. Mother ran to the edge of the garden and called as loud as she cold "Bebe, Bebe come." Swooping out from the trees came her beloved Bebe and back in the house she came for after all she had never weathered a storm before, and this could be traumatic for her. Mother gave her shelter from the storm. It was one more storm in life, one more crisis to pass through and one more time to let go.

Finally, the pain of separation and Bebe left again after the storm. She could now fly on her own. Her nest was empty. Mother walked to Number One son's room, and it was empty. He had left the nest too after many trials and hardships. He had to fly on his own. Mother knelt by his empty bed and prayed for the safe keeping of her son and Bebe.

Fall had made its entrance with the changing of the colors on the trees and the grass was withering. Winter was soon to come. Mother was home alone when she heard a whirring of wind that was rushing and loud. She looked out her back window to witness hundreds, no, maybe thousands of robins flood the trees and the lawn of her back yard.

They swooped in and within a few minutes they swooped up into the air as fast as they had arrived and in only moments the thick cloud of robins disappeared out of sight. It was if they all stopped on their way south to say "goodbye and thank you" for the tender care for Bebe, the precious creature created by a wonderful God Who tells us that Spring is here at the first sighting of a robin.

> *"But the very hairs of your head are all numbered,*
> *Do not fear therefore, you are of more value*
> *than many sparrows" (Even robins)*
> *Luke 12:9 (NKJV).*

IT'S TIME TO FLY

A baby robin red breast
Had fallen from the nest.
So tiny were its feathers
In one of God's little creatures.
We cupped it in our hands
And brought it in our home.
Till it could go and fly out on its own.
Little did we know
How our love for it would grow
And the day would come
When we would have to let it go,
Even though we loved it so!'
It came to me about this time,
That my own son must leave
While in prayer upon my knees
Confessing my sins and heartaches sore.
I confided in God this act and more.
He spoke gently within me,
And said, "My child it is like this, you see.
It's time to let him fly on his own.
It doesn't mean he won't have a home.
I promise I will care for his needs.
For he is your son, your seed."
The tears flowed with heart rendering sobs,
For the nest, evil haunts and robs.
Just as the little robin fell to the ground.
God placed us there for it to be found.
God watches over His creatures big and small.
He cares for them; yes, for them all.
By Joyce A. Leonard 1987

CHAPTER TWENTY-FOUR

Hear No Evil, See No Evil, Speak No Evil

*"Wash yourselves, make yourselves clean.
Put away the evil you are doing
from before My eyes. Cease to do evil"
(Isaiah 1:16).*

There is a dividing line between love and hate, between good and evil. Truth can be taken in, accepted, comprehended, and praised, with the first love experience filled with passion and zeal. But evil walks in very subtle ways even within the church. We must set our boundaries on the side of God to have any protection from the evil that surrounds us. The key to safety is creating a relationship with Jesus.

*"The Angel of the Lord encamps
all around about those who love fear Him
and He delivers them"
(Psalms 34:7).*

As you entered the side door of my mother's home there were placed three monkeys on the entry table which portrayed the title of the chapter. One had his hands over his eyes and the second had his hands over his ears, and the third had his hands over his mouth, expressing the very words, "See no evil, hear no evil, speak no evil." If people did this today, we world have a very different world than we do now.

Depression

Depression is ugly. It is debilitating. It devours and changes one from an adventurous, outgoing spirit to one that is ready to take their own life. It is the work of the enemy, Satan himself wants to destroy God's creation and all He created. Circumstances can do this and so can inherited tendencies. It is important to stay focused on the Life Giver and not the destroyer.

A young woman was depressed. She had suspected her husband to be having Internet affairs and she searched the Internet and found her suspicions to be right. The advertisements present an exciting adventure in finding the "right one" for you though the Internet, a popular way to find the "love of your life." Many do find someone but there are those who prey on either men or women with deceit and lies and they become caught up in a fantasy of believing the lie. Then the one they are married to or have had a long-time relationship with are left wondering what has happened to my spouse or my partner? It is best to be married because marriage makes you one with your partner and God and it is part of the criteria of God's Commandment not to commit adultery.

This young woman fell into depression so deep that she fantasized taking her own life with thoughts like what if while traveling down the highway, she would tumble into a ravine and be killed or meet a tractor trailer truck head on that would end her inner pain. Or even running away to some deserted place and and taking pills, falling asleep forever, and even praying, "Lord let sweet death happen to me."

She had listened to the lies and even heard the man she loved tell the other woman he loved her and could not wait to be with her forever. Yet, he stayed and continued with this heart-breaking pain that overtook this young woman to the point she could not eat, focus, or even function. It excelled even further in this young woman's mind with envisioning her husband having an intimate act with this other woman, but it wasn't just one, it was several, and the burning within her soul as she envisioned these acts between her husband and these other women spiraled her into a depression that became a pit of darkness. The only One to pull her out of this was God.

Subtle Attacks in the Church

A hypothetical story: you begin the experience of crossing the river Jordan, without question, you put your feet in the water's edge and got your feet wet believing God when He says He will make a way for you as you walk. then ground appears. You keep your eyes on the Leader in front of you and you trust Him that everything will be alright. Then without realizing, you begin to take your eyes off the One in front of you and recognize there is a roaring water all around you and you may be overtaken. It is at the very height of the Christian experience that everything begins to happen.

You were chosen to greet those who come into the church each Sabbath with a smile and warm hug or a firm handshake. Confidence grows. You are asked to lead out in song service and then your real talent begins to flourish, and it expands into a prideful feeling. Later you are called to be a division leader and you feel important and self-satisfied. You worked your way up in the church to become clerk, elder, speaker, and your lowly achievements become prestigious.

Silently the attack has been made without you even distinguishing it and you begin to look at the walls that were being built up by the Hand of God and noticed the pebbles on the floor of the riverbed and all the flaws in them. Some looked dirty and needed to be cleaned. You avoided stepping on them. Others were jagged around the edges and when you got near them, they hurt you. You became more satisfied with yourself and patted yourself on the back for your efforts with a self-righteous feeling confirmed by your own opinion. The Leader became obscured to your vision, but you saw the flaws of the followers.

The needs of the church became burdensome and weighed heavily on your mind. You stopped spending as much time in prayer as you had before. Your attitude became negative. Troubles rolled in on every side and your feet began to get wet. You questioned God and His ability to hold back the waters. You blocked your ears from hearing His call and you focused on the cares around you. And one day, you were no longer in church, but outside as one of the scoffers, saying, "Where is the promise of His coming?"

Nice People

There are nice people who are nice to your face and know just how to tell you what you want to hear. They have an ability to defend themselves and their actions with a defense system that is believable. Then when you find out they are liars and are corrupt on every level when you had thought they were nice people. Once upon a time they probably were and then evil forces made their way into their lives and it was easier for them to prey on the unsuspecting victim that had trusted them and were able to take their money, their children, their morals and even worse their salvation.

Love Can Make You Crazy

God is love. Do you accept His love and follow Him, or do you love the world and all it offers? Jesus said, "Let not your heart be troubled; you believe in God, believe also in Me. In My Father's house are many mansions; if it were not so I would have told you. I go to prepare a place for you, and if I go to prepare a place for you, I will come again and receive you unto Myself, that where I am there you may be also" (John 14:1-3 NKJV). Not only are there mansions but it says further—"Eye has not seen, nor ear heard, nor have entered the heart of man the things God has prepared for those who love Him"(I Corinthians 2:9 NKJV).

The love between a man and woman is a resemblance of the love of God. The intimacy between a man and woman is experienced with the love relationship that we are to have with God. The husband is to make the woman feel secure and cherished. The wife who is the help mate is to nurture the husband and work beside him in support and together they become one. If that kind of relationship does not exist, the love that one has for the other is not reciprocated, then disaster begins. God never leaves or forsakes. And this is what is meant for the marriage vow.

God promises us that regardless of whatever we are facing, He will be there for us in all circumstances. He says, He will not leave us, but will continue to love us through the storms of life. When we are faced with one crisis after another, or overwhelmed by circumstances, God's promises are sure. While we go through the trial, He will be an "ever present help in a time of need" (Psalms 46:1), and will hold us with "His right hand of righteousness" (Isaiah 41:10).

God Cannot Lie

As we claim the promises of God and depend on them, we forget that perhaps the one we are praying for has free will. God Who is the Creator of all flesh and can move mountains with the faith of a mustard seed and still must wait on the one He created to accept Him in order for Him to transform him into that beautiful being. Free will means saying "yes" to Jesus. Lust takes on the form of selfishness and hides under the skirts of deceit and control. Unless you keep that ongoing relationship with Jesus you fall short of carrying that message of love to those around you. You begin to see evil, speak evil and hear evil drowning out out the love of God. The promises that man make are broken by the selfishness within us, but the promises of God are not to be confused with being the same promises of friends and loved ones, for God cannot lie.

Jesus Paid it All

We must at all costs be careful of what our ears listen to so evil won't drown out "the still small voice" letting us know which way to go, to the right or to the left (I Kings 19:12 NKJV). We must be careful that our eyes don't wander for the heart walks after what the eye sees (Job 31:7 NKJV). We must be careful of what we say for we are judged by our words for if "you give your mouth to evil, your tongue frames deceit" (Psalms 50:19 NKJV). It is time to "see no evil, hear no evil, speak no evil" for Jesus is waiting for a people that will stand firm and not be ashamed to look up and claim Him as King of kings, Lord of lords. He paid the ransom for your life and mine so we can be with Him forever and ever.

EVIL, EVIL, EVIL ALL AROUND

Have you neglected to whisper a prayer to a dying soul?
Have you instead condemned that one in a judgmental role?
Evil, evil, evil all around—
For when the heart is cold, evil will abound.
Speak no evil, my friend
For you never know what soul you may offend.
Angels hold a listening ear
To words spoken in disdain or cheer.
Have you turned your eyes in a lustful gaze?
Harboring fleshly desire in sinful ways.
Evil, Evil, Evil all around.
For when the heart is cold, evil will abound.
Don't look at evil, my friend;
For you never know what signal your expression may send.
Angels watch and record every action and deed,
For you may be the only Bible someone may read.
Have you entertained gossip or a vulgar joke?
Laughing in ridicule of another's burdened yoke?
For Jesus paid the price for His children to be free
To call upon His holy name so evil won't need to be
He is waiting for His children to search
for Him with all their hearts
To put on His armor to shield the fiery darts,
For we are no match for the evil that lurks all around
But God's Spirit is greater and will gallantly abound
Just look up my friend for the holy city on high
For Jesus coming is soon and your redemption draws nigh.
By Joyce A. Leonard June 16, 2004.

CHAPTER TWENTY-FIVE

His Hand was on Me

"Bless the Lord, O my soul, and forget not all His benefits, Who forgives all your iniquities, Who heals all your diseases" (Psalms 103:2-3 NKJV).

Pressing my lips together and feeling a tingling sensation, I thought there was something in my lipstick causing it. Then I began having incontinence and thought I might need mesh constructed on my bladder due to having a hysterectomy many years ago. I figured since I no longer had a uterus acting as a shelf to hold my bladder, then that was the problem. But the issues didn't stop there. Next it seemed every time I stooped over to pick up something or just to tie a shoelace, I would have a dizzy spell and become light-headed. My hands began to feel numb, and I didn't have the grip I used to have. I had a diagnosis for everything, and this continued for well into a year. I would complain to my co-workers how I felt pain here and there and they suggested I see a Chiropractor. I wasn't certain within myself that a Chiropractor was the way to go so decided to go to an Osteopathic doctor whom I found one and made an appointment.

When I entered Dr. Carey's office he asked why I felt I needed his services, and I began to let him know all my symptoms and what I thought they might be. His words were, "I am not touching you." He immediately called St Mary's Hospital and set up an MRI which I had almost immediately. While waiting for the okay to leave making sure the x-rays to the MRI had come out alright, the Radiologist came out and told me he was ordering another x-ray. I entered another ex-ray room with a white glassed panel up on a step, and stood sideways against it. I was instructed to bend my head forward and then back up again. I almost fell over! My head popped off my spinal column and when I put my had up, it went back on. If at any time it had not gone back on, I would have been paralyzed from the neck down irreversibly. He put a hard brace on my neck immediately. I went directly from there back to Dr. Carey's office and he asked me, "who do you want for a surgeon?"

I was in shock trying to process what was being said. Neurosurgeon? I don't know any neurosurgeons! Names were rattled off to me and the only one I recognized was Dr Franck. The only reason I knew his name was because when I drove bus for Western Maine Transportation, he had done a successful brain surgery on a little boy that was part of the clientele I had transported. I had visited this little boy after his surgery and taken him something at that time and met his mother. His mother was so happy with the outcome of her son's surgery, so remembering this I said I would go with him if he was available.

An appointment was set up and I was in Dr Franck's office within a week. When I entered his office, he took his time to explain in detail to me exactly what he was going to do and assured me that as long as I followed his instructions completely that I would be alright.

Since learning my light-headed dizzy spells were due to my vertebrae were coming off my spinal column when I bent down and when I picked my head back up it popped back on again this would have been a trauma that I may not have been able to endure. God had His hand on me while I had suffered these symptoms for over a year, being totally unaware of the danger I was in. It was not long before the surgery was performed. I returned home wearing a hard neck brace. Bone had been taken from my left hip and fused into my neck C3,4,5,6,7. A steel plate with 8 titanium screws were put in place to hold my neck together.

It became a joke in the family that I would lose my head if it wasn't screwed on. Recovery was long and tedious. My first week home, I was taken by ambulance back to the hospital since I had lost so much blood I could not stand up or sit up without passing out. I did not have a blood transfusion but was there a week to recover and be watched. Then I returned back home. I had to be careful about using my eyes since this affected my recovery. No reading. No watching television. I could not shower. I could not do anything that would impede my recovery in any way. I wore the hard brace for 6 months before I was able to go to a soft one, then I wore the soft brace for another six months.

During this time, a co-worker and friend came faithfully to my rescue every day during the week while my husband was at work and gave me a sponge bath, making sure I was fed, and my needs were met until she had to return to work for her final bus run for the day. I will be forever grateful for her friendship and dedication to my recovery. She was one of God's human angels. I returned to school bus driving after eight months while wearing my soft brace. My only difficulty was turning my neck to the left. There seemed to be a stopper there and I cannot move it beyond a certain point.

It was during this crucial time I began Prayer ministry. When there is nothing else you can do but be still, it is then the verse "Be still and know that I am God" (Psalms 46:10), becomes very real. I began praying for my neighbors and whatever they may be going through, my family and all the struggles they were facing as well as those within the church. I even was able to pray for my enemies or the not so sweet people in our lives. My prayers became more and more thoughtful, as I started interceding for those who seemed distant to God's calling. God began a tremendous work in me with prayer and it not only brought healing to me but I am sure only heaven will reveal the healing that may have taken place in the lives of those I was praying for. This was 1995.

It was 2002 when I began to go through more pain in my lower back. After a school bus run, I would have all I could do to get out of my seat after a two-hour run. Slowly I would have to turn sideways to get out of my seat willing my legs to move so I could get up out of the seat. It came to a point that I knew I must see a doctor.

The first one I went to said he would not do any surgery on me because it was too risky. He expected that I would be in a wheelchair soon for the rest of my life. I came away quite discouraged. But I went for a second opinion to hear the same words from the second doctor's mouth. It was suggested that I go for cortisone shots in my lower spine going up through the base of the spine, I was given a sedative before they were administered this injection as this was very painful procedure. I continued these shots for a year waiting three weeks between sessions before another one could be administered. The relief didn't last. Sometimes relief was a two-week period and then the pain returned. I was put on Lyrica and for the nerve pain from my neck and then on Vicodin.

I had decided one week end to meet my sister the church nearest her in Conway, New Hampshire, where I grew up. On this Sabbath there was a specialist in neurosurgery attending. He knew my sister well and after the worship service we met in the fellowship hall to have lunch together as a church family. Dr Jay Neil was used by God to direct me to where I was to go. As conversation was friendly between my sister and Dr. Neil "What do you specialize in?" I interrupted and blurted out to him, He told me and I quickly rambled out my problem to him. He knew exactly what my health issue was and told me to see Dr Matthias Agren, and tell him that he had sent me. Dr. Neil was on his way to his grandson's bedside to have major surgery in California when his flight was canceled, therefore he decided to attend church in Conway. Dr. Neil told me that day, for us to be there at the same time was a divine appointment. He believed his flight was delayed because of me! God makes a way where there is no way. He orchestrates things that we cannot even imagine that could possibly happen. Dr Neil was certain that Dr Agren could repair my lower back so I would still be able to walk. It was no time before I was in Dr. Agren's office having x-rays that no other doctor had put me through. L3,4,5 needed repair. I went to Maine Medical Hospital in Portland and had surgery.

Hydrocodone was given to me for pain which immediately started me vomiting. I was having an allergic reaction. I reverted to extra strength Tylenol and IB Profen. I was told I could not leave the hospital until I could walk up 3 steps. It took every ounce of strength, will power and determination I had but I did it painfully so I could come home. The following six months a therapist came to my house three times a week to work my legs until I could walk again. The treadmill was a tremendous help in the strengthening my legs to walk again. I began at .3 miles per hour which was about as slow as you could go without standing still completely. Over the course of six months, I worked up to 3 miles an hour. This was 2005

Before both major surgeries I was anointed for healing. God had His hand on me. I have had no doubt during that time to this day that He had a plan for me to work for Him even if it is only to write this book and tell the world about the great HEALER Who still has power in the hem of His garment today as He did then when the woman had faith to touch it to be healed from the issue of blood she had suffered for 12 years (see Matthew 9:20-22). That same HEALING power that was given to the lame man at the pool of Bethsaida is still healing today (see John 5:1-9). The same HEALING power that took the chains of pain and depression, and mental anguish till the Balm of Gilead was administered to the demoniac and is still able to heal the broken lives today and transform them to live actively to be His witness for the world. I am privileged to have gone through the pain and suffering to be part of that healing and become His witness.

PRAYERS AND TEARS

As tears trickle down staining the pages of time,
They are filled in a golden bottle
That overflows and is emptied
Into the rivers, the lakes, yes even the sea;

Each tear blended with fervent prayers,
From bended knee and feeble lips.
There is no greater love than that of God,
And He awaits the sinners request,
Waiting to see if he will pass the test—
And wait

To be healed—restored—and returned
From what the enemy has held captive and spurned.
But we must choose life to receive it,
Otherwise, time runs out and we have lost it all.
Because we didn't listen to the Savior's call.
And the tears still flow,
And prayers continue to grow
Continually being uttered from trembling lips
And the prayer request waits, refusing to lose its grip.
The Savior waits
Until He can wait no more
For not making the choice is the choice
And you may be lost forevermore.
Weighing n the balance life and death
Is the weight the Savior bore.
Are you willing to lose heaven for the bondage of sin?
Are you willing to give up what Chist has prepared for you?
Mistrusting His promises to make all things new?
Are you so fearful that things won't be as you desire?
That you don't want to trust God and answer His call?
Have you forgotten how many times
He spared your life in the past?
That you cannot trust Him with the future at all.
The secret of what God can do with the fervent prayer
Is to help you forgive the unforgiveable and really care.
To be like the unforgettable few
Who like the Father in heaven forgive,
Forgive,

Forgive
And to forgive forgetfully, freely
At an outrageous cost
For His children that are lost
For as we forgive…we are forgiven,
Restored, blessed, and called "sons and daughters of God."
That is what the secret of what prayer can do
For you and me.
(Revised from May 15, 2003, in January
21, 2022 by Joyce A. Leonard)
And because of prayer, God's Hand was on me.

CHAPTER TWENTY-SIX

Profession or a Calling

THE SCHOOL BUS DRIVER

I chose this profession to be with my
children when they were small,
To care for them on days when there was no school at all.
It was the love for mine that developed my love for yours.
It increased my tolerance and opened
insight to otherwise closed doors.
Children are a reflection of their parents' way.
They repeat the vocabulary of what they say.
They act as we did when we were young.
It is the same old generation songs being sung.
When the bus is filled with noisy chatter,
When someone shrieks and makes an awful clatter,
I look to see if someone may be hurt
"Who did that?" annoyed, I blurt.
For if no one is having a pain,
I don't want that outburst to happen again!
While driving in speeding traffic both near and far,

Often re-routing through construction
sites and trucks filled with tar;
I travel in weather conditions of heavy rain to slippery snow,
Summer days of glaring sun and tourists on the go!
I carry a precious cargo of life entrusted to my care,
Expecting me to follow safety and
discipline with all that is fair.
But when I send home the warning slip
That your child has broken rules and given some nasty lip—
Some parents quickly doubt my word
Of the obscenity that I heard.
Some are ready to defend their child to the utter end,
Placing the burden of proof on me
with my character to defend!
I don't try to pick on your child,
This one who manipulates my heart when
my feathers are riled. For when I look deep
into the wide eyes of your little girl,
I see a gem of a cultured pearl.
And when your son looks at me with his big blue eyes,
Sometimes his innocent look overrides his lies.
It isn't easy to write that warning slip,
But safety is the issue on this trip.
Sometimes the din of so many voices distract my thoughts,
So when it is your child's turn for the pick-up or drop—
Occasionally I may claim the insanity of "forget"-
When other times, I may slowly ride by
your stop with blaring horn,
Searching the windows and doors on that early morn,

For the child who may have overslept,
While traffic at bay is kept
For the straggler that may appear,
Dragging their backpack as they make their way clear.
Through the years I have…
Scrubbed crayon marks from the seats
Where busy fingers have left their trademark and treats!
Nursed bloody noses and soothed the fear in their eyes,
Expressed by their whimpers and their cries.
Cleaned vomit off the bus floor,
Band aided boo boos and much much more!
I have listened to the pat-a cake repeated refrains,
Disciplined loud chatter thoughtless and whimsical.
I have listened to savory tales told by your child
Some with wild endings while others quite mild.
I have listened to their woes,
Over life and how some silly thing goes.
I have joined in their laughter too,
And complimented them on something new.
Carefully I watch them in front of my bus cross,
Counting footsteps and watching for
anything that may be lost.
Observing each mirror is a constant must,
Until they safely leave the vigil of my trust.
I recognize the laugh and the tone of their voice,
So when they say, "It wasn't me," they give me no choice,
For I know your child as if they were my own,
And through the years I have watched how they have grown.

I recognize their walk and the coat that they wear,
I try to show in little ways, I really do care.
It is not just a job or a way of living—
It is learning patience, endurance and a lot of giving.
It is not just a profession that I have chose;
It is a calling to serve your child, heaven knows.
For there is a child in all of us,
Especially for those who drive a yellow school bus!
(By Joyce A. Leonard November 1, 1996)

Some Unforgeable Memories

It was the high school run and there was a young man—we will call him Tony, and he was sure to do everything he could against obeying the bus rules. "Tony turn around and face the front please," the bus driver would politely ask as she glanced up and watched him chatting with the students behind him while sitting on the edge of his seat with his feet in the aisle to hold him back from falling. He would turn around and sit properly for a few minutes and in no time, Tony was repeating his actions. The bus driver would repeat the instructions giving more authority in her voice than before he would once again turn in the proper position, but it was an ongoing scenario every day. It didn't stop there. Tony had a fowl mouth and would be loud and obnoxious spewing out obscenities. The bus driver would again continue to ask him to stop with the unnecessary vocabulary. It would stop for a few minutes and then be repeated again as if nothing had been said.

Tony would often reach out and touch one of the girls and she would shriek, "Cut it out, leave me alone." Or another girl might laugh and teasingly dare him to touch her again.

The bus driver would often catch the action just in time as she looked up in the rear view mirror that displayed all the young people riding. Often the bus driver noticed Tony didn't have socks on in the winter time and only shoes to cover his bare feet from the cold. She asked him, "Do you need socks, Tony?" He would reply, "Nah, I don't mind it."

Finally the bus driver had to serve Tony with a written warning. She told him, you cannot ride again until your mother or father have signed this warning. He replied, "I don't have any parents." The driver pressed, "then whoever your guardian is, they must sign it before you can ride again. Tony came back with, I live alone." The driver was determined that he would have to have it signed in order to ride her bus again. "Well, Tony take it to the supervisor at the bus garage and she will have to sign it before you ride again." With that he got off the bus. It was a month before Tony returned to his bus stop. He passed the slip signed by his mother. The driver looked at him and said, "Oh, my, Tony, you found your mother! Congratulations!" But it wasn't long before Tony returned to his old ways and this time, the bus driver said to him as he got off her bus at the high school, "Tony why don't you do both of us a favor and get your license and drive yourself to school." Tony took her advice and the next time she saw Tony, he was driving a small pick up through the school parking lot hanging out his window waving his arm at her while grinning from ear to ear.

The Third Grade Rebel

This boy, we will call Harley. He was a rebel at 9 years old. He was the product of a dad in prison and he thought if he did everything he could to be bad, he could be in prison with his dad. Harley wore muscle shirts in the middle of winter and a bandanna on his head. He would curse and sing songs to me that he would spit on my grave and bury me twelve feet under. He insulted the other students and caused as much unrest as possible during his ride from his home to school with the repeat performance back home in the afternoon.

Often I would have the kids draw pictures and would hang them over the windows down the side of the bus or up front over my mirror. The High school young people were also invited to take part. There was a picture that really caught Harley's eye. It was a picture of a man who looked pretty dark and sinister. Harley wanted that picture, but being good and obeying the rules for a week was more than Harley could do.

I learned the following year that Harley would no longer be on my bus. I was so happy to be done with this little trouble maker. Then throughout the summer, I decided to send the picture to his mother and said at some point she could give it to Harley when she thought he might appreciate it.

That following Fall while waiting at the school where Harley used to go, I saw Harley walking up the driveway to the bus. He came right to my bus and thanked me for the picture and apologized to me for the way he acted. I was so pleased and since then I have wondered what ever happened to Harley. Sometimes the TLC really comes through.

God does not treat us as we deserve but treats us as we would want to be treated if we are in bad circumstances. We are molded and made into what we should be by God's grace. I hope that Harley has learned that by now and found his best friend Jesus who accepts him just as he is. How about you?

Auburn, ME school bus drivers 2000 and Joyce
The elementary students from Joyce's bus during a fire drill

ELEMENTARY BUS DAYS

Busy chatter, busy chatter,
Laughing squealing, talking clatter
Some memories may linger while others may fade
Some left dancing forever where memories are made!
"Sit down, aisle clear, quiet please!"
And many, many more of these
Are words embedded within the mind,
But lost when measured where to find.
The empty seats when summer has begun;
The sing-song cheer "school is out" is being sung,
But caress the time when we have spent
Happy, funny silly thoughts that have come and went.
The Christmas songs we loudly sing,
From sleigh bells ring to what Santa will bring.
Slippery roads with wide-eyed wonder
In Springtime rains with lightening and thunder.
It has been my pleasure to be of service to you,
As we say good bye and wish this school year adieu.

By Joyce A. Leonard
2000

Auburn bus driver doubles as poet

By day, Joyce Leonard drives bus 9 for the Auburn School Department. By night she writes poetry. During National School Bus Safety Week, she combined her talents by writing "Be Cool and Follow the Rules." Fellow bus driver, Wayne Strout, put the poem to music, and Ann Gorhuis played the guitar as students sang the new song that reinforces good behavior on the school bus. Leonard's literary talents were recently recognized when another of her poems was selected for publication in an anthology put together by The National Library of Poetry. Gorhuis is shown accompanying Leonard at a presentation.

October 24, 1995 Lewiston, Maine Sun Journal

Unleashed Promises of Merciful Love

CHAPTER TWENTY-SEVEN

Mothers, Mothers and Mothers

> "Mother—that was the bank
> where we deposited our hurts
> and worries."
> -Dewitt Talmage

Mothers come in all shapes and sizes. They have many challenges on a day to day basis. The don't always make the best choice not because they don't want to but because of circumstances or whatever they may be facing at any given time. Some mothers are disciplinarians, and some are nurturing mothers, sacrificial mothers, and hard working mothers, as well as lazy mothers and sadly there are evil mothers.

The Bible tells us of some of these mothers—like Jochebed, Moses mother. There was a decree to kill all the boys of the Israelites for Pharaoh feared as they got older they would overrun his army, and take over his kingdom so he ordered all the midwives to the Hebrew women to kill all baby boys when they were born. Jochebed hid her son for three months. When she could hide him no longer, she put together a basket making it unsinkable and able to float on the water. Placing her beloved baby boy in the basket to float on the river in the basket she sent his sister to watch over him. When Pharaoh's daughter came to bathe in the river, she found him and wanted to keep him. Miriam went quickly and offered her mother (Moses mother) to care for him until he could return to the princess. This was the beginning of a powerful development for Moses who became a type of god to Pharaoh and was able to bring the Children of Israel out of bondage under Pharaoh's rule delivering God's people. I am sure that Jochebed prayed diligently and fervently for her son.

Then Hannah—who couldn't have children and prayed while sobbing in the temple for a son. When her prayer was answered, she dedicated her son to be a servant of God becoming a prophet of God and God blessed him greatly. Hannah was honored for her sacrifice to give her son for the work in the temple and his service to Eli, the priest and to God.

Much has been said about Mary and the son she carried that was born to be the Savior of the world. God knew her heart and how she would follow what He wanted her to do in bringing up the Son of God to be faithful—even unto the death of the cross.

And Elizabeth, another faithful mother, cousin to Mary, Jesus mother. She brought John the Baptist into the world as a forerunner to Jesus. And then there is the evil and vindictive mother Herodias, who had her daughter dance before King Herod. Because of her beauty and her dance, the king offered her whatever she wanted. Her mother connived that she ask for the head of John the Baptist. And John was beheaded. The account is in Matthew 14. God is faithful and those who misuse the sacred trust of motherhood will pay a price with the loss of eternity for one day He will ask "Where is the flock I gave you?" We as mothers are accountable to how we have brought up our children for their eternal lives are at stake. Children may grow up but to a mother they are still children in her eyes.

JOYCE A. LEONARD

MOTHER'S ARE NOT PERFECT

I cannot "fix" feelings of one without
affecting those of another,
I cannot "kiss away the hurt" as
sanctioned by many a mother.
I am not in control of thoughts and emotions.
I cannot read minds and remedy all notions.
Mother's are not perfect.
No they are not.
They do as they feel best at the time
when life has dealt it's lot.
There is not always an absolute right or wrong.
Circumstances may vary, just as the tune of a song.
Sacrifice and unconditional love in a pot belong,
Spiced and simmered over the years are made strong,
By the mother who rushed to her child's defense,
In serious struggle or utter nonsense.
Mother's are not perfect, oh no they are not!
They do all they can with what life has brought;
Hoping that by giving up pleasure in life
Their children will gain respect for their strife.
And give rewards of joy for all that they have done,
And in their old age bring back some
sort of laughter and fun.
A child may give a scathing rebuke to a
Mother who gave her all;
Setting mother straight and exposing
her sins for salvation's call.
And you wonder O mother, where did you fail
In giving this child the hammer and the nail

Unleashed Promises of Merciful Love

To scourge your character along a bloody trail?
And sentence your morals without allotting bail.
Mothers are not perfect; Oh no they are not!
Yet the sins of their children are deliberately forgot.
The sands of time cannot be erased.
They become altars of experience redeemed by grace;
Forged in the balance of life and then we move on,
Learning lessons even after the children are gone.
Then once in awhile over life's bumpy road,
The burdens get heaver with each new load,
That children lay upon your shoulders heaped with stress,
Sometimes unintentionally but alway plagued with distress.
Yet mother's take all the pain to heart,
Because the "fix it" feeling won't depart.
Oh mother's are not perfect, you know.
They hurt and cry with each new mistake as they grow.
They cover the pain with smiles and silly chatter;
They take on extras with the "wave
of the hand" and "it doesn't
matter."
But when life's trials are said and done,
With some battles lost and others won.
Mother may look to her Savior in thought,
For assurance that her prayers have not been forgot.
His Voice will cheer her when children
have rendered distraught,
When He whispers what His unfailing love has brought.
Forgiveness and peace is what she she has sought,
For mother's are not perfect—Oh mother's are not!
By Joyce A. Leonard July 11, 1996

JOYCE A. LEONARD

COULD I—WOULD I?

Would I have been like Hannah,
Crying pitifully for the Lord to provide the manna
Of a child birth, then willingly after all those tears
Let go of motherhood and let another
nurture the tender years,
Consecrated to a training served by God alone?
Would I have been willingly able to make this loan?
Would I have been like Elizabeth the mother of John,
Knowing my son would pave the way for a purpose forgone?
Could I have dedicated each day to a holy calling?
With training, teaching, and praying without hesitation or
stalling?
Could I have molded my son to travel a wilderness road.~
Being empowered with speech by the mother's touch, a gift
God bestowed?
Could I—Would I?
If I had been chosen for a son of fame to live or die,
Would I have been like Mary,
And could I have been the one chosen to carry
And meet the call of "blessed among
women," a title to endure
Criticism, ridicule, and yet maintain all that is pure?
For the Seed was placed there as God had willed,
And it was there the blessed Savior was to her instilled,
With a path chosen to deny
Burdened with sorrows while hearing a mournful cry.
"The fervent, effectual prayer of a righteous," mother,

Holds the sacred vow bound one with another,
For the child born of the womb,
Some live for Christ and turn away from sin,
While others live without prayer and die within.
So, child of my womb and my vow,
Hear the pleas of this mother now.
I could and I would pray for you.
I could and I would carry your name each day a new
Before the Throne of Grace, mingled with mercy and love,
To envision my mind with God's eyes from above,
Enlightened with promises as you grew
And seeing my precious child as God sees you.
So could I? Would I?
Heed the mother's call to sacrifice and deny,
To pray for you and others
I have taken as my own.
Praying throughout the day and in the
night making petitions known?
Yes, my child, I can and I will,
For you are engraved upon the Hand of God still,
And heaven would be empty if you were not there,
So I could and I would cry out your name in prayer.
By Joyce A. Leonard September 8, 2001

CHAPTER TWENTY-EIGHT

"Don't Worry, Be Happy!"

"Cast all your cares upon Him, for He cares for you"
I Peter 5:7(NKJV).

How did worry first come into existence? Let's begin with Adam and Eve. They had just disobeyed God. When they heard Him coming to meet them in the Garden, they ran and hid themselves out of fear. They were fearful for the first time about seeing Him because they were worried about the consequences of their disobedience. They had been given the gift of choice as we all have, and they made the wrong one when they took the fruit from the tree of Knowledge and Good and Evil, and listened to the serpent, Satan. The account is given in Genesis 3:8-10.

Now the account of Abraham in Genesis 22, when God told him to take his only son Issac and offer him as a burnt offering, even with the faith of this great man, don't you think he may have worried a little bit over this sacrifice that he was asked to give? But he obediently did as God asked, taking the journey to Moriah and then to have to deal with the questions from his son, asking where the burnt offering was that was to be presented to the Lord. Faithful Abraham said, "My

Tempo totale: 25 MIN| Servire: 3

INGREDIENTI:
- 3 strisce di pancetta
- 1 tazza di mozzarella, tritata
- 2 cucchiai di burro
- 6 uova
- Sale e pepe
- ½ avocado, a cubetti
- 1 oz di formaggio cheddar, grattugiato

ISTRUZIONI:
- Cuocere la pancetta fino a renderla croccante, mettere da parte fino al bisogno.
- Riscalda una padella antiaderente e metti 1/3 di tazza di mozzarella nella padella e cuoci per 3 minuti fino a doratura attorno ai bordi. Metti un cucchiaio di legno in una ciotola o in una pentola e usa delle pinze per sollevare il taco al formaggio dalla pentola. Ripeti con il formaggio avanzato.
- Sciogliere il burro in una padella e uova strapazzate; usa pepe e sale per condire.
- Versare le uova in gusci induriti e guarnire con avocado e pancetta.
- Completare con il cheddar e servire.

NUTRIZIONE: Calorie 443 | Grassi totali 36,2 g | Carboidrati netti: 3g | Proteine 25,7 g | Fibre: 1,7 g)

12.Pancetta al formaggio e frittata di erba cipollina

Tempo totale: 30 MIN| Servire: 2

INGREDIENTI:
- 1 cucchiaio di buccia di psillio
- 1 cucchiaino di lievito in polvere
- Sale
- 3 once di formaggio cheddar
- 4 uova, grandi
- 3 cucchiai di farina di mandorle
- 1 cucchiaio di burro, biologico
- 1 cucchiaino di condimento italiano
- 4 cucchiai di parmigiano
- ½ tazza di salsa di pomodoro

ISTRUZIONI:
- Aggiungere tutti gli ingredienti in una ciotola tranne il formaggio e la salsa di pomodoro. Usa un mixer o un frullatore ad immersione per unire fino a ottenere un composto denso.
- Riscalda la piastra per waffle e usa la miscela per fare due waffle.
- Metti i waffle su una teglia foderata e condisci con salsa di pomodoro e formaggio (dividere uniformemente). Cuocere per 3 minuti o fino a quando il formaggio si scioglie.
- Servire.

NUTRIZIONE: Calorie 525,5 | Grassi totali 41,5 g | Carboidrati netti: 5g | Proteine 29g | Fibra 5,5 g)

14.Frittata di acciughe, spinaci e asparagi

Tempo totale: 23 MIN| Servire: 2

INGREDIENTI:
- 2 once di acciughe in olio d'oliva
- 2 uova biologiche
- 3/4 tazza di spinaci
- 4 asparagi marinati
- Sale del Mar Celtico
- Pepe nero appena macinato
-

ISTRUZIONI:
- Preriscalda il forno a 375 F.
- Mettere l'acciuga sul fondo della teglia.
- In una ciotola sbattete le uova e versatele sopra il pesce. Aggiungere sopra gli spinaci e gli asparagi tritati.
- Condite con sale e pepe a piacere.
- Cuocere in forno preriscaldato per circa 10 minuti.
- Servire caldo.

NUTRIZIONE: Calorie 83 | Grassi totali 4,91 g | Carboidrati netti: 2,28 g | Proteine 7,5 g)

15.autunnale alla zucca senza pancia

Tempo totale: 1 ora e 30 minuti | Servire: 2

INGREDIENTI:
- 3 albumi d'uovo
- 1/2 tazza di latte di cocco
- 1 1/2 tazze di farina di mandorle
- 1/2 tazza di purea di zucca
- 2 cucchiaini di lievito in polvere
- 1 1/2 cucchiaino di spezie per torta di zucca
- 1/2 cucchiaino di sale kosher
- Olio di cocco per ungere

ISTRUZIONI:
- Preriscalda il forno a 350F. Ungere una teglia da pane standard con olio di cocco fuso.
- Setacciare tutti gli ingredienti secchi in una ciotola capiente.
- In un'altra ciotola, aggiungi la purea di zucca e il latte di cocco e mescola bene. In una ciotola separata, sbattere gli albumi. Incorporare gli albumi e incorporarli delicatamente all'impasto.
- Stendere l'impasto nella teglia preparata.
- Cuocere il pane per 75 minuti. Una volta pronto, togliere il pane dal forno e lasciarlo raffreddare.
- Affettare e servire.

NUTRIZIONE: Calorie 197 | Grassi totali 16g | Carboidrati netti: 8,18 g | Proteine 7,2 g)

16.Ccino Frozen Zero-Pancia

Tempo totale: 10 MIN| Servire: 1

INGREDIENTI:
- 1 tazza di caffè freddo
- 1/3 di tazza di panna
- 1/4 cucchiaino di gomma di xantano
- 1 cucchiaino di estratto di vaniglia puro
- 1 cucchiaio di xilitolo
- 6 cubetti di ghiaccio
-

ISTRUZIONI:
- Metti tutti gli ingredienti nel frullatore.
- Frullare fino a quando tutti gli ingredienti sono ben amalgamati e diventano lisci.
- Servire e gustare.

NUTRIZIONE: Calorie 287 | Grassi totali 29g | Carboidrati netti: 2,76 g | Proteine 1,91 g)

17. Uova dolci e cremose

Tempo totale: 17 MIN| Servire: 1

INGREDIENTI:

- 2 uova biologiche
- 1/3 di tazza di panna, preferibilmente biologica
- ½ cucchiaio di stevia
- 2 cucchiai di burro biologico
- 1/8 cucchiaino di cannella, macinata

ISTRUZIONI:

- In una piccola ciotola, sbatti le uova, la panna da montare e il dolcificante.
- Sciogliere il burro biologico in una padella a fuoco medio e poi versare il composto di uova.
- Mescolare e cuocere fino a quando le uova iniziano ad addensarsi, quindi trasferirle in una ciotola.
- Cospargere con la cannella in cima prima di servire.

NUTRIZIONE: Calorie 561 | Grassi totali 53,6 g | Carboidrati netti: 6,4 g | Proteine 15g)

18.d'avena senza pancia

Tempo totale : 20 MIN| **Servire: 5**

INGREDIENTI:
- 1/3 di tazza di mandorle, a scaglie
- 1/3 di tazza di scaglie di cocco non zuccherate
- ¼ tazza di semi di chia
- 2 cucchiai di eritritolo
- ¼ tazza di cocco, grattugiato, non zuccherato
- 1 tazza di latte di mandorle
- 1 cucchiaino di vaniglia, senza zucchero
- 10 gocce di estratto di stevia
- ½ tazza di panna da montare pesante, montata

ISTRUZIONI:
- Metti le mandorle e le scaglie di cocco in una pentola e tosta per 3 minuti fino a quando non diventa fragrante.
- Metti gli ingredienti tostati in una ciotola insieme a semi di chia, eritritolo e cocco grattugiato; mescolare insieme per unire.
- Aggiungere il latte e mescolare. Puoi usare latte caldo o freddo in base alle tue preferenze.
- Aggiungere la vaniglia e la stevia, mescolare e mettere da parte per 5-10 minuti.
- Servire guarnito con panna montata.

NUTRIZIONE: Calorie 277 | Grassi totali 25,6 g | Carboidrati netti: 16,4 g | Proteine 5,5 g | Fibre: 7,5 g)

19. Formaggio Cheddar Ricoperto Di Pastella

Tempo totale: 23 MIN| Servire: 1

INGREDIENTI:
- 1 uovo grande
- 2 fette di formaggio Cheddar
- 1 cucchiaino di noci macinate
- 1 cucchiaino di semi di lino macinati
- 2 cucchiaini di farina di mandorle
- 1 cucchiaino di semi di canapa
- 1 cucchiaio di olio d'oliva
- Sale e pepe a piacere

ISTRUZIONI:
- In una piccola ciotola, sbatti un uovo insieme al sale e al pepe.
- Scaldare un cucchiaio di olio d'oliva in una padella, a fuoco medio.
- In una ciotola separata, mescolare i semi di lino macinati con le noci tritate, i semi di canapa e la farina di mandorle.
- Ricoprire le fette di cheddar con il composto di uova, quindi arrotolare il composto secco e friggere il formaggio per circa 3 minuti su ciascun lato. Servire caldo.

NUTRIZIONE: Calorie 509 | Grassi totali 16g | Carboidrati netti: 2g | Proteine 21g)

20. Uova sode al formaggio

Tempo totale: 27 MIN| Servire: 2

INGREDIENTI:
- 3 uova
- 2 cucchiai di burro di mandorle, senza mescolare
- 2 cucchiai di formaggio cremoso, ammorbidito
- 1 cucchiaino di panna da montare
- Sale e pepe a piacere

ISTRUZIONI:
- In una piccola casseruola fai bollire le uova.
- Quando sono pronte, lavate le uova con acqua fredda, sbucciatele e tritatele. Metti le uova in una ciotola; aggiungere il burro, la crema di formaggio e la panna da montare.
- Mescolare bene e aggiungere sale e pepe a piacere. Servire.

NUTRIZIONE: Calorie 212 | Grassi totali 19g | Carboidrati netti: 0,75 g | Proteine 7g)

21. Torta di frittata di salsiccia di cavolo di Mahón

Tempo totale: 40 MIN| Serve: 8)

INGREDIENTI:
- 3 salsicce di pollo
- 2 1/2 tazze di funghi, tritati
- 3 tazze di spinaci freschi
- 10 uova
- 1/2 cucchiaino di pepe nero e semi di sedano
- 2 cucchiaini di salsa piccante
- 1 cucchiaio di aglio in polvere
- Sale e pepe a piacere
- 1 1/2 tazze di formaggio Mahón (o Cheddar)

ISTRUZIONI:
- Preriscaldare il forno a 400 F.
- Tritare sottilmente i funghi e la salsiccia di pollo e metterli in una padella di ghisa. Cuocere a fuoco medio-alto per 2-3 minuti.
- Mentre le salsicce cuociono, trita gli spinaci, quindi aggiungi gli spinaci e i funghi nella padella.
- Nel frattempo, in una ciotola mescolare le uova con pepe nero e semi di sedano, le spezie e la salsa piccante. Mescola bene tutto il composto.
- Mescola spinaci, funghi e salsicce in modo che gli spinaci possano appassire completamente. Condite con sale e pepe a piacere.
- Infine, aggiungi il formaggio in cima.
- Versare le uova sul composto e amalgamare bene.
- Mescola il composto per alcuni secondi, quindi metti la padella nel forno. Cuocere per 10-12 minuti, quindi grigliare la parte superiore per 4 minuti.

● Lasciare raffreddare per un po', tagliare in 8 fette e servire caldo.

NUTRIZIONE: Calorie 266 | Grassi totali 17g | Carboidrati netti: 7g | Proteine 19g)

22. Frittata di pancetta e scalogno di Monterey

Tempo totale: 30 MIN| Servire: 2

INGREDIENTI:

- 2 uova
- 2 fette di pancetta cotta
- 1/4 di tazza di scalogno, tritato
- 1/4 tazza di formaggio Monterey Jack
- Sale e pepe a piacere
- 1 cucchiaino di strutto

ISTRUZIONI:

- In una padella scaldare lo strutto a fuoco medio-basso. Aggiungere le uova, lo scalogno e sale e pepe a piacere.
- Cuocere per 1-2 minuti; aggiungere la pancetta e rosolare 30 - 45 secondi in più. Spegni il fuoco sul fornello.
- Sopra la pancetta mettere un formaggio. Quindi, prendi due lembi della frittata e ripiegali sul formaggio. Tieni i bordi lì per un momento mentre il formaggio deve sciogliersi parzialmente. Procedete allo stesso modo con l'altro uovo e lasciate cuocere in padella tiepida per un po'.
- Servire caldo.

NUTRIZIONE: Calorie 321 | Grassi totali 28g | Carboidrati netti: 1,62 g | Proteine 14g)

23. Muffin con bacon di tacchino affumicato e avocado

Tempo totale: 45 MIN| Serve: 16)

INGREDIENTI:
- 6 fette di pancetta di tacchino affumicata
- 2 cucchiai di burro
- 3 cipollotti
- 1/2 tazza di formaggio cheddar
- 1 cucchiaino di lievito in polvere
- 1 1/2 tazze di latte di cocco
- 5 uova
- 1 1/2 cucchiaio di polvere di metamucil
- 1/2 tazza di farina di mandorle
- 1/4 di tazza di semi di lino
- 1 cucchiaino di aglio tritato
- 2 cucchiaini di prezzemolo essiccato
- 1/4 cucchiaino di peperoncino rosso in polvere
- 1 1/2 cucchiaio di succo di limone
- Sale e pepe a piacere
- 2 avocado medi

ISTRUZIONI:
- Preriscaldare il forno a 350 F.
- In una padella a fuoco medio-basso, cuocere la pancetta con il burro fino a renderla croccante. Aggiungere i cipollotti, il formaggio e il lievito.
- In una ciotola mescolate il latte di cocco, le uova, il Metamucil in polvere, la farina di mandorle, il lino, le spezie e il succo di limone. Spegnete il fuoco e lasciate raffreddare. Quindi sbriciolare la pancetta e aggiungere tutto il grasso al composto di uova.
- Pulire e tritare l'avocado e unirlo al composto.

● Misurare la pastella in un vassoio per cupcake che è stato spruzzato o unto con spray antiaderente e cuocere per 25-26 minuti.
● Una volta pronto, lasciate raffreddare e servite caldo o freddo.

NUTRIZIONE: Calorie 184 | Grassi totali 16g | Carboidrati netti: 5,51 g | Proteine 5,89 g)

24.Peperoni per la colazione al chorizo

Tempo totale: 25 MIN| Servire: 2

INGREDIENTI:
- ½ cucchiaio di burro chiarificato
- 1 cipolla, tritata
- 2 spicchi d'aglio
- 6 uova biologiche
- ¼ di tazza di latte di mandorle, non zuccherato
- 1 tazza di formaggio cheddar, grattugiato
- Sale e pepe a piacere
- 3 peperoni grandi, tagliati a metà, privati del torsolo e dei semi
- ½ libbra salsiccia di chorizo piccante, sbriciolata

ISTRUZIONI:
- Vedi sopra due 350 F.
- Scaldare il burro chiarificato in una padella antiaderente a fuoco medio e cuocere il chorizo sbriciolato. Accantonare
- Usando la stessa padella, aggiungere le cipolle e l'aglio e soffriggere per qualche minuto. Spegnere il fuoco e mettere da parte.
- In una ciotola, mescola le uova, il latte, il cheddar e condisci con sale e pepe.
- Aggiungere il chorizo nella ciotola con le uova e mescolare bene.
- Metti le metà del peperone in una pirofila riempita con ¼ di pollice di acqua.
- Versare il composto di chorizo e uova nei peperoni e mettere la pirofila in forno a cuocere per 35 minuti.
- Servire caldo.

NUTRIZIONE: Calorie 631 | Grassi totali 46 g | Carboidrati netti: 13g | Proteine 44g | Fibra: 3,5 g)

25. Mousse cremosa di cioccolato e avocado

Tempo totale: 50 MIN| Servire: 2

INGREDIENTI:
- 2 avocado maturi
- 1/3 tazza di cacao in polvere
- ½ cucchiaino di semi di chia
- 1 cucchiaino di estratto di vaniglia
- 10 gocce Stevie
- 3 cucchiai di olio di cocco

ISTRUZIONI:
- Mettere tutti gli ingredienti in un frullatore e frullare fino a che liscio.
- Versate il composto in una ciotola e mettete in frigorifero a raffreddare per 40 minuti o più.
- Servire freddo.

NUTRIZIONE: Calorie 462 | Grassi totali 46 g | Carboidrati netti: 15 g | Proteine 6g | Fibra 1,2 g)

26. Frittelle Di Formaggio Con Panna Acida

Tempo totale: 30 MIN| Servire: 2

INGREDIENTI:

- 2 uova
- 1/4 di tazza di crema di formaggio
- 1 cucchiaio di farina di cocco
- 1 cucchiaino di zenzero macinato
- Stevie liquido da 1/2 tazza
- Olio di cocco
- Sciroppo d'acero senza zucchero

ISTRUZIONI:

- In una ciotola profonda, sbatti insieme tutti gli ingredienti fino a che liscio.
- Scaldare una padella con olio a fuoco medio-alto. Mestolo la pastella e versare l'olio caldo.
- Cuocere da un lato e poi girare. Completare con uno sciroppo d'acero senza zucchero e servire.

NUTRIZIONE: Calorie 170 | Grassi totali 13g | Carboidrati netti: 4g | Proteine 6,90 g)

27. Uova strapazzate del Vesuvio con provolone

Tempo totale: 15 MIN| Servire: 2

INGREDIENTI:
- 2 uova grandi
- 3/4 tazza di provolone
- 1,76 once salame essiccato all'aria
- 1 cucchiaino di rosmarino fresco (tritato)
- 1 cucchiaio di olio d'oliva
- Sale e pepe a piacere
-

ISTRUZIONI:
- Soffriggere il salame tritato in una piccola padella con olio d'oliva.
- Nel frattempo in una ciotolina sbattete le uova, poi aggiungete il sale, il pepe e il rosmarino fresco.
- Aggiungere la provola e mescolare bene con una forchetta.
- Versare il composto di uova nella padella con il salame e cuocere per circa 5 minuti. Servire caldo.

NUTRIZIONE: Calorie 396 | Grassi totali 32,4 g | Carboidrati netti: 2,8 g | Proteine 26,1 g | Fibra: 0,3 g)

28. Adorabili muffin ai semi di lino alla zucca

Tempo totale: 25 MIN| Servire: 2

INGREDIENTI:
- 1 uovo
- 1 1/4 tazze di semi di lino (macinati)
- 1 tazza di purea di zucca
- 1 cucchiaio di spezie per torta di zucca
- 2 cucchiai di olio di cocco
- 1/2 tazza di dolcificante a scelta
- 1 cucchiaino di lievito in polvere
- 2 cucchiaini di cannella
- 1/2 cucchiaino di aceto di mele
- 1/2 cucchiaino di estratto di vaniglia
- Sale due chiavi

ISTRUZIONI:
- Preriscalda il forno a 360 F.
- Per prima cosa, macina i semi di lino per alcuni secondi.
- Unite tutti gli ingredienti secchi e mescolate.
- Quindi, aggiungi la tua purea di zucca e mescola per unire.
- Aggiungere l'estratto di vaniglia e le spezie di zucca.
- Aggiungere l'olio di cocco, l'uovo e l'aceto di mele. Aggiungi dolcificante a tua scelta e mescola di nuovo.
- Aggiungi un cucchiaio colmo di pastella a ogni muffin foderato o cupcake e guarnisci con alcuni semi di zucca.
- Cuocere per circa 18 - 20 minuti. Servire caldo.

NUTRIZIONE: Calorie 43| Grassi totali 5,34 g | Carboidrati netti: 3g | Proteine 1g | Fibra: 1 grammo)

29. Prosciutto Cotto E Uova Strapazzate Di Cavolo

Tempo totale: 40 MIN| Servire: 2

INGREDIENTI:
- 5 once di prosciutto a dadini
- 2 uova medie
- 1 cipolla verde, tritata finemente
- 1/2 tazza di foglie di cavolo, tritate
- 1 spicchio d'aglio, schiacciato
- 1 peperoncino verde, tritato finemente
- 4 peperoni già arrostiti
- Pizzicare il pepe di cayenna
- 1 cucchiaio di olio d'oliva
- 1/2 lattina d'acqua

ISTRUZIONI:
- Riscaldare il forno a 360 F.
- Scaldare l'olio in una piccola padella antiaderente. Aggiungere la cipolla verde e cuocere per 4-5 minuti fino a quando non si ammorbidisce.
- Mescolare l'aglio e il peperoncino e cuocere per un altro paio di minuti.
- Aggiungi 1/2 bicchiere d'acqua. Condire bene e aggiungere i peperoni e il prosciutto già arrostiti. Portare a ebollizione e cuocere per 10 minuti.
- Aggiungi il cavolo, mescolando fino ad appassire.
- In una ciotolina sbattete le uova con un pizzico di pepe di Cayenna e versatele nella padella insieme agli altri ingredienti.
- Trasferire la padella nel forno e cuocere per 10 minuti.
- Servire caldo.

NUTRIZIONE: Calorie 251| Grassi totali 15,74 g | Carboidrati netti: 3,8 g | Proteine 22g | Fibra: 0,8 g)

30.Frittata di peperoni e prosciutto

Tempo totale: 30 MIN| Servire: 2

INGREDIENTI:
- 4 uova grandi
- 1 tazza di peperone verde, tritato
- Prosciutto da 1/4 di libbra, cotto e tagliato a dadini
- 1 cipolla verde, a dadini
- 1 cucchiaino di olio di cocco
- Sale e pepe appena macinato a piacere

ISTRUZIONI:
- Lavare e tritare le verdure. Accantonare.
- In una piccola ciotola sbattere le uova. Accantonare.
- Scaldare una padella antiaderente a fuoco medio e aggiungere l'olio di cocco. Versare metà delle uova sbattute nella padella.
- Quando l'uovo si è parzialmente solidificato, aggiungi metà delle verdure e del prosciutto a metà della frittata e continua a cuocere fino a quando l'uovo è quasi completamente rappreso.
- Piega la metà vuota sopra il prosciutto e le verdure usando una spatola.
- Cuocere per altri 2 minuti e poi servire.
- Servire caldo.

NUTRIZIONE: Calorie 225,76 | Grassi totali 12g | Carboidrati netti: 6,8 g | Proteine 21,88 g | Fibra: 1,4 g)

31.Frittelle Di Farina Di Chia

Tempo totale: 25 MIN| Servire: 6

INGREDIENTI:
- 1 tazza di farina di chia
- 2 cucchiaini di dolcificante a scelta
- 1 uovo sbattuto
- 1 cucchiaio di burro di cocco o olio
- 1/2 tazza di latte di cocco (in scatola)

ISTRUZIONI:
- In una ciotola media, unire la farina e il dolcificante. Aggiungere l'uovo, il latte e il burro di cocco. Mescolate bene fino a ottenere una pastella liscia.
- Ungere una padella antiaderente e scaldare a fuoco medio-alto. Metti un cucchiaio colmo di pastella sulla superficie calda.
- Quando si formano delle bollicine sulla superficie degli scones, girateli con una spatola e poi cuoceteli per circa 2 minuti per lato.
- Servire caldo.

NUTRIZIONE: Calorie 59 | Grassi totali 3,5 g | Carboidrati netti: 4,65 g | Proteine 2,46 g | Fibra: 1,78 g)

32. Porridge Chocó Mocha Chia

Tempo totale: 35 MIN| Servire: 6

INGREDIENTI:
- 3 cucchiai di semi di chia
- 1 tazza di latte di mandorle, non zuccherato
- 2 cucchiaini di cacao in polvere
- 1/4 di tazza di lamponi, freschi o congelati
- 2 cucchiai di mandorle, macinate
- Dolcificante a scelta
-

ISTRUZIONI:
- Mescolare e mescolare insieme il latte di mandorla e il cacao in polvere.
- Aggiungere i Semi di Chia nella miscela.
- Mescolare bene con una forchetta.
- Mettere il composto in frigorifero per 30 minuti.
- Servire con lamponi e mandorle tritate sopra (facoltativo)

NUTRIZIONE: Calorie 150,15 | Grassi totali 9,62 g | Carboidrati netti: 15,2 g | Proteine 5,47 g | Fibra: 11,28 g)

33. Colazione da sogno ai semi di lino al caffè

Tempo totale: 10 MIN| Servire: 1

INGREDIENTI:
- 3 cucchiai di semi di lino, macinati
- 2 1/2 cucchiai di scaglie di cocco, non zuccherate
- 1/2 tazza di caffè nero forte, non zuccherato
- Dolcificante a scelta a piacere
- 1/2 bicchiere d'acqua (facoltativo)
-

ISTRUZIONI:
- In una ciotola unire i semi di lino e le scaglie di cocco.
- Aggiungere l'olio di cocco sciolto, quindi versarci sopra il caffè caldo e mescolare.
- Se è troppo denso, aggiungi un po 'd'acqua.
- Alla fine, aggiungi il dolcificante che preferisci a piacere.

NUTRIZIONE: Calorie 246,43 | Grassi totali 22,1 g | Carboidrati netti: 1,52 g | Proteine 1,48 g | Fibra: 0,9 g)

34. Funghi Crimini con Uova Sode Colazione

Tempo totale: 25 MIN| Servire: 6

INGREDIENTI:
- 14 funghi crimini, tritati finemente
- 8 uova grandi, sode, tritate
- 6 fette di guanciale o pancetta
- 1 cipollotto, a dadini
- Sale e pepe nero macinato a piacere

ISTRUZIONI:
- In una padella cuocete la pancetta. Prenota un grasso di pancetta nella padella. Tritare i pezzi di pancetta e metterli da parte.
- In una casseruola profonda, fai bollire le uova. Una volta pronte, lavarle, pulirle, sgusciarle e tagliarle a pezzetti.
- In una padella soffriggere il cipollotto con il restante grasso della pancetta a fuoco medio-alto.
- Aggiungere i funghi Crimini e saltare altri 5-6 minuti.
- Frullare le uova, la pancetta e cuocere insieme. Aggiustare di sale e pepe nero macinato a piacere.
- Servire.

NUTRIZIONE: Calorie 176,15 | Grassi totali 13,38 g | Carboidrati netti: 2,43 g | Proteine 11,32 g | Fibra: 1,5 g)

35. Frittata di albumi e spinaci

Tempo totale: 25 MIN| Servire: 2

INGREDIENTI:
- 5 albumi d'uovo
- 2 cucchiai di latte di mandorle
- 1 zucchina, tritata
- 1 tazza di foglie di spinaci, fresche
- 2 cucchiai di cipollotto, tritato
- 2 spicchi d'aglio
- Olio d'oliva
- Foglie di basilico, fresche, tritate
- Sale e pepe nero macinato a piacere

ISTRUZIONI:
- Lavare e tritare le verdure
- In una ciotola montate a neve gli albumi e il latte di mandorla.
- In una padella unta con olio d'oliva, cuocere le verdure (spinaci, zucchine e cipollotto) solo per uno o due minuti.
- Mettete da parte le verdure, ungete nuovamente la padella con olio d'oliva e versate le uova. Cuocere fino a quando le uova sono sode. Aggiungere le verdure da un lato e cuocere per altri due minuti. Aggiustare di sale e pepe a piacere.
- Decorare con foglie di basilico e servire.

NUTRIZIONE: Calorie 70,8 | Grassi totali 1,56 g | Carboidrati netti: 5,78 g | Proteine 11,08 g | Fibra: 1,58 g)

SNACK E ANTIPASTI

36. Pancetta & Uova

Tempo totale: 25 MIN| Servire: 4

INGREDIENTI:
- 4 grosse fette di pancetta
- 2 uova, ruspanti
- 1 tazza di burro chiarificato, ammorbidito
- 2 cucchiai di maionese
- Sale e pepe nero appena macinato a piacere
- Olio di cocco per friggere

ISTRUZIONI:
- In una padella antiaderente unta, cuocere la pancetta da entrambi i lati per 1-2 minuti. Togliere dal fuoco e mettere da parte.
- Nel frattempo, fai bollire le uova. Per rendere le uova sode occorrono circa 10 minuti. Al termine, lavare bene le uova con acqua fredda e staccare i gusci.
- Mettere il burro chiarificato in una ciotola profonda e aggiungere le uova in quarti. Schiaccia bene con una forchetta. Condirlo con sale e pepe a piacere; aggiungere la maionese e mescolare. Se vuoi puoi versare il grasso della pancetta. Unire e mescolare bene. Mettete la ciotola in frigo per almeno un'ora.
- Togliete dal frigo il composto di uova e formate 4 palline uguali.
- Sbriciolate la pancetta a pezzetti. Rotolate ogni pallina nella pancetta sbriciolata e disponetela su un grande piatto da portata.
- Rimuovi le bombe di uova e pancetta in frigorifero per altri 30 minuti. Servire freddo.

NUTRIZIONE: Calorie 238 | Grassi totali 22g | Carboidrati netti: 0,5 g | Proteine 7,5 g)

37.Pizza Margherita Pancia Zero

Tempo totale: 20 MIN| Servire: 2

INGREDIENTI:
PER L'IMPASTO:
- 2 uova biologiche
- 2 cucchiai di parmigiano grattugiato
- 1 cucchiaio di buccia di psillio in polvere
- 1 cucchiaino di condimento italiano
- ½ cucchiaino di sale
- 2 cucchiaini di burro chiarificato

PER I TOPPING:
- 5 foglie di basilico tritate grossolanamente
- 2 once. mozzarella, affettata
- 3 cucchiai di salsa di pomodoro naturale

ISTRUZIONI:
- Metti tutti gli ingredienti per la crosta in un robot da cucina e pulsa fino a quando non saranno ben combinati.
- Versate il composto in una padella antiaderente calda e inclinatela per stendere la pastella.
- Cuocere fino a quando i bordi sono marroni. Girare dall'altra parte e cuocere per altri 45 secondi. Togliere dal fuoco.
- Distribuire la salsa di pomodoro sopra la crosta, aggiungere sopra la mozzarella e le foglie di basilico e mettere nella griglia per far sciogliere il formaggio per 2 minuti.
- Servire.

NUTRIZIONE: Calorie 459 | Grassi totali 35 g | Carboidrati netti: 3,5 g | Proteine 27g)

38. Facile, facile, pizza al formaggio

40. Sciogliere Pancetta E Formaggio

Tempo totale: 15 MIN| Servire: 2

INGREDIENTI:
- 8 bastoncini di mozzarella a filo
- 8 strisce di pancetta
- Olio d'oliva per friggere

ISTRUZIONI:
- Preriscalda la tua friggitrice a 350 F.
- Avvolgi un bastoncino di formaggio con una striscia di pancetta e fissalo con uno stuzzicadenti. Ripeti fino a quando non hai usato tutta la pancetta e il formaggio.
- Friggere i bastoncini di formaggio nella friggitrice per 3 minuti.
- Rimuovere e posizionare sopra un tovagliolo di carta.
- Servire con una foglia di insalata verde a parte.

NUTRIZIONE: Calorie 590 | Grassi Totali 50g | Carboidrati netti: 0 g | Proteine 34g)

41. Rotolo BLT

Tempo totale: 10 MIN| Servire: 1

INGREDIENTI:
- 4 foglie, lattuga romana
- 4 strisce di pancetta, cotte e sbriciolate
- 4 fette di tacchino
- 1 tazza di pomodorini tagliati a metà
- 2 cucchiai di maionese

ISTRUZIONI:
- Adagiare la fetta di tacchino sopra le foglie di lattuga.
- Spalmare la maionese sulla fetta di tacchino e poi ricoprire con i pomodorini e la pancetta.
- Arrotolare la lattuga e poi fissarla con uno stuzzicadenti.
- Servire subito.

NUTRIZIONE: Calorie 382 | Grassi totali 38,5 g | Carboidrati netti: 11,5 g | Proteine 4,1 g | Fibra 6,3 g)

42. Pizza Portobello

Tempo totale: 25 MIN| Servire: 4

INGREDIENTI:
- 1 pomodoro medio, a fette
- ¼ tazza di basilico, tritato
- 20 fette di peperoni
- 4 cappelli di funghi Portobello
- 4 once di mozzarella
- 6 cucchiai di olio d'oliva
- Pepe nero
- Sale

ISTRUZIONI:
- Rimuovi l'interno dei funghi ed estrai la carne in modo da lasciare il guscio.
- Rivestire i funghi con metà dell'olio e condire con pepe e sale; cuocere per 5 minuti, quindi capovolgere e ricoprire con l'olio rimasto. Cuocere per altri 5 minuti.
- Aggiungere il pomodoro all'interno del guscio e guarnire con basilico, peperoni e formaggio. Cuocere per 4 minuti fino a quando il formaggio si scioglie.
- Servire caldo.

NUTRIZIONE: Calorie 321 | Grassi totali 31g | Carboidrati netti: 2,8 g | Proteine 8,5 g | Fibra 1,3 g)

43.Pizza Basilico e Peperoni

Tempo totale: 30 MIN| Servire: 2

INGREDIENTI:
PER BASE:
- ½ tazza di farina di mandorle
- 2 cucchiaini di crema di formaggio
- 1 uovo
- ½ cucchiaino di sale
- 6 once di mozzarella
- 2 cucchiai di buccia di psillio
- 2 cucchiai di parmigiano
- 1 cucchiaino di condimento italiano
- ½ cucchiaino di pepe nero

PER I TOPPING:
- 1 pomodoro medio, a fette
- 2/3 peperone, affettato
- 4 once di formaggio cheddar, grattugiato
- ¼ tazza di salsa di pomodoro
- 3 cucchiai di basilico, tritato

ISTRUZIONI:
- Preriscalda il forno a 400 F. Metti la mozzarella in un piatto adatto al microonde e sciogliilo per 1 minuto, mescolando di tanto in tanto.
- Aggiungere la crema di formaggio alla mozzarella fusa e unire.
- Mescolare gli ingredienti secchi per la base insieme in una ciotola, aggiungere l'uovo e unire. Aggiungi la miscela di formaggio e usa le mani per unire in un impasto.

- Formate un cerchio, infornate per 10 minuti e togliete dal forno. Condire con salsa di pomodoro, pomodoro, basilico, peperone e formaggio cheddar.
- Rimettere in forno e cuocere per altri 10 minuti.
- Servire caldo.

NUTRIZIONE: Calorie 410 | Grassi totali 31,3 g | Carboidrati netti: 5,3 g | Proteine 24,8 g | Fibra 5,8 g)

POLLAME

44. Torta Di Pollo

Tempo totale: 30 MIN| Servire: 5

INGREDIENTI:
- ½ libbra cosce di pollo disossate tagliate a pezzetti
- 3,5 once di pancetta, tritata
- 1 carota, tritata
- ¼ di tazza di prezzemolo, tritato
- 1 tazza di panna
- 2 porri cipolla, tritati
- 1 bicchiere di vino bianco
- 1 cucchiaio di olio d'oliva
- Sale e pepe a piacere

PER L'IMPASTO
- 1 tazza di farina di mandorle
- 2 cucchiai di acqua
- 1 cucchiaio di stevia
- 1½ cucchiaio di burro
- ½ cucchiaino di sale

ISTRUZIONI:
- Preparare prima la crosta unendo tutti i suoi ingredienti. Accantonare.
- Scaldare l'olio d'oliva in una padella a fuoco medio-alto. Aggiungere i porri tritati e mescolare. Trasferire su un piatto.
- Gettare la carne di pollo e la pancetta e cuocere fino a doratura e aggiungere i porri.
- Aggiungere le carote e versare il vino bianco, quindi ridurre il fuoco a medio.
- Aggiungere il prezzemolo e versare la panna nel mescolare bene. Trasferire in una pirofila.

- Coprire con la crosta preparata e mettere in forno a cuocere fino a quando la crosta diventa dorata e croccante.
- Lasciare riposare per 20 minuti prima di servire.

NUTRIZIONE: Calorie 396| Grassi totali 33g | Carboidrati netti: 6,5 g | Proteine 12,1 g | Fibra: 2,5 g)

45. Parmigiana di pollo classica

Tempo totale: 50 MIN| Servire: 2

INGREDIENTI:
- 2 pezzi di cosce di pollo disossate
- 8 strisce di pancetta, tritate
- ½ tazza di parmigiano grattugiato
- ½ tazza di mozzarella, tritata
- 1 uovo biologico
- 1 pomodoro in scatola a dadini

ISTRUZIONI:
- Impostare il forno a 450 F.
- Ammorbidire il pollo e metterlo da parte.
- Mettere il parmigiano in un piatto.
- Rompi l'uovo in una ciotola e sbattilo. E immergici il pollo.
- Trasferire nel piatto con il formaggio e ricoprire il pollo con il parmigiano.
- Ungere la teglia con il burro, adagiare le cosce di pollo e cuocere in forno per 30-40 minuti.
- Mentre aspetti che il pollo cuocia, cuoci la pancetta.
- Versare i pomodori con la pancetta e mescolare. Riduci il fuoco al minimo e lascia sobbollire e ridurre.
- Togliere il pollo dal forno quando è pronto e versarvi sopra la salsa di pomodoro.
- Cospargere con la mozzarella e rimettere in forno per far sciogliere il formaggio.
- Servire caldo.

NUTRIZIONE: Calorie 826 | Grassi totali 50,3 g | Carboidrati netti: 6,2 g | Proteine 83,2 g | Fibra: 1,2 g)

46. Arrosto di coscia di tacchino

Tempo totale: 1 ora e 20 minuti | Servire: 4

INGREDIENTI:
- 2 cosce di tacchino
- 2 cucchiai di burro chiarificato

PER IL RUB:
- $\frac{1}{4}$ cucchiaino di pepe di Caienna
- $\frac{1}{2}$ cucchiaino di timo essiccato
- $\frac{1}{2}$ cucchiaino di peperoncino ancho in polvere
- $\frac{1}{2}$ cucchiaino di aglio in polvere
- $\frac{1}{2}$ cucchiaino di cipolla in polvere
- 1 cucchiaino di fumo liquido
- 1 cucchiaino Worcestershire
- Sale e pepe a piacere

ISTRUZIONI:
- Impostare il forno a 350 F.
- Unire tutti gli ingredienti per il rub in una ciotola. Sbatti bene.
- Asciugare le cosce di tacchino con un canovaccio pulito e strofinarle generosamente con la miscela di spezie.
- Riscaldare il burro chiarificato a fuoco medio-alto in una padella di ghisa e poi scottare le cosce di tacchino per 2 minuti su ciascun lato.
- Mettere il tacchino in forno a cuocere per un'ora.

NUTRIZIONE: Calorie 382 | Grassi totali 22,5 g | Carboidrati netti: 0,8 g | Proteine 44g | Fibra: 0,0 g)

47. Pollo greco a cottura lenta

Tempo totale: 7 ore 10 minuti | Servire: 4

INGREDIENTI:
- 4 pezzi di cosce di pollo disossate
- 3 spicchi d'aglio, tritati
- 3 cucchiai di succo di limone
- 1 ½ tazza di acqua calda
- 2 cubetti di brodo di pollo
- 3 cucchiai di rub greco

ISTRUZIONI:
- Rivesti la pentola a cottura lenta con uno spray da cucina
- Condire il pollo con lo strofinaccio greco seguito dall'aglio tritato.
- Trasferisci il pollo nella pentola a cottura lenta e cospargilo con il succo di limone.
- Sbriciolate i cubetti di pollo e metteteli nella pentola a cottura lenta. Versare l'acqua e mescolare.
- Coprire e cuocere a fuoco basso per 6-7 ore.

NUTRIZIONE: Calorie 140 | Grassi totali 5,7 g | Carboidrati netti: 2,2 g | Proteine 18,6 g)

48. Pollo arrosto avvolto nella pancetta

Tempo totale: 1 ora e 25 minuti | Servire: 6

INGREDIENTI:
- 1 pollo intero condito
- 10 strisce di pancetta
- 3 rametti di timo fresco
- 2 pezzi di lime
- Sale e pepe a piacere

ISTRUZIONI:
- Impostare il forno a 500 F.
- Sciacquare bene il pollo e farcirlo con i rametti di lime e timo.
- Condire il pollo con sale e pepe e poi avvolgere il pollo con la pancetta.
- Condisci di nuovo con sale e pepe e poi mettilo su una teglia sopra una teglia (assicurati di raccogliere i succhi) e mettilo in forno ad arrostire per 15 minuti.
- Abbassa la temperatura a 350 F e poi arrostisci per altri 45 minuti.
- Togliere il pollo dal forno, coprire con un foglio e mettere da parte per 15 minuti.
- Prendi i succhi dal vassoio e mettili in una casseruola. Portare a ebollizione a fuoco alto e utilizzare una miscelazione ad immersione per mescolare tutte le "cose buone" del succo.
- Servire il pollo con la salsa a parte.

NUTRIZIONE: Calorie 375 | Grassi totali 29,8 g | Carboidrati netti: 2,4 g | Proteine 24,5 g | Fibra: 0,9 g)

49.Pollo al curry croccante

Tempo totale: 60 MIN| Servire: 4

INGREDIENTI:
- 4 pezzi di cosce di pollo
- ¼ tazza di olio d'oliva
- 1 cucchiaino di curry in polvere
- ¼ cucchiaino di zenzero
- ½ cucchiaino di cumino, macinato
- ½ cucchiaino di paprika affumicata
- ½ cucchiaino di aglio in polvere
- ¼ cucchiaino di pepe di Caienna
- ¼ cucchiaino di pimento
- ¼ di cucchiaio di peperoncino in polvere
- Pizzico di coriandolo, macinato
- Pizzico di cannella
- Pizzico di cardamomo
- ½ cucchiaino di sale

ISTRUZIONI:
- Impostare il forno a 425 F.
- Unire tutte le spezie insieme.
- Foderare una teglia con un foglio e adagiarvi sopra il pollo.
- Condire il pollo con olio d'oliva e strofinare.
- Cospargi la miscela di spezie sopra e poi strofina di nuovo, assicurandoti di ricoprire il pollo con le spezie.
- Mettere in forno a cuocere per 50 minuti.
- Lasciare riposare per 5 minuti prima di servire.

NUTRIZIONE: Calorie 277 | Grassi totali 19,9 g | Carboidrati netti: 0,6 g | Proteine 42,3 g)

50. Le perfette ali di pollo al forno

Tempo totale: 60 MIN| Servire: 4

INGREDIENTI:
- 4 pezzi di cosce di pollo
- ¼ tazza di olio d'oliva
- 1 cucchiaino di curry in polvere
- ¼ cucchiaino di zenzero
- ½ cucchiaino di cumino, macinato
- ½ cucchiaino di paprika affumicata
- ½ cucchiaino di aglio in polvere
- ¼ cucchiaino di pepe di Caienna
- ¼ cucchiaino di pimento
- ¼ di cucchiaio di peperoncino in polvere
- Pizzico di coriandolo, macinato
- Pizzico di cannella
- Pizzico di cardamomo
- ½ cucchiaino di sale

ISTRUZIONI:
- Impostare il forno a 425 F.
- Unire tutte le spezie insieme.
- Foderare una teglia con un foglio e adagiarvi sopra il pollo.
- Condire il pollo con olio d'oliva e strofinare.
- Cospargi la miscela di spezie sopra e poi strofina di nuovo, assicurandoti di ricoprire il pollo con le spezie.
- Mettere in forno a cuocere per 50 minuti.
- Lasciare riposare per 5 minuti prima di servire.

NUTRIZIONE: Calorie 277 | Grassi totali 19,9 g | Carboidrati netti: 0,6 g | Proteine 42,3 g)

50.Le perfette ali di pollo al forno

Tempo totale: 40 MIN| Servire: 2

INGREDIENTI:
- 2,5 libbre di ali di pollo
- ½ cucchiaino di bicarbonato di sodio
- 1 cucchiaino di lievito in polvere
- Sale due chiavi
- 4 cucchiai di burro, sciolto

ISTRUZIONI:
- Aggiungi tutti gli ingredienti (tranne il burro) in un sacchetto Ziploc e agita, assicurandoti che le ali siano ricoperte dal composto.
- Mettere in frigo per una notte.
- Quando sei pronto per cucinare, imposta il forno a 450 F.
- Metti le ali su una teglia e cuoci in forno per 20 minuti.
- Girare le ali e cuocere per altri 15 minuti.
- Sciogliere il burro e cospargere le ali.

NUTRIZIONE: Calorie 500 | Grassi totali 0,0 g | Carboidrati netti: 38,8 g | Proteine 44g | Fibra: 34g)

51.Pollo in salsa Kung Pao

Tempo totale: 25 MIN| Servire: 2

INGREDIENTI:
- 2 cosce di pollo disossate tagliate a pezzi più piccoli
- ½ peperone verde, tritato
- 2 cipollotti, affettati sottili
- ¼ di tazza di arachidi, tritate
- 1 cucchiaino di zenzero, grattugiato
- ½ cucchiaio di scaglie di peperoncino rosso
- Sale e pepe a piacere

PER LA SALSA:
- 2 cucchiaini di aceto di vino di riso
- 1 cucchiaio di ketchup senza pancia
- 2 cucchiai di pasta di peperoncino all'aglio
- 1 cucchiaio di salsa di soia a basso contenuto di sodio
- 2 cucchiaini di olio di sesamo
- 2 cucchiaini di stevia liquida
- ½ cucchiaino di sciroppo d'acero

ISTRUZIONI:
- Condisci il pollo con sale, pepe e zenzero grattugiato.
- Metti una padella di ghisa sul fuoco medio-alto e aggiungi il pollo quando la padella è calda. Cuocere per 10 minuti.
- Sbattete tutti gli ingredienti per la salsa in una ciotola mentre aspettate che il pollo si cuocia.
- Aggiungere il peperone verde, i cipollotti e le arachidi nella padella con il pollo e cuocere per altri 4-5 minuti
- Aggiungere la salsa nella padella, mescolare e far bollire.

NUTRIZIONE: Calorie 362 | Grassi totali 27,4 g | Carboidrati netti: 3,2 g | Proteine 22,3 g)

52 Pizza al barbecue di pollo

Tempo totale: 20 MIN| Servire: 4

INGREDIENTI:
- 1 tazza di pollo arrosto, tritato
- 4 cucchiai di salsa barbecue
- ½ tazza di formaggio cheddar
- 1 cucchiaio di maionese
- 4 cucchiai di salsa di pomodoro naturale

PER LA CROSTA DELLA PIZZA
- 6 cucchiai di parmigiano grattugiato
- 6 uova biologiche
- 3 cucchiai di buccia di psillio in polvere
- 2 cucchiaini di condimento italiano
- Sale e pepe a piacere

ISTRUZIONI:
- Vedi sopra due 425 F.
- Mettere tutti gli ingredienti per la crosta in un robot da cucina e frullare fino a ottenere un impasto denso.
- Formare l'impasto della pizza e metterlo in forno a cuocere per 10 minuti.
- Ricoprire la crosta cotta con la salsa di pomodoro seguita dal pollo, il formaggio e un filo di salsa barbecue e maionese in cima.

NUTRIZIONE: Calorie 357 | Grassi totali 24,5 g | Carboidrati netti: 2,9 g | Proteine 24,5 g)

53.Masala di pollo a cottura lenta

Tempo totale: 3 ore 10 minuti | Servire: 2

INGREDIENTI:
- 1 ½ libbre. cosce di pollo disossate, tagliate a pezzetti
- 2 spicchi d'aglio
- 1 cucchiaino di zenzero, grattugiato
- 1 cucchiaino di cipolla in polvere
- 3 cucchiai di masala
- 1 cucchiaino di paprika
- 2 cucchiaini di sale
- ½ tazza di latte di cocco (diviso in 2)
- 2 cucchiai di concentrato di pomodoro
- ½ tazza di pomodori a cubetti
- 2 cucchiai di olio d'oliva
- ½ tazza di panna
- 1 cucchiaino di stevia
- Coriandolo fresco per guarnire

ISTRUZIONI:
- Metti prima il pollo nella pentola a cottura lenta. Aggiungere lo zenzero grattugiato, l'aglio e il resto delle spezie. Mescolata.
- Aggiungere quindi il concentrato di pomodoro e i pomodori a dadini e mescolare ancora.
- Versare la metà del latte di cocco e mescolare, quindi cuocere a fuoco vivo per 3 ore.
- Al termine della cottura, aggiungere il restante latte di cocco, la panna, la stevia e mescolare nuovamente.
- Servire caldo.

NUTRIZIONE: Calorie 493 | Grassi totali 41,2 g | Carboidrati netti: 5,8 g | Proteine 26g)

54.Pollo Al Burro Al Forno

Tempo totale: 1 ora 10 minuti | Servire: 2

INGREDIENTI:
- 4 pezzi di cosce di pollo
- ¼ di tazza di burro biologico ammorbidito
- 1 cucchiaino di rosmarino essiccato
- 1 cucchiaino di basilico essiccato
- ½ cucchiaino di sale
- ½ cucchiaino di pepe

ISTRUZIONI:
- Vedi sopra due 350 F.
- Sbattere tutti gli ingredienti (tranne il pollo) in una ciotola.
- Adagiare le cosce di pollo su una teglia rivestita di carta stagnola e spennellarle generosamente con il composto di burro.
- Mettere il pollo in forno a cuocere per un'ora.
- Servire caldo.

NUTRIZIONE: Calorie 735 | Grassi totali 33,7 g | Carboidrati netti: 0,8 g | Proteine 101,8 g)

55.Parmigiana di pollo

Tempo totale: 25 MIN| Servire: 4

INGREDIENTI:
PER IL POLLO:
- 3 petti di pollo
- 1 tazza di mozzarella
- Sale
- Pepe nero

PER RIVESTIMENTO:
- ¼ di tazza di farina di semi di lino
- 1 cucchiaino di origano
- ½ cucchiaino di pepe nero
- ½ cucchiaino di aglio in polvere
- 1 uovo
- 2,5 once di cotenne di maiale
- ½ tazza di parmigiano
- ½ cucchiaino Sale
- ¼ di cucchiaino di fiocchi di peperoncino
- 2 cucchiaini di paprika
- 1 ½ cucchiaino Brodo di pollo

PER LA SALSA:
- 1 tazza di salsa di pomodoro, a basso contenuto di carboidrati
- 2 spicchi d'aglio
- Sale
- ½ tazza di olio d'oliva
- ½ cucchiaino di origano
- Pepe nero

ISTRUZIONI:

- Aggiungere la farina di lino, le spezie, le cotiche di maiale e il parmigiano in un robot da cucina e macinare fino a quando non saranno combinati.
- Pestare il petto di pollo e sbattere l'uovo con il brodo in un contenitore. In una casseruola mettete tutti gli ingredienti per la salsa, mescolate e fate cuocere a fuoco lento.
- Immergi il pollo nell'uovo e poi ricoprilo con il composto secco.
- Scaldare l'olio in una padella e friggere il pollo, quindi trasferirlo in una casseruola. Condire con salsa e mozzarella e infornare per 10 minuti.

NUTRIZIONE: Calorie 646 | Grassi totali 46,8 g | Carboidrati netti: 4g | Proteine 49,3 g | Fibre 2,8 g)

FRUTTI DI MARE

56. Snapper in agrodolce

Tempo totale: 20 MIN| Servire: 2

INGREDIENTI:
- 4 filetti di dentice
- ¼ tazza di coriandolo fresco, tritato
- 4 cucchiai di succo di lime
- 6 pezzi di litchi, affettati
- 2 cucchiai di olio d'oliva
- Sale e pepe a piacere

ISTRUZIONI:
- Condire i filetti con sale e pepe.
- Scaldare l'olio d'oliva in una padella a fuoco medio e cuocere per 4 minuti per lato.
- Versare il succo di lime sul pesce; aggiungere il coriandolo e i litchi affettati.
- Abbassate la fiamma al minimo e lasciate cuocere per altri 5 minuti.
- Trasferire su un piatto da portata e gustare.

NUTRIZIONE: Calorie 244 | Grassi totali 15,4 g | Carboidrati netti: 0,1 g | Proteine 27,9 g)

57.Eglefino cremoso

Tempo totale: 20 MIN| Servire: 2

INGREDIENTI:
- 5,3 once di eglefino affumicato
- 1/2 acqua bollente
- 1 cucchiaio di burro
- ¼ di tazza di panna
- 2 tazze di spinaci

ISTRUZIONI:
- Scaldare una casseruola a fuoco medio.
- Mescolare l'acqua bollente con la panna e il burro in una ciotola.
- Metti l'eglefino e la salsa nella padella e lascia bollire fino a quando l'acqua evapora, lasciando dietro di sé una salsa cremosa al burro.
- Servire l'eglefino, coperto con la salsa su spinaci freschi o appassiti.

NUTRIZIONE: Calorie 281 | Grassi totali 10g | Carboidrati netti: 15 g | Proteine 18g)

58. Nasello Fritto In Padella

Tempo totale: 15 MIN| Servire: 1

INGREDIENTI:
- 1 cucchiaio di olio d'oliva
- Sale e pepe a piacere
- 1 Tritare il filetto
- Spicchi di limone fresco

ISTRUZIONI:
- Scaldare l'olio d'oliva in una padella capiente a fuoco medio-alto.
- Asciugare il pesce con un tovagliolo di carta da cucina e poi condirlo con sale e pepe su entrambi i lati.
- Friggete i pesci per circa 4-5 minuti per lato, a seconda del loro spessore, o finché non avranno una crosticina dorata e la polpa si sfalderà facilmente con una forchetta.

NUTRIZIONE: Calorie 170 | Grassi totali 8g | Carboidrati netti: 7g | Proteine 18g)

59. Pesto e salmone alle mandorle

Tempo totale: 15 MIN| Servire: 2

INGREDIENTI:
- 1 spicchio d'aglio
- ½ limone
- ½ cucchiaino di prezzemolo
- 2 cucchiai di burro
- Una manciata di frisée
- 1 cucchiaio di olio d'oliva
- ¼ tazza di mandorle
- ½ cucchiaino di sale himalayano
- 12 once. Filetti di salmone
- ½ scalogno

ISTRUZIONI:
- Aggiungere le mandorle, l'aglio e l'olio d'oliva in un robot da cucina e frullare fino a quando il composto diventa pastoso. Aggiungere il prezzemolo, il sale e spremere il succo di limone nel composto e mettere da parte fino al momento dell'uso.
- Condire il salmone con pepe e sale.
- Scaldare l'olio in una padella e mettere la pelle di salmone nella pentola e cuocere per 3 minuti per lato.
- Aggiungi il burro alla padella e scalda fino a quando non si scioglie; ricoprire il pesce con il burro e togliere dal fuoco.
- Servire il salmone con frisée e pesto.

NUTRIZIONE: Calorie 610 | Grassi totali 47g | Carboidrati netti: 6 g | Proteine 38g | Fibre: 1g)

60. Salmone Avocado Lime

Tempo totale: 25 MIN | Servire: 2

INGREDIENTI:
- 1 Avocado
- 2 cucchiai Cipolle rosse (tritate)
- ½ tazza di cavolfiore
- 12 once. Filetti di salmone (2)
- ½ limetta

ISTRUZIONI:
- Metti il cavolfiore in un robot da cucina e pulsa fino a quando la consistenza non è simile al riso.
- Ungere la padella con spray da cucina e aggiungere il riso nella padella, cuocere per 8 minuti con il coperchio.
- Aggiungere gli ingredienti rimanenti tranne il pesce in un robot da cucina e frullare fino a ottenere un composto cremoso e liscio.
- Riscalda l'olio che preferisci in un'altra padella e metti i filetti con la pelle nella pentola. Cuocere per 5 minuti e aggiungere pepe e sale a piacere. Capovolgi e cuoci per altri 5 minuti.
- Servire il salmone con il cavolfiore e guarnire con la salsa di avocado.

NUTRIZIONE: Calorie 420 | Grassi totali 27g | Carboidrati netti: 5g | Proteine 37g | Fibre: 0,5g)

61. Salmone allo zenzero glassato al sesamo

Tempo totale: 40 MIN| Servire: 2

INGREDIENTI:
- 2 cucchiai di salsa di soia
- 1 cucchiaio di aceto di vino di riso
- 2 cucchiaini Aglio, grattugiato
- 1 cucchiaio di ketchup
- Filetto di salmone da 10 once
- 2 cucchiaini Olio di sesamo
- 1 cucchiaino Zenzero, a dadini
- 1 cucchiaio di salsa di pesce
- 2 cucchiai di vino bianco

ISTRUZIONI:
- Unisci salsa di soia, aceto, aglio, zenzero e salsa di pesce in una ciotola e aggiungi il salmone. Marinare per 15 minuti.
- Scaldare l'olio di sesamo in una padella fino a quando non fuma, quindi aggiungere il pesce con la pelle nella padella. Cuocere per 4 minuti, quindi capovolgere e cuocere per altri 4 minuti o fino a cottura ultimata.
- Aggiungere la marinata nella pentola e cuocere per 4 minuti, togliere dalla pentola e mettere da parte.
- Aggiungi il bianco e il ketchup alla salsa e cuoci per 5 minuti fino a quando non si saranno ridotti.
- Servire il pesce con la salsa.

NUTRIZIONE: Calorie 370 | Grassi totali 23,5 g | Carboidrati netti: 2,5 g | Proteine 33g)

62. Gamberi Al Burro

Tempo totale: 25 MIN| Servire: 3

INGREDIENTI:
PER GAMBERETTI IN PASTELLA:
- 2 cucchiai di farina di mandorle
- $\frac{1}{4}$ cucchiaino di curry in polvere
- 1 uovo
- 3 cucchiai di olio di cocco
- 0,5 g Parmigiano Reggiano
- $\frac{1}{2}$ cucchiaino Lievito in polvere
- 1 cucchiaio di acqua
- 12 gamberi medi

PER LA SALSA AL BURRO:
- $\frac{1}{2}$ cipolla, tritata
- 2 peperoncini tailandesi, tritati
- $\frac{1}{2}$ tazza di panna
- Sale
- 2 cucchiai di burro, non salato
- 1 spicchio d'aglio, a dadini
- 2 cucchiai di foglie di curry
- Cheddar maturo da 0,3 once
- Pepe nero
- 1/8 cucchiaino di semi di sesamo

ISTRUZIONI:
- Sbucciare e sgusciare i gamberi; gamberetti asciutti usando un tovagliolo di carta.
- Unire tutti gli ingredienti secchi per la pastella, quindi aggiungere l'acqua e l'uovo e mescolare accuratamente per unire.

- Scaldare l'olio di cocco in una padella, immergere i gamberi nella pastella e friggere fino a doratura. Togliere dalla pentola e mettere da parte a raffreddare.
- Sciogliere il burro in un'altra pentola e soffriggere la cipolla fino a doratura. Aggiungere le foglie di curry, i peperoncini e l'aglio e cuocere per 3 minuti o fino a quando non saranno aromatici.
- Abbassa il fuoco e aggiungi la panna e il cheddar, cuoci finché la salsa non si addensa. Aggiungere i gamberi e mescolare per ricoprire.
- Servire condito con semi di sesamo.

NUTRIZIONE: Calorie 570 | Grassi totali 56,2 g | Carboidrati netti: 18,4 g | Proteine 4,3 g | Fibra 1,4 g)

63. Zero Pancia Friendly

Tempo totale: 25 MIN| Servire: 3

INGREDIENTI:
- 16 once di cavolfiore
- 2 cucchiai di aceto di riso, non stagionato
- 5 fogli Nori
- ½ avocado, affettato
- 6 once di crema di formaggio, ammorbidita
- 1 cucchiaio di salsa di soia
- Cetriolo
- 5 once di salmone affumicato

ISTRUZIONI:
- Mettere il cavolfiore in un robot da cucina e frullare fino a ottenere una consistenza simile al riso.
- Taglia ogni estremità del cetriolo e taglia ogni lato, butta via il centro e taglia i lati a strisce. Mettere in frigo fino al momento dell'uso.
- Scaldare una padella e aggiungere il cavolfiore e la salsa di soia. Cuocere per 5 minuti o fino a cottura completa e leggermente asciugata.
- Trasferire il cavolfiore nella ciotola insieme all'aceto e al formaggio, unire e mettere in frigorifero fino a quando non si raffredda. Tagliare gli avocado e metterli da parte.
- Coprire il rullo di bambù con un involucro di plastica, adagiare un foglio di nori, guarnire con cavolfiore cotto, salmone, cetriolo e avocado. Arrotolare e affettare.
- Servire.

NUTRIZIONE: Calorie 353 | Grassi totali 25,7 g | Carboidrati netti: 5,7 g | Proteine 18,32 g | Fibra: 8g)

64. Avocado ripieno con tonno

Tempo totale: 20 MIN| Servire: 4

INGREDIENTI:
- 2 avocado maturi, tagliati a metà e snocciolati
- 1 lattina (15 once) di tonno bianco solido confezionato in acqua, sgocciolato
- 2 cucchiai di maionese
- 3 cipolle verdi, affettate sottilmente
- 1 cucchiaio di pepe di cayenna
- 1 peperone rosso, tritato
- 1 cucchiaio di aceto balsamico
- 1 pizzico di aglio sale e pepe nero qb
-

ISTRUZIONI:
- In una ciotola, mescola il tonno, la maionese, il pepe di cayenna, le cipolle verdi, il peperoncino e l'aceto balsamico.
- Condire con pepe e sale, quindi confezionare le metà dell'avocado con il composto di tonno.
- Pronto! Servire e gustare!

NUTRIZIONE: Calorie 233,3| Grassi totali 17,77 g | Carboidrati netti: 9,69 g | Proteine 7,41 g | Fibra: 6,98 g)

65. Filetti Di Salmone Al Forno Alle Erbe

Tempo totale: 35 MIN| Servire: 6

INGREDIENTI:

- 2 libbre. filetti di salmone
- 1/2 tazza di funghi freschi tritati
- 1/2 tazza di cipolle verdi tritate
- 4 once. burro
- 4 cucchiai di olio di cocco
- 1/2 tazza di salsa di soia tamari
- 1 cucchiaino di aglio tritato
- 1/4 cucchiaino di timo
- 1/2 cucchiaino di rosmarino
- 1/4 cucchiaino di dragoncello
- 1/2 cucchiaino di zenzero macinato
- 1/2 cucchiaino di basilico
- 1 cucchiaino di foglie di origano

ISTRUZIONI:

- Preriscalda il forno a 350 gradi F. Fodera una teglia grande con un foglio.
- Tagliare a pezzi il filetto di salmone. Metti il salmone nella busta Ziploc con la salsa tamari, l'olio di sesamo e il composto di salsa alle spezie. Refrigerare il salmone e marinarlo per 4 ore.
- Mettere il salmone in una teglia e cuocere i filetti per 10-15 minuti.
- Sciogliere il burro. Aggiungere i funghi freschi tritati e la cipolla verde e mescolare. Togli il salmone dal forno e versa il composto di burro sui filetti di salmone, assicurandoti che ogni filetto sia coperto.
- Cuocere per circa 10 minuti in più. Servire subito.

NUTRIZIONE: Calorie 449 | Grassi totali 34g | Carboidrati netti: 2,7 g | Proteine 33g | Fibra 0,7 g)

66. Salmone in crosta di noci

Tempo totale: 20 MIN| Servire: 2

INGREDIENTI:
- ½ tazza di noci
- ½ cucchiaio di senape di Digione
- 6 once di filetti di salmone
- Sale
- 2 cucchiai Sciroppo d'acero, senza zucchero
- ¼ cucchiaino di aneto
- 1 cucchiaio di olio d'oliva

ISTRUZIONI:
- Vedi sopra due 350 F.
- Metti senape, sciroppo e noci in un robot da cucina e pulsa fino a quando il composto diventa pastoso.
- Scaldare l'olio in una pentola e mettere la pelle rivolta verso il basso nella padella e scottare per 3 minuti.
- Guarniscilo con la miscela di noci e mettilo in una teglia foderata.
- Cuocere per 8 minuti.
- Servire.

NUTRIZIONE: Calorie 373 | Grassi totali 43g | Carboidrati netti: 3g | Proteine 20g | Fibra 1g)

67. Salmone glassato al forno

Tempo totale: 30 MIN| Servire: 2

INGREDIENTI:
- 2 filetti di salmone
- Per la glassa:
- 1 cucchiaio di senape dolce
- 1 cucchiaio di senape di Digione
- 1 cucchiaio di succo di limone
- ½ cucchiaino di scaglie di peperoncino
- 1 cucchiaino di salvia
- Sale due chiavi
- 1 cucchiaio di olio d'oliva

ISTRUZIONI:
- Impostare il forno a 350 F.
- In una ciotola sbattere tutti gli ingredienti per la glassa.
- Disponete i filetti di salmone su una teglia foderata con carta da forno e spennellate i filetti di salmone con la glassa.
- Mettere in forno a cuocere per 20 minuti. Servire caldo.

NUTRIZIONE: Calorie 379 | Grassi totali 24,9 g | Carboidrati netti: 4,3 g | Proteine 35,5 g)

68. Hamburgers al salmone

Tempo totale: 20 MIN| Servire: 4

INGREDIENTI:
- 1 14 once può cuocere i fiocchi di salmone in acqua
- 2 uova biologiche
- 1 tazza di pangrattato senza glutine
- 1 cipolla piccola, tritata
- 1 cucchiaio di prezzemolo fresco, tritato
- 3 cucchiai di maionese
- 2 cucchiaini di succo di limone
- Sale due chiavi
- 1 cucchiaio di olio d'oliva
- 1 cucchiaio di burro chiarificato

ISTRUZIONI:
- Rompi le uova in una ciotola e usa una frusta a mano per sbatterle fino a renderle spumose.
- Aggiungere il pangrattato nella ciotola con l'uovo e amalgamare bene.
- Aggiungere le cipolle, il prezzemolo e la maionese e mescolare nuovamente.
- Aggiungere i fiocchi di salmone e condire con il succo di limone e l'olio d'oliva. Aggiustate di sale e mescolate ancora.
- Dividete il composto in 4 parti e poi create delle polpette con le mani.
- Riscaldare il burro chiarificato in una padella di ghisa a fuoco medio-alto e friggere le polpette fino a doratura.
- Servire con un'insalata a parte.

NUTRIZIONE: Calorie 281 | Grassi totali 25,2 g | Carboidrati netti: 9,1 g | Proteine 6,2 g | Fibra 0,8 g)

ZUPPE E STUFATI

69.Stufato di manzo all'aglio e rosmarino

Tempo totale: 4 ore 20 minuti | Serve: 8)

INGREDIENTI:
- 4 carote medie, affettate
- 4 gambi di sedano, affettati
- 1 cipolla media, a dadini
- 2 cucchiai di olio d'oliva
- 4 spicchi d'aglio, tritati
- 1,5 libbre di carne stufata di manzo (stinco o mandrino)
- Sale e pepe
- $\frac{1}{4}$ di tazza di farina di mandorle
- 2 tazze di brodo di manzo
- 2 cucchiai di senape di Digione
- 1 cucchiaio di salsa Worcestershire
- 1 cucchiaio di salsa di soia
- 1 cucchiaio di xilitolo
- $\frac{1}{2}$ cucchiaio di rosmarino essiccato
- $\frac{1}{2}$ cucchiaino di timo

ISTRUZIONI:
- Aggiungi cipolla, carote e sedano in una pentola a cottura lenta.
- Aggiungere la carne in umido in una ciotola capiente e condire con pepe e sale.
- Aggiungere la farina di mandorle e mescolare la carne fino a ricoprirla bene.
- Soffriggere l'aglio nell'olio bollente per circa un minuto.
- Aggiungi la carne condita e tutta la farina dal fondo della ciotola nella padella.

- Cuocere la carne senza mescolare per qualche minuto per farla rosolare da un lato.
- Capovolgere e ripetere fino a quando tutti i lati della carne sono dorati.
- Aggiungi la carne rosolata nella pentola a cottura lenta e mescola per unirla alle verdure.
- Aggiungi il brodo di manzo, la senape di Digione, la salsa Worcestershire, la salsa di soia, lo xilitolo, il timo e il rosmarino nella padella.
- Mescolare per unire tutti gli ingredienti e sciogliere i pezzetti dorati dal fondo della padella.
- Una volta sciolto tutto, versa la salsa sugli ingredienti nella pentola a cottura lenta.
- Coprire la pentola a cottura lenta con il coperchio e cuocere a fuoco alto per quattro ore.
- Terminata la cottura, togliete il coperchio e mescolate bene lo spezzatino e con una forchetta fate a pezzetti la carne di manzo.

NUTRIZIONE: Calorie 275 | Grassi totali 10g | Carboidrati netti: 24g | Proteine 22g)

70. Stufato di pesce Bouillabaisse

Tempo totale: 6 ore 55 minuti | Servire: 6

INGREDIENTI:
- 1 bicchiere di vino bianco secco
- succo e scorza di 1 arancia
- 2 cucchiai di olio d'oliva
- 1 cipolla grande, a dadini
- 2 spicchi d'aglio, tritati
- 1 cucchiaino di basilico essiccato
- 1/2 cucchiaino di timo essiccato
- 1/2 cucchiaino di sale
- 1/4 cucchiaino di pepe nero macinato
- 4 tazze di brodo di pesce; si può usare anche il brodo di pollo
- 1 lattina di pomodori a cubetti, scolati
- 1 foglia di alloro
- 0,9 lb di filetto di pesce bianco disossato e senza pelle (es. merluzzo)
- 0,9 libbre di gamberi sgusciati e sgranati
- Cozze da 0,9 libbre nei loro gusci
- Succo di 1/2 limone
- 1/4 di tazza di prezzemolo fresco italiano (a foglia piatta).

ISTRUZIONI:
- Scaldare l'olio in una padella capiente.
- Aggiungere la cipolla e soffriggere tutte le verdure fino a renderle quasi tenere.
- Aggiungere l'aglio, il basilico, il timo, il sale e il pepe.

- Versare il vino e portare ad ebollizione. Aggiungere il brodo di pesce, la scorza d'arancia, i pomodori e l'alloro e mescolare per unire.
- Versare tutto in una pentola a cottura lenta, coprire la pentola e cuocere a fuoco basso per 4-6 ore.
- Circa 30 minuti prima di servire, accendi il fornello al massimo. Condire il pesce e i gamberi con il succo di limone.
- Mescolare nel brodo nel fornello, coprire e cuocere fino a quando il pesce cuoce per circa 20 minuti.
- Aggiungere le cozze alla fine e lasciare cuocere a vapore per 20 minuti con il coperchio.

NUTRIZIONE: Calorie 310 | Grassi Totali 30g | Carboidrati netti: 4g | proteine 3g)

71. Stufato Di Manzo E Broccoli

Tempo totale: 2 ore 20 minuti | Serve: 8)

INGREDIENTI:
- 1 tazza di brodo di manzo
- 1/4 di tazza di salsa di soia
- 1/4 di tazza di salsa di ostriche
- Xilitolo da 1/4 di tazza
- 1 cucchiaio di olio di sesamo
- 3 spicchi d'aglio, tritati
- Mandrino di manzo disossato da 2,2 libbre arrosto e affettato sottilmente
- 2 cucchiai di farina di mandorle o buccia di psillio
- 2 teste di broccoli, tagliate a cimette

ISTRUZIONI:
- In una ciotola media, sbatti insieme il brodo di manzo, la salsa di soia, la salsa di ostriche, lo zucchero, l'olio di sesamo e l'aglio.
- Metti la carne in una pentola a cottura lenta. Aggiungi il composto di salsa e mescola delicatamente per unire. Coprire e cuocere a fuoco basso per 90 minuti.
- In una piccola ciotola, sbatti insieme 1/4 di tazza di acqua e farina di mandorle.
- Mescolare la miscela di farina di mandorle e i broccoli nella pentola a cottura lenta.
- Coprite e fate cuocere a fuoco vivace per altri 30 minuti.

NUTRIZIONE: Calorie 370 | Grassi totali 18g | Carboidrati netti: 4g | Proteine 47g)

72. Stufato Di Cozze

Tempo totale: 5 ore 45 minuti | Serve: 8)

INGREDIENTI:
- 1 kg di cozze fresche o congelate, pulite
- 3 cucchiai di olio d'oliva
- 4 spicchi d'aglio tritati
- 1 cipolla grande, tagliata finemente
- 1 cestino di funghi, a dadini
- 2 lattine di pomodori a cubetti
- 2 cucchiai di origano
- ½ cucchiaio di basilico
- ½ cucchiaino di pepe nero
- 1 cucchiaino di paprika
- Dash fiocchi di peperoncino rosso
- 3/4 di tazza d'acqua

ISTRUZIONI:
- Soffriggere cipolle, aglio, scalogno e funghi, raschiare l'intero contenuto della padella nel crockpot.
- Aggiungi tutti gli ingredienti rimanenti nella tua pentola a cottura lenta tranne le cozze. Cuocere a fuoco basso per 4-5 ore o a fuoco alto per 2-3 ore. Stai cucinando fino a quando i tuoi funghi sono teneri e fino a quando i sapori si fondono insieme.
- Una volta che i funghi sono cotti e la salsa è pronta, alza il crockpot al massimo. Aggiungi le cozze pulite nella pentola e chiudi bene il coperchio. Cuocere per altri 30 minuti.
- Versate le vostre cozze in ciotole con abbondante brodo. Se qualche cozza non si è aperta durante la cottura, butta anche quelle

NUTRIZIONE: Calorie 228 | Grassi totali 9g | Carboidrati netti: 32g | Proteine 4g)

73. Stufato cremoso di pollo e zucca

Tempo totale: 5 ore| Servire: 6

INGREDIENTI:
- Petto di pollo disossato da 1,3 libbre di pollo
- 1 1/4 tazze di brodo di pollo
- 1 lattina di latte evaporato (panna intera)
- 1/3 di tazza di panna acida o crème fraiche
- 1 cucchiaio di aglio tritato
- ½ tazza di formaggio cheddar stagionato grattugiato
- Zucca tritata finemente fresca o surgelata
- Sale e pepe a piacere

ISTRUZIONI:
- In una pentola di terracotta unire tutti gli ingredienti.
- Coprire e girare la pentola di coccio in basso. Cuocere per 4,5 ore a fuoco basso o fino a quando sia il pollo che la zucca sono cotti e morbidi.
- Mescolare la salsa in una pentola di coccio prima di servire.

NUTRIZIONE: Calorie 321 | Grassi totali 12g | Carboidrati netti: 17g | Proteine 35g)

74. Stufato di patate dolci

Tempo totale: 6 ore 20 minuti | Servire: 6

INGREDIENTI:
- 2 tazze di patate dolci a cubetti
- 4 petti di pollo disossati
- 4 cosce di pollo disossate
- 2 tazze di brodo di pollo
- 1 ½ tazza di peperoni verdi tritati
- 1 ¼ tazza di pomodori freschi a dadini
- ¾ tazza può mix di pomodori, cipolla e peperoncino
- 1 cucchiaio di condimento cajun o curry
- 2 spicchi d'aglio, tritati
- ¼ tazza di noci cremose
- Coriandolo fresco
- Noci tostate tritate

ISTRUZIONI:
- In una pentola a cottura lenta patate dolci, pollo, brodo, peperoni, pomodori a dadini, pomodori e peperoncini verdi mescolati, condimento Cajun e aglio.
- Coprire e cuocere a fuoco basso per 10-12 ore o a fuoco alto per 5-6 ore.
- Rimuovere 1 tazza di liquido caldo dal fornello. Sbattere il liquido con il burro di noci in una ciotola. Aggiungi la miscela nel fornello.
- Servire condito con coriandolo e, se lo si desidera, arachidi.

NUTRIZIONE: Calorie 399 | Grassi totali 21g | Carboidrati netti: 13,5 g | Proteine 37g)

75. Stufato Di Stinco Di Manzo

Tempo totale: 3 ore 25 minuti | Serve: 8)

INGREDIENTI:
- 2 libbre. stinco di manzo di qualità, a cubetti
- 4 cucchiai di olio d'oliva
- 2 cipolle rosse, sbucciate e tritate grossolanamente
- 3 pezzi di carote, sbucciate e tritate grossolanamente
- 3 gambi di sedano, mondati e tritati grossolanamente
- 4 spicchi d'aglio, non sbucciati
- qualche rametto di rosmarino fresco
- 2 foglie di alloro
- 2 tazze di funghi
- 2 tazze di zucchine
- Sale e pepe a piacere
- 1 cucchiaio di buccia di psillio
- 2 lattine di pomodori
- ⅔ Bottiglia di vino rosso

ISTRUZIONI:
- Preriscalda il forno a 360 F.
- In una casseruola resistente al forno dal fondo pesante, scaldare l'olio d'oliva e soffriggere le cipolle, le carote, il sedano, l'aglio, le erbe aromatiche e i funghi per 5 minuti fino a quando non si ammorbidiscono leggermente.
- Nel frattempo, arrotolare la carne nella buccia di psillio.
- Quindi aggiungere la carne nella casseruola e mescolare fino a quando tutti gli ingredienti sono mescolati.
- Aggiungere i pomodori, il vino e un pizzico di sale e pepe e portare a bollore.

- Una volta raggiunto il bollore, spegnere il fuoco e coprire la casseruola con carta stagnola a doppio spessore e il coperchio.
- Metti la casseruola nel forno per cuocere e sviluppare il sapore per 3 ore o fino a quando la carne può essere separata con un cucchiaio.
- Assaggiate e aggiungete altro sale se necessario.
- Servire e gustare.

NUTRIZIONE: Calorie 315 | Grassi totali 7g | Carboidrati netti: 7g | Proteine 20g)

76. Stufato Di Tonno

Tempo totale: 25 MIN| Servire: 2

INGREDIENTI:
- 1 scatoletta di tonno in acqua, sgocciolato
- 1 cucchiaio di burro
- ¼ di cipolla piccola, tritata finemente
- 1 spicchio d'aglio, tritato
- 1 cucchiaino di zenzero fresco, grattugiato
- ½ scatola di pomodori, tritati finemente
- 1 tazza di spinaci, tritati finemente
- 1 carota piccola, grattugiata
- 1 cucchiaino di curry in polvere 1 cucchiaino di curcuma
- ½ cucchiaino di pepe di cayenna (facoltativo)
- Sale e pepe a piacere

ISTRUZIONI:
- Soffriggere la cipolla, l'aglio e lo zenzero nel burro.
- Aggiungere i pomodori una volta che le cipolle sono morbide.
- Pezzi e acqua quanto basta per fare uno stufato per gli spinaci, la carota e il tonno. Cuocere a fuoco basso per circa 15 minuti.
- Non cuocere troppo gli spinaci.
- Cuocere a vapore 2 tazze di cavolfiore, schiacciare e aggiungere 1 cucchiaio di burro. Servire lo stufato sopra il caulimash.

NUTRIZIONE: Calorie 253 | Grassi totali 5g | Carboidrati netti: 7g | Proteine 25g | Fibre: 2g)

77.Zuppa di cavolfiore e formaggio

Tempo totale: 30 MIN| Servire: 4

INGREDIENTI:

- 4 tazze di cimette di cavolfiore, tritate
- 4 strisce di pancetta
- 1 cucchiaio di burro biologico
- 2 spicchi d'aglio, tritati
- 1 cipolla, tritata finemente
- ¼ di tazza di farina di mandorle
- 4 tazze di brodo di pollo a basso contenuto di sodio
- ½ tazza di latte
- ¼ di tazza di panna chiara
- 1 tazza di cheddar, tritato
- Sale e pepe a piacere

ISTRUZIONI:

- Cuocere la pancetta in una pentola capiente. Togliere dalla pentola a cottura ultimata e mettere da parte.
- Usando la stessa pentola, imposta il fuoco a fuoco medio e aggiungi le cipolle. Cuocere per 3 minuti, quindi aggiungere l'aglio e le cimette di cavolfiore e cuocere per altri 5 minuti.
- Aggiungere la farina nella pentola e sbattere continuamente per un minuto.
- Versare il brodo di pollo, il latte e la panna leggera e mescolare per 3 minuti.
- Lasciare sobbollire per 15 minuti e poi spegnere il fuoco.
- Aggiungi il formaggio cheddar nella pentola, condisci con sale e pepe e mescola di nuovo.
- Servire con sopra la pancetta tritata.

NUTRIZIONE: Calorie 268 | Grassi totali 15,9 g | Carboidrati netti: 11,9 g | Proteine 19,5 g | Fibra: 3,1 g)

78. Zuppa Di Pancetta Di Pollo

Tempo totale: 8 HR s10 MIN| Servire: 5

INGREDIENTI:
- 4 spicchi d'aglio - tritati
- 1 porro - pulito, mondato e affettato
- 2 sedano ribes a cubetti
- 1 cestino di funghi champignon - affettati
- 2 cipolle dolci medie - affettate sottilmente
- 4 cucchiai di burro
- 2 tazze di brodo di pollo
- 6 petti di pollo disossati e senza pelle, imburrati
- 8 once. crema di formaggio
- 1 tazza di panna
- 1 pacchetto di pancetta striata - cotta croccante e sbriciolata
- 1 cucchiaino di sale
- 1 cucchiaino di pepe
- 1 cucchiaino di aglio in polvere
- 1 cucchiaino di timo

ISTRUZIONI:
- Seleziona l'impostazione bassa sulla tua pentola a cottura lenta.
- Metti 1 tazza di brodo di pollo, cipolle, aglio, funghi, porri, sedano, 2 cucchiai di burro, sale e pepe nella pentola a cottura lenta.
- Metti il coperchio e cuoci gli ingredienti a fuoco basso per 1 ora.
- Rosolare i petti di pollo in una padella con 2 cucchiai di burro.
- Aggiungi la restante 1 tazza di brodo di pollo.

- Raschiare il fondo della padella per rimuovere il pollo che potrebbe essersi attaccato al fondo.
- Togliere dalla padella e mettere da parte, versando il grasso dalla padella sul pollo.
- Aggiungi il timo, la panna, l'aglio in polvere e la crema di formaggio nella tua pentola a cottura lenta.
- Mescolare il contenuto della pentola a cottura lenta fino a quando la crema di formaggio non si è sciolta nel piatto.
- Tagliare il pollo a cubetti. Aggiungi la pancetta e i cubetti di pollo nella pentola a cottura lenta. Mescolare gli ingredienti e cuocere a fuoco basso per 6-8 ore.

NUTRIZIONE: Calorie 355 | Grassi totali 21g | Carboidrati netti: 6,4 g | Proteine 28g)

DOLCI

79. Torta Zefiro del mattino

Tempo totale: 40 MIN| Serve: 8)

INGREDIENTI:
- 3 cucchiai di olio di cocco
- 2 cucchiai di semi di lino macinati
- 8 cucchiai di mandorle, macinate
- 1 tazza di yogurt greco
- 1 cucchiaio di cacao in polvere per spolverare
- 1 tazza di panna da montare pesante
- 1 cucchiaino di lievito in polvere
- 1 cucchiaino di bicarbonato di sodio
- 1 cucchiaino di pura essenza di vaniglia
- 1 pizzico di sale rosa
- 1 tazza di dolcificante stevia o eritritolo

ISTRUZIONI:
- Preriscalda il forno a 350 gradi F.
- Nel frullatore aggiungere prima le mandorle tritate, i semi di lino macinati e il lievito e il bicarbonato di sodio. Frullare per un minuto.
- Aggiungere il sale, l'olio di cocco e frullare ancora un po'. Aggiungere il dolcificante e frullare per 2-3 minuti.
- Aggiungere lo yogurt greco e frullare per un minuto circa, fino a raggiungere una consistenza fine.
- Prendi la pastella in una ciotola e aggiungi l'essenza di vaniglia e mescola con una mano leggera.
- Imburrate la teglia e versateci dentro l'impasto.
- Cuocere per 30 minuti. Lascia raffreddare su una gratella. Servire.

NUTRIZIONE: Calorie 199,84 | Grassi totali 20,69 g | Carboidrati netti: 3,22 g | Proteine 2,56 g | Fibra 1,17 g)

80. Palline Di Burro Di Arachidi

Tempo totale: 22 MIN| Serve: 16)

INGREDIENTI:
- 2 uova
- 2 1/2 tazze di burro di arachidi
- 1/2 tazza di cocco grattugiato (non zuccherato)
- 1/2 tazza di xilitolo
- 1 cucchiaio di puro estratto di vaniglia

ISTRUZIONI:
- Preriscaldare il forno a 320 F.
- Impastare tutti gli ingredienti con le mani.
- Dopo che gli ingredienti sono ben amalgamati, formare delle palline delle dimensioni di un cucchiaio colmo e pressarle in una teglia foderata con carta da forno.
- Cuocere in forno preriscaldato per 12 minuti.
- Quando è pronto, lascia raffreddare su una gratella.
- Servire e gustare.

NUTRIZIONE: Calorie 254,83 | Grassi totali 21,75 g | Carboidrati netti: 8,31 g | Proteine 10,98 g | Fibra 2,64 g)

81. Blondie di semi di lino alle noci pecan

Tempo totale: 40 MIN| Serve: 16)

INGREDIENTI:
- 3 uova
- 2 1/4 tazze di noci pecan, arrostite
- 3 cucchiai di panna
- 1 cucchiaio di sciroppo di caramello salato
- 1/2 tazza di semi di lino, macinati
- 1/4 di tazza di burro, sciolto
- 1/4 di tazza di eritritolo, in polvere
- 10 gocce di stevia liquida
- 1 cucchiaino di lievito in polvere
- 1 pizzico di sale

ISTRUZIONI:
- Preriscalda il forno a 350F.
- In una teglia arrostire le noci pecan per 10 minuti.
- Macina 1/2 tazza di semi di lino in un macinaspezie. Metti la polvere di semi di lino in una ciotola. Macina l'eritritolo in un macinino per spezie fino a ridurlo in polvere. Mettere nella stessa ciotola della farina di semi di lino.
- Metti 2/3 delle noci pecan tostate nel robot da cucina e lavora fino a formare un burro di noci liscio.
- Aggiungi le uova, la stevia liquida, lo sciroppo di caramello salato e un pizzico di sale alla miscela di semi di lino. Mescolare bene. Aggiungi il burro di noci pecan alla pastella e mescola di nuovo.
- Schiacciare le restanti noci pecan tostate a pezzetti.
- Aggiungi le noci pecan tritate e 1/4 di tazza di burro fuso nella pastella.

- Mescolare bene la pastella e quindi aggiungere la panna e il lievito. Amalgamate bene il tutto.
- Mettere l'impasto nella teglia e cuocere per 20 minuti.
- Raffreddare leggermente per circa 10 minuti.
- Tagliare a quadretti e servire.

NUTRIZIONE: Calorie 180,45 | Grassi totali 18,23 g | Carboidrati netti: 3,54 g | Proteine 3,07 g | Fibra 1,78 g)

82.Gelato al cioccolato alla menta piperita

Tempo totale: 35 MIN| Servire: 3

INGREDIENTI:
- 1/2 cucchiaino di estratto di menta piperita
- 1 tazza di panna
- 1 tazza di crema di formaggio
- 1 cucchiaino di estratto di vaniglia puro
- 1 cucchiaino di estratto di stevia liquida
- Cioccolato Fondente 100% per topping

ISTRUZIONI:
- Metti la coppa del gelato nel congelatore.
- In una ciotola di metallo, aggiungi tutti gli ingredienti tranne il cioccolato e sbatti bene.
- Rimettete in freezer per 5 minuti.
- Montare la gelatiera e aggiungere il liquido.
- Prima di servire guarnire il gelato con scaglie di cioccolato. Servire.

NUTRIZIONE: Calorie 286,66 | Grassi totali 29,96 g | Carboidrati netti: 2,7 g | Proteine 2,6 g)

83. Waffle gonfi al cocco

Tempo totale: 20 MIN| Serve: 8)

INGREDIENTI:

- 1 tazza di farina di cocco
- 1/2 tazza di panna (da montare).
- 5 uova
- 1/4 cucchiaino di sale rosa
- 1/4 cucchiaino di bicarbonato di sodio
- 1/4 di tazza di latte di cocco
- 2 cucchiaini di sciroppo Yacon
- 2 cucchiai di olio di cocco (sciolto)

ISTRUZIONI:

- In una ciotola capiente aggiungere le uova e sbattere con uno sbattitore elettrico per 30 secondi.
- Aggiungi la panna (da montare) e l'olio di cocco alle uova mentre stai ancora mescolando. Aggiungere il latte di cocco, la farina di cocco, il sale rosa e il bicarbonato di sodio. Mescolare con il frullatore a immersione per 45 secondi a bassa velocità. Accantonare.
- Riscalda bene la tua macchina per waffle e prepara i waffle secondo le specifiche del produttore.
- Servire caldo.

NUTRIZIONE: Calorie 169,21 | Grassi totali 12,6 g | Carboidrati netti: 9,97 g | Proteine 4,39 g | Fibra 0,45 g)

84. Crema di cioccolato al lampone

Tempo totale: 15 MIN| Servire: 4

INGREDIENTI:
- 1/2 tazza di cioccolato fondente al 100%, tritato
- 1/4 di tazza di panna
- 1/2 tazza di crema di formaggio, ammorbidita
- 2 cucchiai di sciroppo di lamponi senza zucchero
- 1/4 tazza di eritritolo

ISTRUZIONI:
- Sciogliere a bagnomaria il cioccolato tritato e la crema di formaggio. Aggiungere il dolcificante Erythritol e continuare a mescolare. Togliere dal fuoco, lasciare raffreddare e mettere da parte.
- Quando la crema si è raffreddata aggiungere la panna e lo sciroppo di lamponi e mescolare bene.
- Versare la crema in ciotole o bicchieri e servire. Da tenere in frigorifero.

NUTRIZIONE: Calorie 157,67 | Grassi totali 13,51 g | Carboidrati netti: 7,47 g | Proteine 1,95 g | Fibra 1g)

85. Biscotti Di Cacao Crudo Di Nocciola

Tempo totale: 6 ore| Serve: 24)

INGREDIENTI:
- 2 tazze di farina di mandorle
- 1 tazza di nocciole tritate
- 1/2 tazza di cacao in polvere
- 1/2 tazza di lino macinato
- 3 cucchiai di olio di cocco (sciolto)
- 1/3 di tazza d'acqua
- 1/3 di tazza di eritritolo
- 1/4 cucchiaino di Stevia liquida

ISTRUZIONI:
- In una ciotola mescolate la farina di lino e di mandorle, il cacao in polvere.
- Mescolare olio, acqua, agave e vaniglia. Quando sarà ben amalgamato, aggiungete le nocciole tritate.
- Formare delle palline, appiattirle con i palmi e posizionarle sugli schermi del disidratatore.
- Disidratare un'ora a 145, quindi ridurre a 116 e disidratare per almeno cinque ore.
- Servire e gustare.

NUTRIZIONE: Calorie 181.12 | Grassi totali 15,69 g | Carboidrati netti: 8,75 g | Proteine 4,46 g | Fibra: 3,45 g)

86. Muffin cheesecake alla zucca senza peccato

Tempo totale: 15 MIN| Servire: 6

INGREDIENTI:
- 1/2 tazza di purea di zucca
- 1 cucchiaino di spezie per torta di zucca
- 1/2 tazza di noci pecan, macinate finemente
- 1/2 tazza di crema di formaggio
- 1 cucchiaio di olio di cocco
- 1/2 cucchiaino di estratto di vaniglia puro
- 1/4 cucchiaino di sciroppo di Yacon puro o eritritolo

ISTRUZIONI:
- Preparare uno stampo per muffin con i pirottini.
- Metti alcune noci pecan macinate in ogni stampo per muffin e crea una crosta sottile.
- In una ciotola mescolate il dolcificante, le spezie, la vaniglia, il cocco e la purea di zucca. Aggiungere la crema di formaggio e sbattere fino a quando il composto è ben combinato.
- Versare circa due cucchiai di composto di ripieno sopra ogni crosta e levigare i bordi.
- Mettere in freezer per circa 45 minuti.
- Togliere dallo stampo per muffin e lasciare riposare per 10 minuti. Servire.

NUTRIZIONE: Calorie 157,34 | Grassi totali 15,52 g | Carboidrati netti: 3,94 g | Proteine 2,22 g | Fibra: 1,51 g)

87. Biscotti Sour Nocciola Con Tè Arrowroot

Tempo totale: 50 MIN| Serve: 12

INGREDIENTI:

- 1 uovo
- 1/2 tazza di nocciole
- 3 cucchiai di olio di cocco
- 2 tazze di farina di mandorle
- 2 cucchiai di tè alla radice di freccia
- 2 cucchiaini di zenzero
- 1 cucchiaio di cacao in polvere
- 1/2 tazza di succo di pompelmo
- 1 buccia d'arancia di mezza arancia
- 1/2 cucchiaino di bicarbonato di sodio
- 1 pizzico di sale

ISTRUZIONI:

- Preriscaldare il forno a 360 F.
- Prepara il tè alla radice di freccia e lascialo raffreddare.
- Frullare le nocciole in un robot da cucina. Aggiungere gli altri ingredienti e continuare a frullare fino a quando non saranno ben amalgamati. Con le mani formate dei biscotti con la pastella.
- Mettere i biscotti su carta da forno e cuocere per 30-35 minuti. Quando è pronto, togliere la teglia dal forno e lasciarlo raffreddare.
- Servire caldo o freddo.

NUTRIZIONE: Calorie 224,08 | Grassi totali 20,17 g | Carboidrati netti: 8,06 g | Proteine 6,36 g | Fibra 3,25 g)

88. Biscotti al tartaro senza pancia

Tempo totale: 35 MIN| Serve: 8)

INGREDIENTI:

- 3 uova
- 1/8 cucchiaino di cremor tartaro
- 1/3 di tazza di crema di formaggio
- 1/8 cucchiaino di sale
- Un po' di olio per ungere

ISTRUZIONI:

- Preriscaldare il forno a 300 F.
- Rivestite la teglia con carta da forno e ungetela con un filo d'olio.
- Separare le uova dai tuorli. Metti entrambi in ciotole diverse.
- Con uno sbattitore elettrico, inizia a montare gli albumi fino a renderli spumosi. Aggiungere la crema di tartaro e sbattere fino a formare picchi rigidi.
- Nella ciotola del tuorlo d'uovo, aggiungi la crema di formaggio e un po 'di sale. Sbattere fino a quando i tuorli d'uovo sono di un giallo pallido.
- Unire gli albumi al composto di crema di formaggio. Mescolare bene.
- Prepara i biscotti e posizionali sulla teglia.
- Cuocere per circa 30-40 minuti. Quando saranno pronte, fatele raffreddare su una gratella e servite.

NUTRIZIONE: Calorie 59,99 | Grassi totali 5,09 g | Carboidrati netti: 0,56 g | Proteine 2,93 g)

89.Gelato Di Fragoline Di Bosco

Tempo totale: 5 MIN| Servire: 4

INGREDIENTI:
- 1/2 tazza di fragoline di bosco
- 1/3 di tazza di crema di formaggio
- 1 tazza di panna
- 1 cucchiaio di succo di limone
- 1 cucchiaino di estratto di vaniglia puro
- 1/3 di tazza del tuo dolcificante preferito
- Cubetti di ghiaccio

ISTRUZIONI:
- Mettere tutti gli ingredienti in un frullatore. Frullare fino a incorporare bene il tutto.
- Mettere in frigo per 2-3 ore prima di servire.

NUTRIZIONE: Calorie 176,43 | Grassi totali 17,69 g | Carboidrati netti: 3,37 g | Proteine 1,9 g | Fibra 0,39 g)

90.Mini cheesecake al limone

Tempo totale: 5 MIN| Servire: 6

INGREDIENTI:
- 1 cucchiaio di scorza di limone grattugiata
- 1 cucchiaino di succo di limone
- ½ cucchiaino di stevia in polvere o (Truvia)
- 1/4 di tazza di olio di cocco, ammorbidito
- 4 cucchiai di burro non salato, ammorbidito
- 4 once di crema di formaggio (crema pesante)

ISTRUZIONI:
- Frullare tutti gli ingredienti con una frusta a mano o un frullatore fino a ottenere un composto liscio e cremoso.
- Preparare uno stampo per cupcake o muffin con 6 pirottini di carta.
- Versare il composto nello stampo preparato e metterlo in freezer per 2-3 ore o fino a quando non si rassoda.
- Cospargere le tazze con altra scorza di limone. Oppure prova a usare noci tritate o cocco tritato e non zuccherato.

NUTRIZIONE: Calorie 213 | Grassi totali 23g | Carboidrati netti: 0,7 g | Proteine 1,5 g | Fibra: 0,1 g)

91.Quadrati morbidi al burro di arachidi

Tempo totale: 10 MIN| Serve: 12

INGREDIENTI:
- 1 tazza di burro di arachidi cremoso tutto naturale
- 1 tazza di olio di cocco
- 1/4 di tazza di latte di mandorle alla vaniglia non zuccherato
- un pizzico di sale marino grosso
- 1 cucchiaino di estratto di vaniglia
- 2 cucchiaini di stevia liquida (opzionale)

ISTRUZIONI:
- In una ciotola adatta al microonde, ammorbidisci insieme il burro di arachidi e l'olio di cocco. (Circa 1 minuto a fuoco medio-basso.)
- Unire il burro di arachidi ammorbidito e l'olio di cocco con gli altri ingredienti in un frullatore o robot da cucina.
- Frullare fino a completa combinazione.
- Versare in una teglia da pane 9X4 "rivestita con carta pergamena.
- Refrigerare fino a quando non viene visto. Circa 2 ore.
- Godere.

NUTRIZIONE: Calorie 292 | Grassi totali 28,9 g | Carboidrati netti: 4,1 g | Proteine 6g | Fibra 1,4 g)

92.Quadrati di limone e crema di cocco

Tempo totale: 1 ora 5 minuti | Serve: 8)

INGREDIENTI:
BASE:
- 3/4 di tazza di scaglie di cocco
- 2 cucchiai di olio di cocco
- 1 cucchiaio di mandorle tritate

CREMA:
- 5 uova
- 1/2 succo di limone
- 1 cucchiaio di farina di cocco
- Dolcificante Stevia da 1/2 tazza

ISTRUZIONI:
PER LA BASE
- Preriscaldare il forno a 360 F.
- In una ciotola mettete tutti gli ingredienti base e con le mani pulite impastate bene il tutto fino a renderlo morbido.
- Ungere una pirofila rettangolare con olio di cocco. Versare l'impasto in una teglia. Cuocere per 15 minuti fino a doratura. Mettere da parte a raffreddare.

PER LA CREMA
- In una ciotola o in un frullatore, sbatti insieme: uova, succo di limone, farina di cocco e dolcificante. Versare uniformemente sulla torta cotta.
- Metti la teglia nel forno e cuoci altri 20 minuti.
- Quando è pronto mettete in frigo per almeno 6 ore. Tagliare a cubetti e servire.

NUTRIZIONE: Calorie 129 | Grassi totali 15g | Carboidrati netti: 1,4 g | Proteine 5g | Fibra 2,25 g)

93. Ricca torta al burro di mandorle e salsa al cioccolato

Tempo totale: 10 MIN| Serve: 12

INGREDIENTI:
- 1 tazza di burro di mandorle o mandorle ammollate
- 1/4 di tazza di latte di mandorle, non zuccherato
- 1 tazza di olio di cocco
- 2 cucchiaini di dolcificante Stevia liquido a piacere

TOPPING: SALSA AL CIOCCOLATO
- 4 cucchiai di cacao in polvere, non zuccherato
- 2 cucchiai di burro di mandorle
- 2 cucchiai di dolcificante Stevia

ISTRUZIONI:
- Sciogliere l'olio di cocco a temperatura ambiente.
- Aggiungere tutti gli ingredienti in una ciotola e mescolare bene fino a quando combinato.
- Versare il composto di burro di mandorle in un piatto foderato di pergamena.
- Mettere in frigorifero per 3 ore.
- In una ciotola, sbatti insieme tutti gli ingredienti per la farcitura. Versare sopra la torta di mandorle dopo che è stata impostata. Tagliare a cubetti e servire.

NUTRIZIONE: Calorie 273 | Grassi totali 23,3 g | Carboidrati netti: 2,4 g | Proteine 5,8 g | Fibra 2g)

94. Torta al burro di arachidi ricoperta di salsa al cioccolato

Tempo totale: 10 MIN| Serve: 12

INGREDIENTI:
- 1 tazza di burro di arachidi
- 1/4 di tazza di latte di mandorle, non zuccherato
- 1 tazza di olio di cocco
- 2 cucchiaini di dolcificante Stevia liquido a piacere

TOPPING: SALSA AL CIOCCOLATO
- 2 cucchiai di olio di cocco, sciolto
- 4 cucchiai di cacao in polvere, non zuccherato
- 2 cucchiai di dolcificante Stevia

ISTRUZIONI:
- In una ciotola per microonde mescolare olio di cocco e burro di arachidi; sciogliere in un forno a microonde per 1-2 minuti.
- Aggiungi questa miscela al tuo frullatore; aggiungere il resto degli ingredienti e mescolare bene fino a quando combinato.
- Versare il composto di arachidi in una teglia o piatto da portata foderato di pergamena.
- Refrigerare per circa 3 ore; più lungo è, meglio è.
- In una ciotola, sbatti insieme tutti gli ingredienti per la farcitura. Versare sopra la caramella di arachidi dopo che è stata fissata. Tagliare a cubetti e servire.

NUTRIZIONE: Calorie 273 | Grassi totali 27g | Carboidrati netti: 2,4 g | Proteine 6g | Fibra 2g)

FRULLATI

95. Frullato al cocco verde

Tempo totale: 10 MIN| Servire: 2

INGREDIENTI:
- 1 tazza di latte di cocco
- 1 mela verde, privata del torsolo e tritata
- 1 tazza di spinaci
- 1 cetriolo
- 2 cucchiai di cocco a scaglie
- 1/2 bicchiere d'acqua
- Cubetti di ghiaccio (se necessario)

ISTRUZIONI:
- Metti tutti gli ingredienti e il ghiaccio in un frullatore; pulsare fino a che liscio.
- Servire subito.

NUTRIZIONE: Calorie 216,57 | Grassi totali 16,56 g | Carboidrati netti: 8,79 g | Proteine 2,88 g | Fibra: 4g)

96. Frullato del diavolo verde

Tempo totale: 10 MIN| Servire: 2

INGREDIENTI:
- 3 tazze di cavolo, fresco
- 1/2 tazza di yogurt al cocco
- 1/2 tazza di broccoli, cimette
- 2 gambi di sedano, tritati
- 2 tazze d'acqua
- 1 cucchiaio di succo di limone
- Cubetti di ghiaccio (se necessario)

ISTRUZIONI:
- Frullare tutti gli ingredienti fino a ottenere un composto liscio e leggermente spumoso.

NUTRIZIONE: Calorie 117.09 | Grassi totali 4,98 g | Carboidrati netti: 1,89 g | Proteine 4,09 g | Fibra 6.18g)

97.Frullato senza pancia Green Dream

Tempo totale: 10 MIN| Servire: 4

INGREDIENTI:
- 1 tazza di cetriolo crudo, sbucciato e affettato
- 4 tazze d'acqua
- 1 tazza di lattuga romana
- 1 tazza di avocado Haas
- 2 cucchiai di basilico fresco
- Dolcificante a scelta (facoltativo)
- Una manciata di noci
- 2 cucchiai di prezzemolo fresco
- 1 cucchiaio di zenzero fresco grattugiato
- Cubetti di ghiaccio (opzionale)

ISTRUZIONI:
- In un frullatore, unire tutti gli ingredienti e frullare fino a che liscio.
- Aggiungere il ghiaccio se utilizzato. Servire freddo.

NUTRIZIONE: Calorie 50,62| Grassi totali 3,89 g | Carboidrati netti: 1,07 g | Proteine 1,1 g | Fibra 2,44 g)

98. di sedano e noci senza pancia

Tempo totale: 10 MIN| Servire: 2

INGREDIENTI:
- 2 gambi di sedano
- 1 tazza di foglie di spinaci, tritate grossolanamente
- 1/2 tazza di pistacchi (non salati)
- 1/2 avocado, tritato
- 1/2 tazza di lime, succo
- 1 cucchiaio di semi di canapa
- 1 cucchiaio di mandorle ammollate
- 1 tazza di acqua di cocco
- Cubetti di ghiaccio (opzionale)

ISTRUZIONI:
- Aggiungere tutti gli ingredienti in un frullatore con alcuni cubetti di ghiaccio e frullare fino a che liscio.

NUTRIZIONE: Calorie 349,55 | Grassi totali 17,88 g | Carboidrati netti: 5,01 g | Proteine 11,08 g | Fibra 9,8 g)

99. Frullato di lime e menta piperita

Tempo totale: 5 MIN| Servire: 4

INGREDIENTI:
- 1/4 di tazza di foglie di menta fresca
- 1/4 di tazza di succo di lime
- 1/2 tazza di cetriolo, tritato
- 1 cucchiaio di foglie di basilico fresco, tritate
- 1 cucchiaino di semi di chia (opzionale)
- Una manciata di semi di chia
- 3 cucchiaini di scorza di lime
- Dolcificante a scelta a piacere
- 1 tazza di acqua, divisa
- Ghiaccio quanto basta

ISTRUZIONI:
- Mettere tutti gli ingredienti in un frullatore o in un robot da cucina. Pulsare fino a che liscio.
- Riempi i bicchieri di ghiaccio, versa la limeade in ogni bicchiere e divertiti.

NUTRIZIONE: Calorie 28.11 | Grassi totali 1,16 g | Carboidrati netti: 0,75 g | Proteine 0,84 g | Fibra 1,98 g)

100. Frullati di cavolo al pompelmo rosso

Tempo totale: 10 MIN| Servire: 4

INGREDIENTI:

- 2 tazze di melone
- 1/4 di tazza di fragole fresche
- 8 once di yogurt al cocco
- 2 tazze di foglie di cavolo, tritate
- 2 cucchiai di dolcificante a piacere
- 1 Ghiaccio quanto basta
- 1 tazza d'acqua

ISTRUZIONI:

- Pulite il pompelmo e privatelo dei semi.
- Unire tutti gli ingredienti in un frullatore elettrico e frullare fino a che liscio. Aggiungere il ghiaccio se utilizzato e servire.

NUTRIZIONE: Calorie 260,74 | Grassi totali 11,57 g | Carboidrati netti: 2,96 g | Proteine 4,42 g | Fibra 7,23 g)

CONCLUSIONE

Mentre concludiamo questo viaggio di trasformazione, speriamo che il libro di cucina Zero Pancia ti abbia ispirato ad abbracciare un approccio nutriente ed equilibrato al cibo. Le ricette e i principi condivisi in questo libro di cucina sono progettati per aiutarti a ottenere un corpo più sano e una vita più felice ed energica.

Con Zero Pancia Cookbook, hai gli strumenti per apportare cambiamenti positivi alle tue abitudini alimentari. Ogni ricetta è realizzata con cura per fornirti i nutrienti di cui hai bisogno supportando la tua perdita di peso e gli obiettivi di salute generale. Abbracciando l'approccio Zero Pancia, non stai solo adottando una dieta a breve termine, ma piuttosto uno stile di vita a lungo termine che promuove salute e benessere sostenibili.

Quindi, mentre continui il tuo percorso verso una persona più sana, lascia che il libro di cucina Zero Pancia sia il tuo fidato compagno, fornendoti ricette nutrienti, consigli utili e un senso di potere. Abbraccia il potere di ingredienti genuini, un'alimentazione consapevole e un approccio equilibrato alla nutrizione. Ogni pasto che prepari da questo libro di cucina è un'opportunità per nutrire il tuo corpo e fare scelte che supportano il tuo benessere generale.

Possa la tua cucina riempirsi degli aromi di ingredienti nutrienti, della gioia di cucinare e della soddisfazione di nutrire il tuo corpo con pasti deliziosi. Saluti a te più sano e a una vita di vitalità e benessere!

www.ingramcontent.com/pod-product-compliance
Lightning Source LLC
LaVergne TN
LVHW021658060526
838200LV00050B/2413